# Classroom Discourse

## The Language of Teaching and Learning

### Courtney B. Cazden

HEINEMANN • Portsmouth, NH

**Heinemann**
A division of Reed Elsevier Inc.
361 Hanover Street
Portsmouth, NH 03801–3912
www.heinemann.com

*Offices and agents throughout the world*

The author and publisher wish to thank those who have generously given permission to reprint borrowed material:

Excerpts reprinted from *The Language of Learning: How Children Talk, Write, Draw, and Sing Their Understanding of the World* by Karen Gallas. Copyright © 1994 by Teachers College, Columbia University. Reprinted by permission of Teachers College Press, New York. All rights reserved.

Chapter 2: From C. B. Cazden, "What Is Sharing Time For?" *Language Arts* 62 (1985), pp. 182–88. Reprinted with permission of the publisher.

Figure 3–1: Transcription of birthplaces from initiation 5 through initiation 34. Reprinted by permission of Hugh Mehan.

Figure 3–2 is reprinted from "Reevaluating the IRF Sequence: A Proposal for the Articulation of Theories of Activity and Discourse for the Analysis of Teaching and Learning in the Classroom" by G. Wells in *Linguistics and Education,* Volume 5, Copyright © 1993. Reprinted by permission of Reed Elsevier Science, Oxford, England.

Excerpts from "Agreeing to Disagree: Developing Sociable Mathematical Discourse" by M. Lampert, P. Rittenhouse, and C. Crumbaugh in *The Handbook of Education and Human Development: New Models for Learning, Teaching and Schooling* edited by D. R. Olson and N. Torrance. Reprinted by permission of Blackwell Publishers, Oxford, England.

*(credits continued on page 209)*

**Library of Congress Cataloging-in-Publication Data**
Cazden, Courtney B.
    Classroom discourse : the language of teaching and learning / Courtney B. Cazden.—2nd ed.
        p.   cm.
    Includes bibliographical references (p. ) and index.
    ISBN 0-325-00378-5 (alk. paper)
    1. Communication in education. 2. Interaction analysis in education. 3. Verbal behavior. 4. Teacher-student relationships. I. Title.
LB1033.5 .C34 2001
371.102'2—dc21

                                                                                    2001039162

*Editor:* William Varner
*Production editor:* Sonja S. Chapman
*Cover design:* Jenny Jensen Greenleaf
*Manufacturing:* Steve Bernier

Printed in the United States of America on acid-free paper
05   04   03            VP            3   4   5

*For all teachers
and teacher researchers:
In the end, it's your
work that counts.*

# Contents

Chapter One
**Introduction**
1

Chapter Two
**Sharing Time**
10

Chapter Three
**Traditional and
Nontraditional Lessons**
30

Chapter Four
**Classroom Discourse
and Student Learning**
60

Chapter Five
**Variations in Discourse Features**
81

Chapter Six
**Talk with Peers and Computers**
109

Chapter Seven
**Differential Treatment
and Cultural Differences**
137

Chapter Eight
## New Contexts for Students' Language Development
169

## Afterword
181

## References
183

## Subject Index
201

## Name Index
205

# Chapter One

# Introduction

## Introduction to the First Edition

My interest in the study of classroom discourse comes from my experience as a primary grades' teacher as well as a university researcher. Before becoming a graduate student and then a university professor, I had been a primary teacher for nine years. Then, in the fall of 1974, I took a leave from my job at the Harvard Graduate School of Education to become again, for one year, a fully certified, full-time teacher of young children at a public school. After thirteen years in the university, it was time to go back to children, to try to put into practice some of the ideas about children's language and education that I had been teaching and writing about,[1] and to rethink questions for future research.

I left Cambridge to teach in San Diego in order to collaborate with sociologist Hugh ("Bud") Mehan. Bud and I met at Berkeley in 1968, when we were both participants in an interdisciplinary summer-long seminar—"Language, Society, and the Child." We kept in touch, and when I decided to go back to a primary classroom and wanted someone there looking over my shoulder, I knew Bud would be the ideal observer. A couple of years, and many negotiations, later that collaboration came to pass.

I taught in a section of San Diego that was one of the lowest in income and school achievement in the city, a community that was then about evenly divided between black and Chicano families. I had twenty-five black and Mexican American children in a combined first, second, and third grade. They will appear in this book—Prenda, Caroline, Wallace, Greg, Veronica, and others.[2]

Also in 1974, just as I was setting off for San Diego, the National Institute of Education assembled a set of panels to propose an agenda for research on teaching. One panel, which I chaired, was on teaching as a linguistic process in a cultural setting. British researcher, Douglas Barnes wrote a paper for that conference even though, at the last minute, he was unable to attend. In part, his paper said:

> Speech unites the cognitive and the social. The actual (as opposed to the intended) curriculum consists in the meanings enacted or realized by a particular teacher and class. In order to learn, students must use what they already know so as to give meaning to what the teacher presents to them. Speech makes available to reflection the processes by which they relate new knowledge to old. But this possibility depends on the social relationships, the communication system, which the teacher sets up.[3]

The study of classroom discourse is the study of that communication system.

Any social institution can be considered a communication system. In the words of one linguist, Michael Halliday: "Its very existence implies that communication takes place within it; there will be sharing of experience, expression of social solidarity, decision making and planning, and, if it is a hierarchical institution, forms of verbal control, transmission of order, and the like."[4] But while other institutions, such as hospitals, serve their clients in nonlinguistic ways, the basic purpose of school is achieved through communication.

Several features of educational institutions make communication so central. First, spoken language is the medium by which much teaching takes place, and in which students demonstrate to teachers much of what they have learned. As the quotation from Barnes says so profoundly, through the actual curriculum enacted between teacher and students, "speech unites the cognitive and the social."

Second, classrooms are among the most crowded of human environments. Few adults spend as many hours per day in such crowded conditions. Classrooms are similar in this respect to restaurants and buses or subways. But in such places simultaneous conversations are normal, whereas in classrooms one person, the teacher, is responsible for controlling all the talk that occurs while class is officially in session—controlling not just negatively, as a traffic officer does to avoid collisions, but also positively, to enhance the purposes of education.

Third, and perhaps least obviously, spoken language is an important part of the identities of all the participants. Variation in ways of speaking is a universal fact of social life. Schools are the first large institution to which children come from their families and home neighborhoods, and in which they are expected to participate individually and publicly (in contrast, for example, to simply sitting and standing at appropriate times and joining in prayers and songs in church). Especially during the period of school consolidation and desegregation, and the continuing migration across state and national borders, classrooms usually include people—adults and children—from different linguistic backgrounds.

Differences in how something is said, and even when, can be matters of only temporary adjustment, or they can seriously impair effective teaching and accurate evaluation. For all these reasons, it is essential to consider the classroom communication system as a problematic medium that cannot be ignored, or viewed as transparent, by anyone interested in teaching and learning.

Readers familiar with linguistics will recognize in these three features of classroom life—the language of curriculum, the language of control, and the language of personal identity—the following tripartite core of all categorizations of language functions:

- the communication of propositional information (also termed the referential, cognitive, or ideational function)
- the establishment and maintenance of social relationships
- the expression of the speaker's identity and attitudes

For short, we can call these the propositional, social, and expressive functions.

More will be said throughout this book about all three functions. It is important to note at the outset, however, that they are functions of language, not functions of separate utterances. Any one utterance can be, and usually is, multifunctional. In each and every utterance, speech truly unites the cognitive and the social.

The study of classroom discourse is thus a kind of *applied linguistics*— the study of situated language use in one social setting. I hope that this study will answer important educational questions. Three questions in particular are prominent in the chapters that follow:

- How do patterns of language use affect what counts as "knowledge," and what occurs as learning?
- How do these patterns affect the equality, or inequality, of students' educational opportunities?
- What communication competence do these patterns presume and/ or foster?

This book discusses research—my own and others'—that attempts to answer these questions. The book begins, in Chapters 2 and 3, with the talk of primary-school children and their teachers. But in later chapters, examples are drawn from classrooms at other levels, from preschool through high school. Most of the research describes classrooms in the United States and England, but whenever possible I have included examples and commentary from other countries.[5]

I have tried to write both for people who see themselves primarily as teachers (or teacher educators and supervisors) and for those who see themselves primarily as researchers. Notes at the end of each chapter give references, and sometimes additional comments (addressed mostly to researchers). The entire book can be read without referring to the notes at all.

The task for both teachers and researchers is to make the usually transparent medium of classroom discourse the object of focal attention. Because of the importance of language to the goals of schools, some aspects of language in education are subject to explicit language planning—such as decisions about whether to have some kind of bilingual education, which language tests to administer, and which language competencies to require for professional employment.

Other aspects of language in education are the result of nondeliberate, usually nonconscious, choice at the moment of use. It is these nonconscious aspects of language use in the classroom that this book is about.

—1988

## Introduction to the Second Edition

Everything said in the first edition's Introduction applies to this revised edition. Classroom discourse is even more important now than it was when that book was written. Therefore our understanding of it—with all its problems and potentialities—is even more important too. Reasons for this enhanced importance converge from changes in many aspects of social and intellectual life.

Socially, there have been significant changes in the nature of the workplace and of civil society. In the changing workplace, two educational economists' study of the abilities required of high school graduates to get decent, high-wage jobs speaks for many such studies. Here is their list of "new basic skills" graduates need:

- The ability to read at the ninth-grade level or higher
- The ability to do math at the ninth-grade level or higher
- The ability to solve semi-structured problems where hypotheses must be formed and tested
- The ability to work in groups with persons of various backgrounds
- The ability to communicate effectively, both orally and in writing
- The ability to use personal computers to carry out simple tasks like word processing[6]

*Civil society* is one term for the web of activities that extend beyond the family and close friends, and beyond the workplace and formal political structures, to the informal and voluntary activities that contribute so much to the vitality and democracy of each community. At the very time when institutional structures maintained by local and federal governments are being shrunk, the need for activities on behalf of the social good by ordinary people is growing. At the same time, the challenges of deciding, planning, and acting together across differences of race, ethnicity, and religion are growing too. For these reasons, two of the abilities necessary to get good jobs in the changing economy are also necessary for participation in a changing society: effective oral and written communication and the ability to work in groups with persons from various backgrounds. In other words, schools have a responsibility to create not only individual human capital for a healthy economy, but collective social capital for healthy communities as well.

Intellectually, there have been significant changes in conceptions of knowledge and learning. To oversimplify, curriculum standards now place less emphasis on products, facts, or procedures to be learned by heart and, correspondingly, more emphasis on processes and strategies for learning and doing. So teachers are being asked to deliberately give up relying so heavily on the traditional three-part pattern of classroom lessons—Initiation/Response/Evaluation (IRE)—that best fits the transmission of facts and routinized procedures. They are being asked to add nontraditional discussions that serve better to stimulate and support "higher-order thinking" across the curriculum.[7] This is the focus of Chapters 2 through 6.

Increasing the challenge for teachers, these changes are being advocated, loudly and widely, for *all* students. Finding ways to decrease the achievement gap among ethnic and social class groups has become a national priority. Teachers cannot be expected to accomplish this societal goal by themselves. Many decisions about crucial resource allocations are beyond their control: decisions about which families have a livable income and health benefits, and which schools get how many computers or have how many Advanced Placement classes, for example. But resource allocations occur within classrooms as well.

If the potentialities of classroom discourse, in which students talk more and in more varied ways, are significant for all students, then we have to pay careful attention to who speaks and who receives thoughtful responses. In the interest of simplicity, the book's title remains the same; but an expanded title could be: *Classroom Discourse: The Drama of Teaching and Learning With Speaking Parts for All.* Equity issues are the special focus of Chapter 7.

It is no wonder that teaching to accomplish such complex goals is sometimes called "adventurous teaching" and that classroom discourse is central to this adventure. More than twenty-five years ago, in his Introduction to one of the first books to present research on language in the classroom, anthropologist and linguist Dell Hymes said: "Language should be studied . . . in its social context, in terms of its organization to serve social ends."[8] The social ends of education are changing; therefore our responsibilities for discourse—whether as teachers, teacher educators, or researchers—must change too.

Now, we understand better than we did when Hymes urged such study that learning different patterns of language use—different "ways with words"—involves changing more than words alone. It entails taking on new roles, and the new identities they express—for students as well as teachers.[9] It has always been the case that formal schooling requires forms of discourse that are different from the informal talk of home and street. The more different these new forms are, the more attention we have to pay to helping all students learn to enact the new roles. Educators from different perspectives, such as Britain's Douglas Barnes and African American Lisa Delpit, urge us to be explicit with students about the "ground rules" (Barnes) of these oral and written "discourses of power" (Delpit).[10] In other words, part of the new curriculum has to be not only individual cognitive processes of learning but the social processes of discourse itself. The Introduction to this book's first edition, near the end says: "The task for both teachers and researchers is to make the usually transparent medium of classroom discourse the object of focal attention." We now realize that sometimes it needs to become the object of focal attention for students as well. This is the special focus of the last chapter, Chapter 8. That's another reason for us to understand classroom discourse more deeply ourselves.

Fortunately, another significant change in the context in which this second edition is written is the movement among teachers to become more "reflective practitioners" by engaging in research in their own classrooms. As a tool for research on classroom discourse, I want to urge the use of recorders, audio or video. Common tools for academic researchers for a long time, tape recorders also have great value for teacher researchers, whether they work individually or in collegial groups.

I realize that some teachers find taping in their classroom a daunting chore. But I still highly recommend it, influenced in part by members of the Brookline Teacher Research Seminar—a teacher-led group in the Boston area. The group has been meeting regularly for more than a decade, sustained for most of these years only by their own desires to be more effective teachers with their increasingly diverse students.[11] Because they closely attend to matters of classroom discourse and because they were familiar with the first edition of this book, I asked the group for their suggestions for revision.

Among their strongest recommendations was the value for teachers of grounding their own discussions of learning and teaching in transcriptions of audiotape recordings of moments of talk in their classrooms. One teacher explained:

> There's no other way to honestly get back at that moment in time and know what was going on without having a transcript. There's no other way to do it. You can take notes afterwards and that's helpful, but it's not as honest and powerful—as real—as having a transcript. . . .

> There's nothing else that can even come close—putting yourself back there. . . . It's the only way to bring everybody else with you as well. Not only do *you* go back there, but *we* get to be there. It's always worth the price.

While reading other people's ideas can suggest new visions, as I hope this book will do, only audiotapes, or less commonly videotapes, and transcripts make possible close attention to the words of a particular classroom.

Another member of the group, who works with even younger children, pointed out that taping validates the children as well.

> Where I am taping or where I am listening closely to what's going on, there's something that happens as I investigate. [The kids] kind of feel like that's important. . . . They're not uncomfortable with it. It makes them feel like people are learning from *them*.[12]

Some teachers have even played excerpts from the tapes with their students to engage them in diagnosing problems, such as marked gender differences in classroom participation, and suggesting ways to change. This book, even more than the first edition, is written not just for university researchers and teacher educators, but for teachers and teacher researchers as well.

In all the chapters, I have been deliberately eclectic in drawing on diverse theories, analytic strategies, and kinds of empirical research. With a focus as complex as classroom discourse in all its many forms, no single perspective can be adequate. Each illuminates some features for attention, while hiding others in shadows. As in the first edition, notes at the end of each chapter give references and sometimes additional comments. As with the first edition, reading these notes is optional.

To avoid overloading the notes, given the great expansion of relevant literature in recent years, I need to explain my criteria for selection based on three overlapping but separate criteria: (1) the importance of how the researchers did their research and what they found, (2) their prominence in professional dialogues, and (3) their position and perspectives as members of underrepresented groups. So that readers will understand these selections throughout the chapters, more, but still brief, information is given about authors in this edition, sometimes including their ethnicity. Admittedly, identifying authors of color leaves white authors, like myself, as the unmarked category; but the fairer alternative of identifying the rest as "white" seemed too cumbersome.[13]

In all writing, choice of personal pronouns is a subtle way of identifying oneself and others, and I need to explain who "we" refers to throughout the book. Sometimes it refers simply to all readers; but sometimes it refers only to teachers (in which I include myself as a former primary teacher) who have to imagine themselves speaking in new roles. At other times "we" refers to the even more specific group of *white* teachers and other readers (again including myself) who have to work especially hard on the equity issues of "speaking parts for all." I hope that readers will be able to interpret these shifts from their local contexts.

As with the first edition, this revision draws on what I have learned from many colleagues. In addition to debts acknowledged in the footnotes, I owe special thanks since my 1995 retirement from the Harvard Graduate School of Education to the Spencer Foundation for a Senior Scholar Grant for travel within "the English writing world" that has contributed much to my understanding of oral discourse and its relationship to writing; to students and faculty at the Bread Loaf School of English for rich ongoing discussions of teaching and learning; and to the staff of the Harvard Graduate School of Education Library for superb service.

# Notes

1. Cazden 1972; and Cazden, John, and Hymes 1972.

2. Mehan 1979 reports his analyses; Cazden 1976 contains my personal account.

3. National Institute of Education 1974, 1.

4. Halliday 1978, 230–231.

5. Cazden 1986a details the recent history of research on classroom discourse; and Cazden 1986b discusses assumptions of various research perspectives. In my own research, I am grateful for past support from the Ford Foundation, Carnegie Foundation, Spencer Foundation, and the National Institute of Education.

6. Murnane and Levy 1996, 32.

7. Two teachers reading this introduction noted the passive role of teachers in "being asked to" change their ways with classroom words (with thanks to JoAnn Ross Cunningham and Scott Mackey, Oxford, England, August 1998). Some of the influential players in this aspect of school reform will be identified in the chapters that follow, but the overall picture of teachers under pressure is, I think, accurate. What's unfortunate is that, in too many school districts, teachers are being expected to change in the face of conflicting pressures for short-term gains on norm-referenced, multiple-choice tests.

8. Cazden, John, and Hymes 1972, xviii.

9. *Ways with Words* is the title of Heath's 1983 book. The relationships among discourse, role, and identity are discussed in detail by Gee 1996. He differentiates between *discourse,* coherent sequences of language longer than a sentence; and *Discourse,* the integration of words, actions, and values into a social identity. In this second edition, I will not try to maintain Gee's distinction by capitalization, but I will expand the meaning of the term in his "big D" direction.

10. Sheeran and Barnes 1991; Delpit 1995; *see also* New London Group 1996.

11. Gallas, K., et al. 1996.

12. From the transcript of a meeting held on November 8, 1996. Barnes and Todd 1995, Ch. 5 includes helpful advice to teachers about taping in their own classrooms.

13. Two excellent general references on classroom discourse that complement this book are Edwards and Westgate 1994 (on research methodology) and Hicks 1995 (on relationships to student learning).

# Chapter Two

# Sharing Time

### Paper Boat

**Jerry:** Ummmm. [*Pause*] Two days ago, ummm, my father and my father's friend were doin' somethin' over the other side and my sister wanted, uhhh, my father's friend to make her a little boat outta paper 'n' the paper was too little. He used his dollar and, umm, my sister un-doed it and we, ah, bought my father and mother Christmas presents.

**T:** A man made a boat out of a dollar bill for you?!! Wow! That's pretty expensive paper to use! [1]

*Sharing time* is a common activity in many primary classrooms that is organized to answer the teacher's seemingly ordinary question: "Who has something to tell us this morning?" The question, however phrased, is an invitation to the children to "share" a personal experience narrative about their out-of-school lives. Jerry is such a first-grade sharer.

The participation structure of traditional sharing time varies from classroom to classroom, but only in the details. [2] Someone, usually the teacher, calls on children to speak; sharers usually come to the front of the room, often standing at the teacher's side; the teacher comments at the end, as Jerry's teacher did, and sometimes interpolates questions into the children's narration; and sometimes other children are invited to comment or question as well. In some classrooms, there are limits on possible topics: no retelling of movies or TV programs, for example; and describing an object, such as a birthday present (from which the name "Show and Tell" is derived), may be allowed only on certain days. Thus, sharing is a true speech event in the technical sense: recurring, bounded with a clear beginning and end, with consistent patterns of participation in each classroom.

Even though more classroom activities are now giving children longer turns to talk, as we will see in the next chapter, sharing time continues to be special. It may still be the only opportunity during the official classroom "air time" for children to compose their own oral texts, and to speak on a self-chosen topic that does not have to meet criteria of relevance to previous discourse. Sharing time may also still be the only time when recounting events from personal, family, and community life is considered appropriate in school. Otherwise, talking to the teacher about personal experiences may be restricted to transition moments such as before school or while waiting in line; in fact, a teacher shift from listening to not listening to such stories can be a clear marker that school has officially begun: "I can't listen now, Sarah, we have to get started." That is, "We have to enter a different discourse world in which what you're talking about, no matter how important to you, is out of bounds." [3]

Given the significance of what might seem a routine and unimportant part of the school day, important questions can be asked: What kind of sharing-time narratives do children tell? How do teachers respond? In a series of studies of traditional sharing time, begun in the 1980s by Sarah Michaels in California and continued together in the Boston area, we tried to answer these questions and to suggest possible influences on both children and teachers.[4] More recently, teacher researchers who were aware of this research have deliberately changed the ground rules for sharing time in their classrooms with important results.

## Traditional Sharing Time

Common features of children's narratives indicate that sharing time is a unique activity for the children themselves. Typically, the narratives begin with information about time; for example, in *Paper Boat*, "Two days ago"; then the key agents are introduced, "my father and my father's friend . . . and my sister"; and the action begins. Here are some other typical openings:

- "At Thanksgiving, when I went to my grandma and grandpa's, we . . . "
- "Last Christmas, my mom . . . "
- "When I slept over my mother's, the cat—in the middle of the night—she . . . "
- "Last Friday, my mother and grandmother went out, and they . . ."

One difference is between what we have come to call topic-centered and episodic narratives. Topic-centered narratives focus on a single object or event. *Paper Boat* is one; *A Hundred Dollars* is another. (The titles for all narratives are ours, for easier reference.)

### A Hundred Dollars

**Carl:**  Well / last night / my father was at work /
he / every Thursday night they have this thing /
that everybody has this dollar /
and it makes up to a hundred dollars /
and my / and you've gotta pick this name out /
and my father's name got picked /
so he won a thousand dollars // a hundred dollars //

**T:**  Tell us what he's gonna do with it /

**Child leader:**  Donald [*Calling on next child*]

**T:**  Wait a minute // He's gonna tell us what he's /
what his father's gonna do with it //

**Carl:**  He's gonna pay bills //

Conventions for transcribing classroom discourse vary from re-searcher to researcher, depending on the focus of the research. I have included a variety of such conventions in this book to exemplify possibilities and show that there is no one best way to capture oral speech in written form. Whereas Dorr-Bremme uses conventional punctuation for *Paper Boat,* Michaels uses a single slash (/) to represent the oral equivalent of a comma, signaling more to come, and a double dash (//) to represent the equivalent of a period, a full stop. To get a richer sense of the narratives as spoken, try reading the transcriptions aloud.[5]

Episodic narratives always include shifting scenes and, as a result, are usually longer. Here is Leona's episodic story, *At Grandmother's,* with line spaces inserted to separate the three episodes.

### At Grandmother's

**Leona:**  On George Washington's birthday /
I'm goin / ice / my grandmother /
we never / haven't seen her since a long time /

and / and she lives right near us /!
and / she's / and she's gonna /
I'm gonna spend the night over her house /

and one day I spoiled her dinner /
and we was having / we was /
she paid ten dollars /
and I got eggs / and stuff /
and I didn't even eat anything / /

## *The Teacher's Response*

In answering the teacher's invitation to "share," child narrators face the problem of speaking to a dual audience. Peers are visually obvious, but it is often only the teacher who responds, and peers and teachers may hear stories very differently. In informal conversation, storytelling places special obligations on the audience. As linguist Pratt puts it:

> We waive our right to preempt the floor until the storyteller himself offers to give it up (with his narrative coda). . . . We can, of course, interrupt to request clarification or details, but we do not thereby put an end to the storyteller's turn. More than nearly any other speech act, I believe, narratives, once begun, are immune to control by other participants in a conversation.[6]

But in school, sharing-time narratives, although about out-of-school experiences and unrelated to the rest of the curriculum, are not immune to such control.

Most teachers make some response to each narrative, and their responses can express appreciation, confusion, or criticism. Jerry's teacher was enthusiastic about *Paper Boat:* "A man made a boat out of a dollar bill for you?!! Wow! That's pretty expensive paper to use!" Appreciation may be combined with a question or comment to encourage the child to say more. So, after *A Hundred Dollars,* the teacher asks Carl to "tell us what he's gonna do with it."

Sometimes an extended teacher–child collaboration results in a more complete description of an object or event than the child would have produced alone. This happened with *Making Candles.*

### Making Candles

**Mindy:** When I was in day camp / we made these candles / /

**T:** You made them?

**Mindy:** And I—I tried it with different colors / with both of them but/
one just came out / this one just came out blue /
and I don't know / what this color is / /

**T:** That's neat-o / / Tell the kids how you do it from the very start / /
Pretend we don't know a thing about candles / /
OK / / What did you do first? / / What did you use? / /
Flour? / /

**Mindy:** There's some hot wax / some real hot wax /
that you / just take a string / and tie a knot in it / /
and dip the string in the wax /

**T:** What makes it have a shape? / /

**Mindy:** You just shape it / /

**T:** Oh / you shaped it with your hand / / mm / /

**Mindy:** But you have / first you have to stick it into the wax /
and then water / and then keep doing that until it gets to the
size you want it / /

**T:** OK / / who knows what the string is for? / / . . .

Especially with the episodic narratives, the teacher's response may express her perplexity, her inability to understand the significance that the story has for the child. When Leona told *My Puppy,* a long and complex episodic story about three same-sex characters—her father, the puppy, and the doctor who "put him asleep"—her teacher finally interrupted to ask, "*Who's* in the hospital, Leona?"[7] When Leona explained that her puppy is there because he's "vicious," the teacher initiated a discussion about what "vicious" means and ended Leona's turn with words about dogs' need for toilet training.

Finally, some responses express a conflict between child and teacher over the significance of the child's topic. *Old Ironsides,* from the same classroom as Joe's *Paper Boat,* shows a conflict about what constitutes reportable highlights of a family outing.

### Old Ironsides

**Nancy:** I went to Old Ironsides at the ocean.

[*Led by a series of teacher questions, Nancy explains that* Old Ironsides *is a boat and that it's old. The teacher herself offers the real name,* The Constitution. *Then Nancy tries to shift the focus of her story.*]

**Nancy:** We also spent our dollars and we went to another big shop.

**T:** Mm. Nancy, what did you learn about Old Ironsides?

[*Again led by teacher questions, Nancy supplies more information about the furnishings inside and the costumes of the guides, and then tries to shift focus again.*]

**Nancy:** I also went to a fancy restaurant.

**T:** Haha! Very good!

**Nancy:** And I had a hamburger, french fries, lettuce and a—

**T:** OK. All right, what's—Arthur's been waiting and then Paula, OK?

Nancy wanted to talk about the other places she had gone, including what she had eaten at the "fancy restaurant," but the teacher wanted her to tell more about the historic ship.

Deena's teacher expressed an even more negative reaction to *Deena's Day.* In this transcription, Michaels uses a vertical bracket to indicate simultaneous speech by Deena and her teacher.

### Deena's Day

**Deena:** I went to the beach Sunday /
and / to McDonald's / and to the park /
and I got this for my / birthday / / [*holds up purse*]
my mother bought it for me /
and I had two dollars for my birthday /
and I put it in here /
and I went to where my friend / named Gigi /
I went over to my grandmother's house with her /
and she was on my back /

and I / and we was walking around / by my house /
and she was HEAVY / /
she was in the sixth or seventh grade / /
**T:** ⌐OK I'm going to stop you / /
I want you to talk about things that are really, really very important / /
that's important to you but can you tell us things that are sort of different
/ / can you do that? / /

Then, having stopped Deena from telling the story as she wanted to tell,
T asks a question about her first sentence, "Tell us what beach you went
to over the weekend." Jerry's teacher expressed a similarly negative
evaluation of one of Jerry's classmates: "If you have something that was
special for you, that you would like to share with us, but we don't want
to hear about TV shows and regular things that happened."

While watching a video of "morning news" in one New Zealand
classroom, I noticed that when a white (Pakeha) child showed her doll,
the teacher asked several appreciative questions for more information;
but a few minutes later when a Maori or Pacific Island boy showed a new
scrapbook with a rock-and-roll singer on the cover, it was acknowledged with a very brief, unappreciative, comment. General awareness
of such differential experiences is suggested in an editorial "Farewell to
Peanuts" on the day that the comic strip ended after almost fifty years:

> "It is Charlie Brown, after all, who brings a little red fire truck to show
> and tell on the same day that Linus brings a homemade facsimile of
> the Dead Sea Scrolls." [8]

## Possible Influences on Child and Teacher

As these transcripts show, children and teachers don't always agree on
what to talk about during sharing time and how to share. We have spec-
ulated about several possible influences on these interactions, especially
with the children who tend to tell episodic stories.

One explanation of the teacher's comprehension problems that we
eliminated is that the child narrators are "egocentric" or otherwise not
taking the needs of their audience into account. Both our prototypical
episodic narrators, Deena in California and Leona in Massachusetts, include in their tellings the kind of spontaneous self-corrections that demonstrate both syntactic competence and concern for their listeners. In
*My Puppy*, for example, after Leona has referred to her puppy as "he,"
she self-corrects her reference to "my father" and then also self-corrects
from indirect "he" to direct, quoted discourse "you" (with her self-
corrections in italics):

and / my puppy / he always be followin' me /
and he said / *my father* said / "he—*you* can't go"
[*i.e., the puppy can't follow Leona to school*] [9]

I realize that researchers' appreciation of the children's narratives comes from time-consuming analyses of tapes and transcripts. To teachers who have to respond in real time, the experience is inevitably very different. I only hope this close look will make it more likely, when children fail to meet a teacher's expectations, that the cause will be sought in reasons other than deficiencies in the children themselves.

**Length and complexity of children's narratives.** Episodic stories are, almost by definition, longer than topic-centered ones. Sheer length alone can create problems for the teacher, whose attention is inevitably divided between listening to the speaker of the moment and thinking (even worrying) about the rest of the class: Are they getting restless? How many more children will want a turn? What time is it getting to be anyway?

Episodic stories are also more complex, with shifting scenes and multiple events in various temporal relationships to each other (as in many current novels and films), creating a greater cognitive load on narrators who are still developing their abilities to meet these task demands.[10] Moreover, the increased cognitive load caused by these complex tasks may result in a greater incidence of false starts; repeated or corrected words; and other disfluencies that, in turn, increase the comprehension problems of listeners.

**Topic.** Teachers are inherently at some disadvantage when trying to understand young children's stories about their out-of-school experiences. Some stories, such as *A Hundred Dollars,* are about widely shared experiences with publicly familiar scripts. Carl's explanation about lotteries has extensive problems with vague vocabulary—"this thing," "it makes up to," "this name." But adult listeners would be able to hear through this vagueness to infer some kind of lottery.

Other stories, more often the episodic ones, are about idiosyncratic events of family life, such as when Leona sleeps over at her grandmother's, and how Deena tried to carry an older and heavier friend on her back, which makes it much harder for the listening teacher to make connections and clarify relationships from extra-text knowledge. When we asked Leona's teacher about her problems in understanding sharing time stories, she spoke about an important difference between being a parent and being a teacher:

> It's confusing when you listen, because their time frame is not the same as ours. When my son was six, we would suddenly talk about something from months earlier, and I could understand because I'd been there; I could make the connection. It's different in class. It's hard to make the connection with so many different individuals.

In their comparison of young children's conversations at home and at school, British psychologists generalize this contrast:

> Familiarity helps adults to interpret little children's meanings, and their communications. It also enables them to help children connect together different aspects of their experience. In my study of four year olds at home and at school, I was able to show how the mother's familiarity with her child allowed her to relate the child's present experiences to past and future events, and in this way give added meaning to them. In contrast, the nursery staff, who were relatively unfamiliar with the children, . . . often had difficulty in communicating with them.
>
> Familiarity thus facilitates not only attachment, but responsiveness . . . [and] responsiveness also plays an important part in learning—it is essential if an interactive sequence is to be sustained and if a high level of social skills is to be developed. . . . *Aspects of children's intellectual functioning thus seem to be intimately related to the social relationships in which they are embedded* [*emphasis added*].[11]

We will see throughout this book how true that last sentence is: children's intellectual functioning, at school as at home, is intimately related to the social relationships in which it becomes embedded.

Teachers' lack of familiarity with children's out-of-school lives is especially important in the primary grades. Older students can, and should, take more responsibility for explicating their ideas to teachers and peers. After all, one of the functions of the public school is to give students opportunities to develop their abilities to communicate with a wider world. But the teacher, for her part, has to convey genuine interest and a willingness to learn.

Teachers undoubtedly try to make their comments relevant to the child's story in some way. But as Karen Tracy points out, a conversational maxim "to be relevant" does not tell us what "relevant" means. Is a relevant remark one that responds to anything in the immediately prior discourse? By what criteria can relevancy be judged? In a series of experiments, Tracy presented conversational stories to adult subjects and asked them to evaluate them, or to produce responses. She found that if the story is comprehensible, the preferred response is to the main idea, the point of the story.[12] Among sharing-time narratives, the teachers' responses to *Paper Boat* and *A Hundred Dollars* can be put in this category. But when the stories were more difficult to understand, Tracy found that listeners were more apt to respond with a query or comment about some detail, as the teachers did to Leona's *My Puppy* and *Deena's Day*, that may be relatively unimportant to the child narrator.

**Cultural differences between child and teacher.** In both California- and Boston-area classrooms, the teachers' lack of comprehension and/or appreciation was related to cultural differences between children and teachers. In the California classroom, Mindy is white and Deena is black; in the Boston-area classroom, Carl is white and Leona is black; both teachers are white.[13] We found this pattern to be more general than these two contrasting pairs. In one classroom, for example, 96 percent of the white children's narratives were topic-centered but only 34 percent of the black children's were; and only 27 percent of narratives told by black girls were topic-centered.[14]

We have no certain explanation for these differences in narrative style. In classrooms, as in American life in general, differences in ethnicity are correlated with differences in social class and with experiences with what is loosely referred to as more oral versus more written cultures. Originally, we spoke in terms of the black–white difference simply because that aspect of the speakers' identities was obvious in the classrooms we observed. Since then, we have found related descriptions of black rhetorical style. For example, African American scholar Gineva Smitherman speaks of black adult narrative style as "concrete narrative . . . [whose] meandering away from the 'point' takes the listener on episodic journeys."[15]

To further explore a possible ethnic basis for teachers' responses, Michaels and I conducted a small experiment in which mimicked versions of children's topic-centered and episodic narratives were played for five black and seven white adult informants, all students at the Harvard Graduate School of Education. The mimicked versions, all recorded by a single speaker, maintained the child's rhythm and intonation contours, while changing black dialect grammatical features to standard English (e.g., "we was having" to "we were having" in Leona's *At Grandmother's*), and possible social-class indicators to more neutral expressions (e.g., "down the Cape" to "at the beach" in another story). The adult informants were asked to comment on how well-formed the story was and to evaluate the probable academic success of the child narrator.[16]

The responses of the two groups, though small in number, were strikingly different. White adults were much more likely to find the episodic stories hard to follow, while black adults were much more likely to evaluate positively both topic-centered and episodic stories, noticing differences but appreciating both.

*At Grandmother's* evoked the most divergent responses. White adults were uniformly negative, with comments such as "terrible story," "incoherent," "This kid hops from one thing to the next." When asked to make a judgment about this child's probable academic standing, without exception, they rated her below children who told topic-centered accounts. The black adults' responses were very different. They found this story well-formed, easy to understand, and interesting, "with lots of detail and description." Three of the five selected it as the best of the five stories they heard. All five commented on the "shifts" and "associations" or the "nonlinear" qualities of the story, but this did not appear to disorient them. Two expanded on what the child meant, explaining that the holiday is just like the weekend because it's an occasion when she gets to visit her grandmother who is an important figure in her life. One informant commented that if you didn't make this inference, you missed the entire point—this was exactly the case for the white adults. All but one of the black adults rated the child as highly verbal, very bright, and/or successful in school.[17]

Why these differences? What are the sources of their contexts in the mind, their expectations about topic and form, that black and white professional adults bring to the listening task? Are the black children using systematic intonational and rhythmic cues that white listeners either misinterpret or simply do not hear? Are the black children's story themes, such as staying at grandmother's, or their stylistic features, such as a humorous twist at the end, more immediately familiar to adults from the same cultural background? Do black adults have greater appreciation for a good oral story, regardless of how well or poorly it could be communicated in written form?

Narratives are a universal meaning-making strategy, but there is no one way of transforming experience into a story. In the words of British educator Harold Rosen, narratives are "first and foremost a product of the disposition of the human mind to narratize [*sic*] experience and to transform it into findings which as social beings we may share and compare with those of others." But while "the story is always out there,"

> the important first step still has to be taken. The unremitting flow of events must first be selectively attended to as holding relationships, causes, motives, feelings, consequences—in a word, meanings. To give order to this otherwise unmanageable flux we must take another step and invent, yes, invent, beginnings and ends, for out there are no such things. . . . This is the axiomatic element of narrative: it is the outcome of a mental process which enables us to excise from our experience a meaningful sequence, to place it within boundaries, to set around it the frontiers of the story, to make it resonate in the contrived silences with which we may precede and end it. The narrative ruthlessly edits the raw tape.

Our potential and disposition to construct narratives, Rosen claims, is similar to our potential and disposition to acquire language:

> If we are programmed to learn a language, we must still be exposed to a language in order to learn it and its socially constituted use. In the same way, however universal our human bent for narratizing experience we encounter our own society's modes for doing this. There is no one way of telling stories; we learn the grammars of our society, our culture.[18]

**The teacher's agenda.** In planning for sharing time and in responding at the moment, teachers need to answer a question for themselves:
What is the purpose of sharing time anyway? Some teachers seem to
consider it an opportunity for children to practice a kind of discourse
style that is valued in school, what Michaels calls "an oral preparation
for literacy"—an opportunity for children to compose an oral text that
is as similar as possible to a written composition.

In Michaels' analysis of *Making Candles,* when Mindy's teacher says:
"Tell the kids how you do it from the very start. Pretend we don't know
a thing about candles," she seems to be speaking from an implicit model
of literate discourse. With the help of questions asked by the teacher (or
in some classrooms by other children), sharers are encouraged to be
clear and precise, putting more and more information into words rather
than relying on shared background knowledge (about candle making)
or contextual cues (the candles Mindy is holding) to communicate part
of the intended message. According to this analysis, Mindy is given an
opportunity for practice that some children in the same class, such as
Deena, do not get:

> Sharing time, then, can either provide or deny access to key literacy-
> related experiences depending, ironically, on the degree to which
> teacher and child start out "sharing" a set of discourse conventions and
> interpretive strategies.[19]

Other teachers use traditional sharing time as an opportunity to
teach particular academic frames of reference, shifting children's discourse not only toward putting more of their experiences into words, but
toward different aspects of that experience, thereby hoping to influence
not only conventions of form but also conventions about meanings that
are valued in school. Remember Nancy and her teacher's conflict about
which were the most reportable aspects of her trip to *Old Ironsides* in Boston Harbor. Nancy wanted to talk about the other places she had gone,
including what she had eaten at a "fancy restaurant," while the teacher
wanted her to tell about what she had learned about the historic ship.

Researchers have also noted this kind of topic conflict when the
child starts with dynamic social events and the teacher shifts to more
static attributes of material objects. In a classroom in Appalachia, when
first-grader Nicholas started to talk about the new shirt he had on that
his daddy had given him, the teacher was very appreciative and then
asked what color it was. When Nicholas tried to switch back to family
events—his grandparents coming to visit and going swimming—the
teacher shifted back to the shirt, this time to its snaps (presumably instead of buttons).[20]

Vygotskian scholar James Wertsch reports another example from
an upper-middle class Chicago suburb when Danny shows his piece of

lava. I have deleted unrelated talk from Wertsch's transcription (noted with elipses— . . .) and renumbered the turns.

1 **T:** Danny, please come up here with what you have.
  [*Danny, with piece of lava in his hand, approaches T.*]
  . . .

2 **C:** Where did you get it?

3 **Danny:** From my mom. My mom went to the volcano to get it.
  . . .

4 **T:** Is there anything you want to tell about it?

5 **Danny:** I've had it ever since I was . . . I've always . . . I've always been, um, taking care of it.

6 **T:** Umhum.

7 **Danny:** It's never fallen down and broken.

8 **T:** Umhum. OK. Is it rough or smooth?

9 **Danny:** Real rough and it's . . . and it's . . . and it's sharp.

10 **T:** OK. Why don't you go around and let the children touch it. OK?
  [*Danny takes it around the group, which is sitting on the floor.*]
  Is it heavy or light?

11 **Danny:** It's heavy.

12 **T:** It's heavy.

13 **Danny:** A little bit heavy.

14 **T:** In fact, maybe they could touch it and hold it for a minute to see how heavy it is.
  . . .

  [*While Danny is passing the lava around, another child shares a picture from her dictionary. When she finishes, T borrows the dictionary to look up* volcano *and then* lava, *and reads aloud about how the hot lava cools into hard rock.*]

15 **Danny:** And it's . . . Know what? And it's still . . . it's still . . . Look . . . Shows from where it got . . . from where it was burned.[21]

Danny, like Nancy and Nicholas, starts to tell about events that are part of his personal life history (numbers 5 and 7); the teacher shifts perspective to ask only about qualities of the object, qualities that can here be expressed in binary category systems (rough or smooth in 8, heavy or light in 10).

In Vygotsky's terms, the shift is from Danny's personal and idiosyncratic "sense" and "spontaneous" experiential concepts to the teacher's more systematic, "scientific" concepts, expressed in "explicit standardized taxonomies." Note that Danny followed the teacher into the changed frame, while Nancy and Nicholas did not; and none of the African American children achieved the kind of interaction with the teacher in which such shifts would even have been possible.[22] Wertsch makes a general statement about the significance of this referential perspective in classroom discourse:

> [T]he way teachers often organize classroom discourse reflects the assumption that this [nonexperiential] speech genre *should* be used to describe objects and events. Even if another form of description—or perspective—could be used to describe an object or event accurately and usefully in a particular problem setting, teachers send a strong implicit message that the speech genre of formal instruction is the appropriate one to use in this context. This is part of the classroom's system of "cognitive values."[23]

These traditional (and maybe still typical) sharing-time examples exemplify a pervasive teaching dilemma: How to validate a student's present meaning, often grounded in personal experience, while leading the child into additional meanings, and additional ways with words for expressing them that reflect more public and educated forms of knowledge. This is a dilemma all teachers face throughout the school day and the school years. It is especially acute during sharing time at the beginning of a child's school career.

## Teacher Research on Sharing-Time Innovations

Teachers reading this chapter will have realized that the research reported so far is limited in two important ways: It presents the interaction between child and teacher as a snapshot taken at only one point in time, and it provides only a close-up portrait that ignores the rest of the children. Researchers can be selective in ways teachers cannot. By their very role, teachers want a dynamic picture of children's development over time, and they can never completely block out the whole classroom community. Not surprisingly then, two teachers' research on innovations for sharing time in their classrooms, in a small town in Maine and in a Boston suburb, extends beyond both of these limitations.

### Sharing Time in a Maine Town

Susan Stires reports on the development of sharing time as it evolved over the six years she taught grades K–2 in a small independent "mainstream middle-class" Maine school of which she was one of the cofounders.[24] "*Oral share* . . . was a time for formal presentational talk based on the kids' interests" through which students teach each other what they know and care about and thereby "expand our community."

Some features of oral share stayed the same over the years. Each child was assigned a particular day of the week, four shared each day, and they were expected to prepare for their talk at home. Each child had about ten minutes to talk and respond to questions and comments. Stires sat behind the circle of children taking notes (and videotaping during the final three years) and occasionally participated after the children had finished.

Other features evolved and changed. Because Stires taught a combined grade, K–1 or 1–2, with the younger children staying with her for a second year, traditions initiated by children one year often continued and were added to in the next. When children started asking why the sharer had selected the particular object or event to tall about, sharers began to end with "I brought it for share because . . . " When one second-grade girl provided a title, her classmates quickly adopted titles, and that convention was continued the following year. In keeping with Stires' purpose of oral share as formal presentational talk, she points out that "Having a title attached an importance to the oral text and signified that it was not conversation."

## Sharing Time in Suburban Boston

Karen Gallas was teaching first and second grades in a Boston suburb that deserves its reputation as a community that cares about good schools but whose reality is more mixed in social class and ethnicity than its white, middle-class image. Among its school children, the mix is increased by the presence of African American children from inner city Boston who have been participating in the twenty-five-year-old voluntary METCO program that buses students to suburban schools. In a community that sees itself as progressive, both politically and educationally, the too-frequent underachievement of the African American children has been a continuing concern. Gallas is a long-time member of a teachers' research group that has focused attention on classroom discourse since its inception.[25]

Gallas reports on the development of Jiana, an African American six-year-old, who had moved into a homeless shelter near the school after a traumatic home life and only a few months of kindergarten.[26] Academically she was at a pre-K level, and even had a hard time speaking. "Her speech was filled with stops and starts, long hesitations, and incredible difficulty at finding words for simple objects and ideas." Rather than referring her out of the classroom for clinical help, Gallas decided to wait and see.

Before Jiana appeared in her class, Gallas had already decided to organize sharing time differently this year from last by letting children take more control. Early in the school year, she set up the new sharing-time structure. Each child had a designated day of the week when he or she could share. Each sharer sat in the teacher's chair, first narrating and then fielding questions and comments from peers. Gallas herself sat at the back of the room, participating as little as possible. What ensued, and was captured in Gallas' notes, was a series of transformations in the way the children talked and listened to each other.

The development of Jiana's voice, and that of some of her peers as well, can be glimpsed through a series of four of her stories over the school year. In the beginning, Jiana's narratives were hardly intelligible; but she persevered, and Gallas' attentive listening seemed to keep the rest of the class listening as well. Here is an early story about a half-finished bookmark ("Karen" is the teacher; LEDP is an after-school program).

**Jiana:** I made this at LEDP.

**T:** I don't think they can hear you honey.

**Jiana:** I got this in LEDP, and . . . and I made it . . . and I didn't want it so . . . I'm going to give it to Karen.

**T:** Do you want to tell more before you take questions?

**Jiana:** Questions or comments? . . . Fanny.

**Fanny:** What are you going to make it out of ? What are you going to make it out of?

**Jiana:** I'm not gonna make it.

**Fanny:** But it's not finished . . . Well, you're going to have to show Karen how to do it because she doesn't know how to do it. And also, I think you need a needle for that.

**Jiana:** I know.

**Fanny:** Oh, do you have a needle?

**Jiana:** No.

**Fanny:** A fat one.

As Gallas sat and watched, by their questions, the "other children like Fanny began to teach Jiana how to fill in her narratives."

Three months later, Jiana was taking the sharing chair with a more upright posture and a stronger voice. Here is her recount of a trip she took with her after-school group to the New England Aquarium:

**Jiana:** Oh. Um, and we saw the rainforest, we saw um, um, there was a um, thing on . . . like a say, tree, and there was a, . . . a fake snake, and everybody, and, and some it was a fake snake but it was long and somebody was moving it in back of the thing, and and everybody thought it was a snake and everybody screamed.

**Donald:** Did you scream?

**Jiana:** No! Because . . . 'cause, a a snake couldn't be . . . yellow.

**Several:** Sure it could. It can.

**Jiana:** . . . And we saw, . . . and we saw um, . . . little kinds of shells and we went to the pickup thing, where we pick up um, um, um, this big crab. . . . We get to pit it, pit it, we get to pit it up, and we pitted, picked it up, with some little things and they have a lot of legs.

**Several:** Starfish! Starfish!

**Jiana:** Yeah. Starfish.

About this time, after other children's stories Jiana also began commenting more, telling how, for example, she had cats too. Although Gallas didn't believe all Jiana's "me too" extensions, she kept quiet.

Another month later, Jiana told the class some details about her personal life:

**Jiana:** My father was on stage talking to his friends, and he did it, he was in this program. My father doing it . . . did something bad, and he's in a program, and I can't tell you why. . . . It's something white. . . . It starts with a *c* but, I don't want to tell. And it's called . . . cocaine. . . . And that's why he's in the program, and he'll never come out.

**Robin:** What do you mean by what you said, your father's doing it? I don't understand.

**Jiana:** It's like something bad, like mommy goes in a closet . . . and I say, "what are you doing?" She says, "You don't need to know," and she's sneaking a cigarette. And I say, "That's not good for you. . . ."

Gallas describes the scene:

> The children listened carefully to her explanations, and there was a feeling of extreme seriousness in the group. They wanted to understand and questioned her closely about the meaning of the words. They empathized, and they gave support; and as the discussion expanded, I was not uncomfortable because Jiana was very composed. She wasn't ashamed. She was just telling her story . . . .

In the middle of the school year, Jiana started telling stories that were clearly fantasy—for example, about a trip to the zoo when the zookeeper took gorillas out for her mother to pet. Gallas' immediate response was to blurt out a reminder, which she later regretted, that sharing time was for "true" stories. But Jiana persisted, and on subsequent days, a few children tried to tell similar stories, while others followed Gallas' example in criticizing their peers. Gallas finally asked herself why she had defined the sharing narrative to mean only true stories; she apologized to Jiana and announced that during the next month, children could tell stories that were either true or "fake"—the children's word for fantasy.

Again, Jiana led the way into a new sharing-time transformation. As her fluency and responsiveness to and from her peers increased, she told a fantasy story that included as characters the teacher and every child in the class:

**Jiana:** When I went to Mars, um, Karen and Karen K., um, they had little pieces of hair sticking up [*laughter*] and, um, and Karen, uh, Karen [*whispers to me, pointing to the rosebud necklace I am wearing, "What are those?" I answer, "Roses . . . rosebuds, rosebuds"*] and when Karen had the rosebuds on, she had her little kid with her . . .

**Others:** She doesn't have one!

**Jiana:** And it was Robin . . .
**Others:** Ahhhhh . . .

These fictional and inclusive narratives flourished, much to the enjoyment of most of the class. Most but not all. Gallas noticed that some
of the Caucasian children, especially the boys, were uncomfortable with
this new type of story. They muttered, "This isn't funny," became openly
inattentive, and refused to try to tell fictional stories themselves. Jiana
kept trying to include those boys, carefully and courteously; and Gallas
increased the pressure on "some very competent mainstream speakers"
to try:

> William, for example, . . . absolutely would not make any attempt at
> the fantasy format. I literally had to force him to try it by refusing to
> let him share some X-rays of his brother's broken arm until he told us
> a fake story. After I realized how different and challenging the fictional
> narratives were, I asked every child to try at least one fake story be-
> fore they returned to a showing format.

By the end of the year, when Jiana herself had vanished, it was clear
that all the children had expanded their narrative discourses, "and continued to work on these skills long after Jiana had left us."

In her conclusions, Gallas emphasizes the relationship between storytelling and the development of a classroom culture. Citing both U.S.
kindergarten teacher Vivian Paley and Russian literary theorist Mikhail
Bakhtin,[27] she argues that it was the inclusive classroom community,
which the stories both came from and built, that enabled the children
to learn from each other:

> Jiana's strong desire to master the sharing discourse was completely
> bound up with her desire to become part of our community. . . . In the
> same way, the other children in the class, in trying to understand her
> speech plan, further pulled her into the discourse, making it easier for
> her to appropriate their language forms to her purposes.

Note the work—listening and intervening—that Gallas had to do
to try to keep the mix of sharing-time discourse styles in balance. The
children, whatever their discourse background, spoke in a single discourse forum. But just immersing children from different discourse
communities in that shared forum was not enough. The teacher had to
make it welcoming and respectful for all speakers. Then, with their equal
status within the group sustained by the teacher, and the availability of
alternative models actively encouraged, and even scheduled, the children could reciprocally appropriate discourse models from each other.
In the process, they transformed the relational aspects of their own
identities as well.

In a later book about other children she has taught, Gallas makes it
clear that such transformations of relationships and identities don't hap-

pen quickly or easily.[28] While working on that book, she responded to my summary of her work with Jiana:

> I think since doing that work that I have found out more about the process. The goal of sustaining equal status is one I aspire to, but it is such a difficult one to achieve. . . . Metaphorically, [for the child] "I stand up to be acknowledged as myself, and then to be embraced by my friends." It is a hopeful sort of quest, one that certainly requires faith that the teacher will make it safe, but one that also knows safety is not a given. And in the end, it is that desire that pushes the child to take the plunge and develop new ways of talking, thinking and being.
>
> I realize that I came to this awareness in the process of researching and then writing my new book. Much of the children's social work was done in that sharing-time space, and I was not in total control of it; I could not make it completely safe or maintain that equal status. And I have to say that was a very painful realization at first. Later I was able to see the function of the space not being totally safe. It is real-life learning. (Personal communication, December 1997)

## Further Thoughts

To see if their objectives are being achieved, teachers need to decide what their objectives are for this particular time in the classroom day, and then monitor what happens over time in the interrelated development of children's discourse and their social relationships within the classroom community. The sharing-time participant structures described here should not be taken as models, but rather as imagined alternatives for reflection, adaptation, and further research by teachers or classroom observers.

Some other classroom activities are similar and different in important ways. Writing conferences in which the teacher responds to a student's written text are a more private form of interaction, but they can entail the same tension between the child's intended meaning and the teacher's valued form. Dialogue journals change the medium of teacher–student interaction to writing, and they may have a more fixed and specialized purpose, depending on the subject of the journals.[29] But the development of oral- and written-language competencies, and of social relationships and personal identities, permeate each and every school day.

## Notes

1. From Dorr-Bremme 1982.

2. By *traditional* sharing time, I have in mind primarily classrooms in the United States, and secondarily what is called "morning news" in England

(Dinsmore 1986), Australia (Christie 1990) and my observations. Poveda [in press] compares "la ronda" in Spain with sharing time in the U.S.A.

3. In his study of "morning news" time in England, Dinsmore (1986) mentions in passing interesting differences between official news time and unofficial, informal conversations that take place as children arrive at school. A comparison of the same event narrated in these contrasting contexts could yield important information about how young children shift between them and their perceptions of the kind of language appropriate for each one. A teacher researcher, hearing an informal telling of an interesting experience, could say to the narrator: "How interesting! Why don't you tell everyone about that in morning news?"

4. Michaels 1981; Michaels and Cazden 1986; Cazden, Michaels, and Tabors 1985.

5. For further discussions of transcription forms and functions, see Baker 1997; Edwards and Westgate 1994, 60–74; and, more theoretically, Ochs 1979.

6. Pratt 1977, 103–104.

7. Several of Leona's episodic narratives have been reformatted and reanalyzed by Gee (1985, 1986), Gee et al. (1992), and Hymes (1996, Ch. 8). These elegant linguistic analyses, made from tapes and earlier transcriptions, show Leona using linguistic and literary devices that attest to her considerable resources, even if expressed in forms that no one listening on the spot, moment to moment, is likely to hear. Solsken et al. 2000 contrast the interpretations of another child's oral stories by teacher and researchers. The traditional sharing-time interactions can also be considered an example of a more general phenomenon present in the non-school world: a tension between narrative structure and a question–answer format required by a particular institutional setting. Linde (1999) analyzes interviews in a social service agency; other institutional settings include doctor's offices and courtrooms.

8. Editorial, *New York Times* January 1, 2000, p. A22.

9. Cazden, Michaels, and Tabors 1985 give more examples.

10. Berman and Slobin et al. (1994) give a detailed and cross-linguistic analysis of children's developing narrative abilities from age three through nine; Berman (1995) includes a short summary of that book. Bartlett and Scribner (1981) look specifically at children's developing ability to make clear references to multiple same-sex characters, as in Leona's *My Puppy.*

11. Tizard 1986, 29–30. Tizard and Hughes (1984) is a book-length version of this research.

12. Tracy 1984.

13. I happen to know that Jerry and Nancy's teacher, observed in Dorr-Bremme 1982, is white; her children's ethnicities are not given.

14. See also Heath's contrasting descriptions of children's stories in (black) Trackton and (white) Roadville communities in Appalachia (1983, 294–310); especially, see Nellie's story (Table 8–30) that, like Leona's, happens to be about her puppy.

15. Smitherman 1977 (1986). I adopted the adjective "episodic" from Smitherman, hoping it would seem less pejorative than Michaels' "topic-associating." In their edited book on Ebonics, Perry and Delpit recommend Smitherman's book as "still the best introduction to the study of Black Language available. It is required reading for teachers who work with African American children" (1998, 205).

16. This "match guise" experimental research technique has been used extensively to reveal language attitudes in bilingual settings; Lambert et al. (1960) give an early description.

17. Perez and Tager-Flusberg 1998 compared the responses of clinicians from hospital and community health clinics to transcriptions of narratives from European American, African American, and Latino children. They found that clinicians' ethnicity did not matter, and that the clinicians as a group responded most negatively to the Latino children's narratives. They conclude that "clinicians trained and practicing in the United States tend to adopt a Euro-American perspective" and "seem to be penalizing [Latino children] for not conforming to the Euro-American structure" (181).

18. Rosen 1984, 12–14. Martin, a teacher of Native American Arapaho children in Wyoming, provides another culturally based contrast with topic-centered narratives and an Arapaho elder's explanation of the traditional style (1987, 166–67).

19. Michaels 1981, 423. This first article by Michaels is her most complete analysis from this perspective.

20. Danielewicz et al. 1996.

21. Wertsch 1991, 113–18.

22. A remarkably similar example comes from a Danish study (with translated excerpts) reported by Chaudron 1980. When a third grader relates an experience with a blackbird nest in a discussion about birds, the teacher asks a series of questions about the nest's height.

23. Wertsch 1991, 116.

24. Stires 1998, manuscript.

25. Gallas et al. 1996.

26. Gallas 1992.

27. Gallas cites Paley (1990), one of her many accounts of her early childhood classrooms starting in 1979; Bakhtin 1981.

28. Gallas 1998.

29. Among the many descriptions of writing conferences, two focus on this tension: Michaels 1985b and Diamondstone (2000). Dialogue journals were first analyzed by Staton et al. 1988, and then as assistance to English language learners by Peyton and Staton 1993. Teacher researchers Reddy et al. (1998) have built on that work in using dialogue journals for the development of children's discourse about science, discussed in Chapter 7.

# Chapter Three

# Traditional and Nontraditional Lessons

**T:** Where were you born, Prenda?

**P:** San Diego.

**T:** You were born in San Diego, all right. Can you come up and find San Diego on the map?

**P:** (goes to the board and points)

**T:** Right there okay.

---

**T:** "Three quarters of the crayons in Mrs. R.'s box are broken. How many unbroken crayons are there?"

**S:** Sean offers to show his solution. "It would be four." [He draws and talks at the chalkboard.]

**T:** "Why . . . " I begin to ask, but Sean interrupts, changing his mind [redraws four groups of three]. Riba, waving her hands, disagrees.

**T:** I ask for other students' reactions.[1]

Anyone hearing the sequence of talk in the top dialogue will recognize it immediately as a traditional lesson. The three-part sequence of teacher Initiation, student Response, and teacher Evaluation (IRE) or teacher Feedback (IRF), may still be the most common classroom discourse pattern at all grade levels. It is certainly the oldest, with a long and hardy life through many decades of formal Western-type schooling. Even traditional sharing time, discussed in Chapter Two, fits this participant structure:

- Teacher calls on a child to share.

- Nominated child tells a narrative.

- Teacher comments on the narrative.

30

In linguistic terminology, IRE, or IRF, is the *unmarked* pattern; in computer terminology, it is the *default option*—doing what the system is set to do "naturally" unless someone makes a deliberate change. Sometimes it is called *recitation*, but I will refer to it simply as the talk of "traditional lessons" to stress, for now, only the fact of longevity.

In contrast, the sequence of talk in the bottom dialogue is obviously different; it is the result of a change in educational goals and therefore in the nature of classroom discourse. Taken from a kind of lesson widely advocated during the 1990s, in deliberate contrast to the IRE/IRF model, these lessons are referred to by a variety of names—"reform," "ambitious," "inquiry" or "discourse-intensive". No one name has been adopted generally. To contrast with *traditional,* I will refer to such lessons simply as *nontraditional.*

Excerpts from both traditional and nontraditional lessons are presented in this chapter, plus a discussion of significant structural and functional features. Chapter Five contains further discussion of the dimensions of difference—dimensions that can serve as components of lesson design for teachers and the focus of lesson analysis by researchers.

## Traditional Lessons

### *Example One: Birthplaces*

The first example comes from Mehan's analysis of nine lessons in the primary classroom I taught in San Diego twenty-five years ago.[2] I have kept this admittedly old example for two reasons: Mehan still provides the most detailed analysis of traditional lesson structure; and because I was the teacher in these lessons, I can be more frankly critical of their limitations from the perspective of our current more complex and ambitious educational goals than if I presented only talk from other teachers' classrooms.

The nine lessons Mehan analyzed took place from September to January. Included here is an excerpt from a November lesson that he calls "Birthplaces," which includes the interaction on the top at the beginning of this chapter. It was part of a social studies unit that had two objectives. One objective was for the children to make and begin to understand maps. They had made individual maps of the classroom, including their and their peers' desks, and a group map of the school. Now we changed the scale again and were locating where individual children and their parents were born on a commercial wall map of the United States and northern Mexico.

The second purpose was more personal. I hoped to lessen the social distance between myself as a visiting teacher from Massachusetts and the California children by displaying on the map the shared experience, via parents or grandparents, of geographical mobility: We or our families had all come to San Diego from somewhere else.[3]

After the children were seated facing the map, the teacher (T, as I will refer to the person in that role) explained:

**T:** Some people did some good homework last night in finding out where they were, were born or where your family, your parents came from. . . . If you know where your parents came from, we're going to put their names up with green paper and pin them right on the map [*demonstrating*]. Now some people were already telling me as soon as they came into school this morning that they had some, that they had some, they knew some things to put on the, to put on the map.

Prenda was the first child called on. (She is African American and all of her peers are either African American or Mexican American.) Figure 3–1 gives a transcript of the sequence about Prenda's family. The assignment of turns to the three IRE columns, and the comments in the fourth column, are Mehan's. I have added horizontal lines to separate his Topically Related Sets.

According to Mehan's analysis, in this lesson the essential "basic" sequence includes "determining each student's (or family member's) birthplace, locating that place on the map, and placing that information on the map." Discussion of Prenda's birthplace (turns 5–7) has only that basic sequence, but discussions of where Prenda's mother and father were born extend beyond the basic sequence to optional "conditional" sequences about the basis of student knowledge (12–17) or the relative distance between cities (31–34). Mehan calls the combination of basic plus conditional sequences a Topically Related Set (TRS). In these lessons, the T's evaluations always occur at the end of sets, but not necessarily after each student response within them. While many other analyses of traditional lesson structure have found the IRE triadic sequence, Mehan was the first to identify the higher TRS structure, and many citations to his work fail to mention this structural unit.

Anyone reading this transcription can speculate about alternative assignments of utterances to columns. For example, the following coding of sequences 22 through 25 seems plausible.

| *Initiation* | *Response* | *Evaluation* |
|---|---|---|
| **T:** I don't, I wonder if anybody knows. | **C:** It's on there with a B, huh? | **T:** Um, well, yes, it is on here with a B. |
| **T:** Uh, Prenda's father [*writing on paper*]. | **C:** I see it— | |

**Figure 3–1**
Transcript of lesson segment about Prenda's family

| Initiation | Response | Evaluation | Comments |
|---|---|---|---|
| 5 **Teacher:** Uh, Prenda, ah, let's see if we can find, here's your name. Where were you you born, Prenda? | **Prenda:** San Diego. | **Teacher:** You were born in San Diego, all right. | 5 Individual nomination of Prenda |
| 6 **Teacher:** Um, can you come up and find San Diego on the map? | **Prenda:** *(goes to board and points)* | **Teacher:** Right there, okay. | 6 Teacher acknowledges answers, even to questions for which only Prenda knows the answer. |
| 7 **Teacher:** So, we will put you right there *(pins paper on map).* | | | |
| 8 **Teacher:** Now, where, where did, where was your mother born, where did your mother come from? | **Wallace:** *(raises hand)* <br><br> **Prenda:** Oh, Arkansas. | **Teacher:** Okay. | 8 Wallace bids nonverbally at end of basic sequence but does not get the floor. Instead Prenda's turn continues. |
| 9 **Teacher:** Prenda's mother *(writes on paper).* | | | |
| 10 **Teacher:** Um, now we *(pause)* I did point out Arkansas on the map yesterday. | **Prenda:** I know where Arkansas is. | | 10 A two-part IR sequence |
| 11 **Teacher:** Can you, do you know where it is, Prenda? | **Wallace:** *(points from his seat toward Arkansas on the map).* <br><br> **Prenda:** *(goes to the board and points).* | **Teacher:** Yeah, good for you. | |

*(continued)*

**Figure 3–1**

Transcript of lesson segment about Prenda's family (*continued*)

| Initiation | Response | Evaluation | Comments |
|---|---|---|---|
| 12 **Teacher:** How did, how did you come, how did you know that? | | | 12 A metaprocess question that asks child to reflect on the basis of knowledge. The teacher's evaluation is simultaneously a negative sanction of Carolyn for interrupting, and a request to Prenda to repeat, though neither is explicit in the words of her utterance. |
| | **Prenda:** [Cause I—<br><br>**Carolyn:** [—this morning. | **Teacher:** Wait a minute, wait a minute. I didn't, couldn't hear what Prenda said. | |
| 13 **Teacher:** What? | **Prenda:** *(Turns head away)* | | |
| 14 **Teacher:** Who told you? Who told you? | **Prenda:** Carolyn did she told me where it was, where Arkansas was. | | |
| 15 **Teacher:** Carolyn, how did you remember where it was? It's kind of in the middle of the country and hard to find out. | **Carolyn:** Uh, cuz, cuz, all three of the grandmothers *(pause)* cuz, cuz, miss Coles told us to find it and she said it started with an A and I said there *(pointing)* and it was right there. | **Teacher:** Uh hum. | |
| 16 **Prenda:** Little Rock | | **Teacher:** Yes, and I thought maybe you remembered, | |

(*continued*)

*(continued)*

| Initiation | Response | Evaluation | Comments |
|---|---|---|---|
| | | because, Carolyn, you mentioned Little Rock yesterday. | |
| 17 **Teacher:** Okay, well so this is green for your mother or your father, and we'll put that *(pins card to map).* | | **Prenda:** My father wasn't born there. | 17 Prenda's evaluation also functions to initiate sequence of talk about father, the logical next topic. |
| 18 **Teacher:** Well that says mother. | | | |
| 19 **Teacher:** Do you know where your father was born? | **Prenda:** *(nod yes)* | | |
| 20 **Teacher:** Where was he born? | **Prenda:** Baltimore, Maryland. | **Teacher:** Really, oh good! | |
| 21 **Carolyn:** Where's that at? | | **Teacher:** Now, where's that at? That's a good question, Carolyn. | 21 Carolyn's question is both well slotted in timing and appropriate in content and receives a meta evaluation (on talk itself) from teacher. |
| 22 **Teacher:** I don't, I wonder if anybody knows. | | | |
| 23 **Carolyn:** It's on there with a B, huh? | **Teacher:** Um, well, yes, it is on there with a B. | | |
| 24 **Teacher:** Uh, Prenda's father *(writing on paper).* | | | |
| 25 **Carolyn:** I see it— | | | |

*(continued)*

**Figure 3–1**

Transcript of lesson segment about Prenda's family (*continued*)

| *Initiation* | *Response* | *Evaluation* | *Comments* |
|---|---|---|---|
| 26 **Teacher:** I think I'll have to tell you that because I don't think there's any way that you would know. It's way over . . . here.⌐ <br> **Carolyn:** Here. | | | |
| 27 **Teacher:** Maryland is MD, and there's Baltimore. | | | |
| 28 **Teacher:** Can you see it from where you are with a B? | **Many:** ⌐Yeah. <br> **Carolyn:**└There it is right there. <br> **Many:** [*Noise*] | | |
| 29 **Teacher:** [*Beckons Prenda to map*] | **Prenda:** [*Goes to map, locates Baltimore*] | **Teacher:** Baltimore and that circle. | |
| 30 **Teacher:** Now, now let's . . . | | | |
| 31 **Wallace:** That's ten times farther than . . . | | | 31 Wallace initiates verbally at a reasonable place—preceding sequence is completed and teacher *now* indicates a new beginning. The content of his comment is unexpected in contrast to Carolyn's (21) but relevant. |
| 32 —: Can I do it? | | | |
| 33 **Teacher:** And now, now let's what were somebody was saying something about ten times or something what? | **Wallace:** That's ten times, and that, far from, ah, San Diego. | **Teacher:** Yes, it is, far from San Diego. | |
| 34 **Teacher:** Uh, Prenda, who came, who came from a, who came farther: your mother from Arkansas to San Diego or your father from Baltimore to San Diego? | **Prenda:** My father. | **Teacher:** Yes, he came ah, he came a long, a long way. | |

Plus, I would consider Prenda's utterance in 16—"Little Rock"—as an additional response to T's initiation in 15 rather than a student initiation. But such small changes do not diminish the value of Mehan's overall TRS structural analysis.

**Topical relationships among utterances.** Tying parts of a sequence of talk together can hold across a considerable stretch of discourse within the larger TRS structure, not just between immediately consecutive utterances. "How did you know that?"—asked at the beginning of sequence 12 about Prenda's ability to locate Arkansas on the map— is not answered until sequence 16, ten turns later, and Carolyn's question in 21 about the location of Baltimore isn't answered until 27 through 29. This means that at any moment criteria of "relevance" may be more complex—for students and teacher alike—than if governed only by the immediately preceding utterance.[4]

**The dual dimensions of discourse structure.** So far, we have been talking about the sequential dimension of lessons (and many other human events): What functional categories are expected to follow after each other (initiation, then response, and so on). There is also a selectional dimension, which constrains the particular actions that are acceptable in each functional slot, in these same events.

Consider the structure of a typical American restaurant menu. There is a set of categories (with names like "appetizer" or "dessert") in a particular order. The appetizer is never at the end nor is dessert at the beginning, and permissable variations are rare. Only the beverage, and sometimes the salad, can be moved about in the sequence to suit individual or cultural differences in taste. That's the sequential dimension. Then, within each of the categories, there are options: a choice of appetizers, main courses, and so on. That's the selectional dimension of the menu structure.[5]

Another cultural product illustrating these two dimensions is the set of three spaces on many application forms into which the date is to be inserted. The sequential dimension is the series of these three spaces; the selectional dimension consists of the particular numbers to be inserted in each slot. People who have filled in such forms outside the United States may have realized that there are cultural differences in the conventional sequence: month-day-year in the United States, but day-month-year in England and many other countries. Culturally based expectations about event structure and expected behaviors built on experience, often out-of-our-awareness, can lead to mistakes in a new environment. Making a mistake in writing the date is a trivial example of a profoundly important aspect of classroom discourse in an increasingly diverse world that we will explore further in later chapters.

We can ask questions about selectional aspects of Birthplaces. How is it that in sequence 6, T's question to Prenda—"Can you come up and find San Diego on the map?"—is understood immediately and un-equivocally not as a yes/no question (which grammatically it is) but as a command to act (which Prenda follows). Sinclair and Coulthard, two British linguists, have focused much of their analysis of classroom discourse on such form–function relationships. Their answer would be the following:

- The subject of the utterance, *you,* is the addressee, Prenda.
- The action, *getting up to find a city on the map,* is permissable.
- The utterance contains a modal verb, *can.*
- The form is a closed yes/no question (not an open wh- question).
- The question refers to an *action* that is feasible at the moment (and, one could add, obviously appropriate to the lesson as T introduced it).

Thus, Prenda's immediate interpretation of the teacher's intended meaning is as a directive for action.[6]

As Sinclair and Coulthard point out, preconditions for the inter-pretation of such indirect directives in abstract speech–act theory—"B (addressee) has the ability to do X" and "A" (speaker) has the right to tell "B to do X"—can, in lessons, be derived from the culturally under-stood rights and obligations of classroom participants. They do not need to be invoked separately for the interpretation of a particular utterance. To take another example in which grammatical form does not corre-spond to communicative intent, in 12 the teacher's evaluation consists of a repeated imperative, "Wait a minute," plus a declarative statement, "I didn't, couldn't hear what Prenda said." Functionally, these utter-ances tell Carolyn to stop speaking out of turn and request Prenda to repeat what she had just said.

In secondary science lessons, Lemke found other examples of such complex form–function relationships. "I can't hear you, Ian," spoken after the nominated student Ian's turn is overlapped by another student, Rosie, is intended by the teacher as a request to Ian to repeat what he has just said and an admonition to Rosie. And "C'mon. I mean I was looking at you when you did it. Be a little subtle," said to a student who had just thrown a paper wad, invokes not only the norm against throw-ing things but also the "deeply implicit convention that violations done 'while teacher is looking' may be presumed deliberate challenges to teacher's authority, acts of defiance, and not just lapses from rules."[7]

These indirect directives exemplify two features of all discourse: the lack of one-to-one correspondence between syntactic form and inter-actional function, and the expression of social meaning in the choice of any particular formal alternative. Teachers have to make many demands on students, demands both to act in certain ways and to refrain from acting in other ways. Conventions of language use give speakers many ways of requesting action from another person in addition to bald imperatives, and teachers take advantage of these options in complex ways, hoping that students will both correctly interpret and willingly comply with their intended requests.

**Structure and improvisation.** Descriptions of human behavior require both searching for repeated patterns and acknowledging, even with admiration, the inevitable improvisation. The repeated patterns— which we call the *structure* of the event, or the *rules* that the participants seem to tacitly follow—can be formally analyzed. But that is only part of Mehan's analysis.

If we were trying to describe the competence of jazz musicians, for example, we would have to attend to both their knowledge of a musical system (a set of notes constituting a scale, and rules for combining them sequentially and simultaneously), and their ability to use that knowledge in creative ways at particular moments. The same is true of speakers: They act on more than the general rules. In the words of Mehan and one of his colleagues, classroom discourse can be characterized as "negotiated conventions—spontaneous improvisations on basic patterns of interaction."[8] During the extended discussion about Prenda's family, Carolyn's question, "Where's that at?" (21, about Baltimore) is an unexpected student initiation, and Wallace's later comment about relative distances from San Diego (31) is unexpected with respect to topic as well. Both can be considered improvisations that contribute substantively to the lesson and prompt T to equally improvised responses.

Frederick Erickson, an educational anthropologist who is also an accomplished musician, makes improvisation more than a metaphor in his rhythmic analysis in the form of musical notation of variations on a theme (patterns of behavior) in a primary classroom's math lesson. At the end, he comments:

> From examination of a number of instances of the performance of a small lesson sequence, an underlying ideal model [canonical form] was inferred. . . . Looking closely at the performance of an instance of the lesson sequence, however, one sees that it is generally discrepant in some features of specific organization from the general, inferred model. If one is not simply to regard these discrepancies as random error (free variation), one has at least two options: to elaborate the formalization of the model by stating an embedded system of optional rules; or to assume that what is happening is adaptive variation, specific to the immediate circumstances of practical action in the moment of enactment.[9]

In his analysis of lesson structure, Mehan (like Erickson) has chosen the second alternative.

Like a group of musicians improvising together, speech events, including classroom discourse, can only be accomplished by the collaborative work of two or more persons. In this sense, *school* is always a performance that must be constituted through the participation of a group of actors. Teacher and students may have different visions of how the performance should be performed, so the teacher assumes the dual role of stage director and chief actor. She may even consider herself the only "native speaker" in the classroom culture, yet she has to depend on "immigrant" students for help in enacting a culturally defined activity.

Descriptions of both the structure and the improvisational quality of traditional lessons not only sharpen our understanding of such events but also constitute a claim about the communicative competence of the participants—what it is a member knows in knowing how to participate. In this case of lessons, these descriptions constitute a claim and a hypothesis, about the communicative competence of teacher and students.

For the teacher, we can assume that, in its canonical form, the traditional lesson acts as an idealized script in the teacher's head that is the residue of her teaching experience and her many years of an "apprenticeship of observation" as a student herself.[10] But the communicative competence of students, especially in the early school years, develops gradually—about discourse expectations for school in general, for each teacher in particular, even for each subject area. Just as a description of a language (a grammar) asserts hypotheses about what the speaker of a language must learn, so a structural description of a lesson asserts hypotheses about what children must learn in order to participate fully and be judged as competent speakers and students.

### Example Two: Measuring Time

A more recent analysis of traditional lessons consists of two science lessons from Gordon Wells' research in a multilingual and mixed-social-class school in Toronto.[11] The focus of Wells' article is a reevaluation of this traditional lesson structure—which he calls *I*nitiation, *R*esponse, *F*eedback (IRF)—in the face of continuing controversy over its function and value.

The two lessons are part of a larger, six-week science unit about measuring time in a combined grades 3 and 4 class. According to the teacher's objectives for the unit as a whole, the students should gain first-hand experience with the practical problems of measuring time by working through specific measuring problems in an imagined world without clocks and watches; they should also supplement their hands-on activities with reference books and keep a science journal. "In addition to conferences with small groups about work in progress, [the teacher] also intended to have meetings with the whole group in order to plan and review the work they were doing and to relate what they were discovering to their existing knowledge and experience."[12] The lessons excerpted here focus on planning and then on reviewing and reflecting. Although Wells does not give the teacher's name, he refers to "her," and I will also.

Figure 3–2 shows Wells' transcription of a small-group planning conference with three girls—Emily and Lily are Chinese Canadians, Veronica is a Caucasian Canadian. Wells presented the discourse in a single column as in the examples at the beginning of this chapter and numbered the turns. He uses periods between words to indicate short pauses, and no periods at the end of sentences. I have added horizontal lines suggesting boundaries between TRSs, using topic shifts as the criterion.

This planning excerpt can be divided into two TRSs—how to measure time for the bottle to empty (sequences 1–9) and how to do a fair test (9–36)—that then become the assignments for small-group work.

At the end of the unit, T leads a review discussion with the whole group. Here, according to Wells, the T's intention

> was to consolidate the learning that had been taking place in the small groups by talking it over in the group as a whole, thereby making it "common knowledge" . . . [and moving the students] to a more principled understanding of some of the key ideas they had encountered. . . . At the same time, however, she wanted to hear and validate the students' opinions both because she considered them to be important in their own right and because she wanted the common knowledge that was constructed to develop from the sense that *they* had made as well as from the conventionally accepted beliefs in the scientific community."[13]

T opens the review by asking, "What have you learned about time?"

Figure 3–3 presents a section of this review that returns to the theme of experimental methodology, here in relation to an activity on pendulums. Again, I have added suggestions for four TRSs: why we control variables (sequences 41–45), which variables Tema's and Veronica's groups controlled (45–49 and 49–73), and the general scientific significance of fair tests (73–75). Substantively, all are aspects of the developing "common knowledge" of the class about doing science.

**The third slot as Feedback, not just Evaluation.** We can see from these two transcriptions why Wells believes Feedback, rather than Evaluation, is a more apt name for the third part of the triadic dialogue. In

**Figure 3–2**

Transcript of a small-group planning conference

---

Immediately before this episode, the teacher (T) and students (Emily, Lily, Veronica) have been looking at the textbook they are using, in which instructions are given for performing the activity.

  1 **T:** Here the picture (a cartoon of children doing the activity) suggests that you can clap, but are there other ways that you can use to figure out how long it takes for the bottle to empty?

  2 **E:** Stamp your feet.

  3 **T:** Stamp your feet, good. another way?

  4 **E:** Er snap

  5 **T:** Snap . . .

  6 **L:** (*Stopwatch*)

  7 **T:** No, you're not supposed to use a clock and a watch

  8 **V:** \*\*\*\*

  9 **T:** OK, so I put the problem to you: Think of as many ways as you can . to figure out the time it takes . for you [Emily] to empty the bottle compared to her [Lily], compared to er Veronica

---

Now the next problem I would like you to think about is . . what are— what the three of you are doing . is it a fair test? The meaning of "fair test" is if you empty a bottle—say if you [Emily] fill the bottle half. and Veronica fills her bottle full . would it be a fair test?

 10 **V:** No

 11 **E:** No . you have to—if I filled my bottle half and to make that a fair test she would fill her bottle half

 12 **T:** That's right . and what about Lily's bottle?

 13 **E:** She would fill her bottle *half*

 14 **T:**                                          *half*

So all your three bottles must have the same amount of water
Now how do you ensure the same amount of water?

 15 **E:** Well .

 16 **T:** Do you just estimate?

 17 **E, V:** No

 18 **T:** Ah-ha!

(*continued*)

*(continued)*

---

Do we have measuring jugs?

19 **E, V:** (nod)

20 **T:** Ah-hah!
So maybe you need to use a measuring jug and say—use the measuring jug, you're going to fill each bottle two hundred and fifty milliliters of water . so then you all have the same amount of water
What's the second *fair test?*
If you use a pop bottle [to Emily] and you use a milk bottle [to Veronica] and she [Lily] uses a pop can, would it be a fair test?

21 **E, V, L:** No

22 **T:** No, why? Because *the*—

23 **E:**                     *the* * of the pop bottle may be bigger,
                    *than* my bottle or the milk bottle

24 **V:**                     *hers*

25 **T:** That's right. that might not be a fair test either
Not so much that the bottle is bigger but—
Let's take the three things and have a look
*(The girls each pick up the bottle they have chosen)*

26 **T:** Are they the same size? *(indicating the bottle mouths)*

27 **V:** No

28 **T:** Are they the same size? (to Emily)

29 **E:** No

30 **T:** Would water fall— flow—
How would water flow through these two?

31 **E:** ***

32 **T:** What would you predict? Which would be faster?

33 **V:** That one would be faster *(pointing to one of the bottles)*

34 **T:** Right

35 **E:** * * * *

36 **T:** So for a fair test for the three of you you must make sure . that even if the bottles are different shapes that they have the same—they look—they release the water at the same . time . . the mouth of the bottle must be more or less the same size
So it would be good if the three of you take Five Alive bottles or the three of you take pop bottles

---

**Figure 3–3**

Transcript of a review discussion

---

41 **T:** OK, why must we control our variables?

42 **Te:** Because if we don't, the time won't be accurate and so you won't get the correct timing

43 **T:** Not so much the time is not accurate, what is not accurate?

44 **Bi:** It's not a fair test

45 **T:** It's not a fair test . a fair test (*writing*)
Your experiments are your test . the fair test—or your science experiment (*writing*) . . . or what you call your science testing—your testing— all your various methods would not be . fair, "fair" here meaning (*writing*) . . consistent, right? . .

---

Remember when you did the pendulum, when one group did the bob. changing the weight of the bob, one group changing the type of bob, one group changing the release height . and all of us did changing the length . that—what— when you want to change the release height what was constant? What was the variable we held constant? Your group? [to Tema]

46 **Te:** Our group . we um. Had to change it and we kept on skipping the same amount

47 **T:** No, you're not listening to my question, Tema I said when we were testing—finding out whether . the release height made a difference, what was—what were the variables you kept constant? . . .

48 **Te:** What we kept constant was the same— the same length of string, the same um amount of bob * * *

49 **T:** *That's right*, the same bob, and the same length of string . and what you would change was your . release height.

---

In your group, what was— what was the one you did? Veronica?

50 **V:** Um we did er the same thing and we had to add them on

(*continued*)

the planning conference, T uses her turn in this slot not only to evaluate student responses to the problems posed for the activities they are to carry out and the predictions they are asked to make, but also uses the Feedback turn to extend their responses. It is especially important to reinforce the criteria for a "fair test" (in 20 and 36). As Wells also points out, T incorporates some of the specialized science *register* into both Initiations and Feedback: for example, "fair test" (4, 6, 7), "compared to" (3), "estimate" (5), "measuring" and "millileters" (5), and "predict" (7).[14]

**Figure 3–3** (*continued*)

51  **T:** Mm?

52  **E:** *Add the—*

53  **V:** *Add* the er washers on

54  **T:** So, the weight of the bob
       So what did you keep constant? What were the variables you kept constant
       so that it was a fair test every time?

55  **E:** We kept the same bob. like *

56  **X:**                                    *

57  **T:** No, you were testing—

58  **Bi:** It was the—it—we—the same type of bob

59  **T:** The same type of bob, washer
       What else did you keep constant?

60  **J**: Um the height

61  **T:** The height . *the* release height—

62  **J:**                *the release*

63  **T:** What else did you keep constant?

64  **E:** The length of the string

65  **T:** The length of the pendulum . just to find out whether the weight of the
       bob makes a difference

\* \* \*

73:  **T:** So that is an example of what we mean by "a fair test"

       And that— do you . think about variables and fair test not just in pen-
       dulums, but in everything you do?

74  **Ch:** Yes.

75  **T:** Yes its very important in science
       Those are some of the science processes you have to think about . OK?

In the whole class review discussion (for which T seems to be acting as scribe as well), T again uses the Feedback slot to reinforce the processes of doing science by drawing out the significance of the students'
own work. And, in the choice of language, she now uses even more of
the specialized discourse register of science:

- "experiment" (45)
- definition by means of a synonym: "fair here meaning consistent,
  right?" (45) in contrast to the planning conference in which "fair
  test" was defined by an example: "say if you . . . "

- the critical question about "What was the variable we held constant?"—a recurring theme as "fair test" was in the planning conference (45, 47, 54, 59, 63)
- a complex noun phrase, "release height" (49), typical of scientific registers.

Whereas no child used any of this scientific register in her or his own language in the planning conference, even in this short segment from the review discussion Tema incorporates one word from the teacher's technical language into her response: "What we *kept constant* was . . . " (48).

**The nature of teacher questions.** The most pervasive criticism of the IRE/IRF lesson structure is that the teacher asks only "display" questions to which she already knows the answer. The questions are, in short, "inauthentic." Either T is simply testing student knowledge, so the criticism goes, or is co-opting students to participate in what could otherwise be a lecture—transforming a monologue into a dialogue by eliciting short items of information at self-chosen points.[15] On the basis of such criticisms, teachers are frequently admonished to ask "authentic" questions more typical of informal conversation. Both example lessons, Birthplaces and Measuring Time, show that these criticisms are oversimplified and they miss important points.

In Birthplaces, T could not have given a lecture because only the students had the knowledge required for the map activity. Most of the teacher's questions are, in that sense, "authentic", the exceptions being the questions about relative distance to which T does know the answer. The purpose of asking them is to get certain information onto the shared public space of the map. A more significant criticism of the questions in Birthplaces is that the kind of knowledge being elicited is limited to facts that can be stated in short answers. Exceptions are the "How did you know/remember?" questions (12 and 15). These questions, which Mehan calls *metaprocess* questions, ask for different kinds of knowledge and prompt longer and more complex responses. But such questions are rare in Mehan's nine lessons: only 8 out of 480 elicitations, or 1.7 percent. The rest ask for factual products or brief opinions.

In both of the Measuring Time lessons, T does know the answer, but to rush to judgment for that reason is to oversimplify again. As Wells puts it:

> The teacher knows what information she is trying to elicit. She had, after all, been present during the experiments and discussed what they were doing with each group. However, this is not a quiz. . . . Rather, the purpose is to establish an agreed account of what they did that will

serve as an instantiation of the practice of controlling the independent variables to ensure that it is a fair test."[16]

"An agreed account of what they did" is part of what Wells calls "common knowledge," after Edwards and Mercer's influential book by that name.[17]

## Further Comments on Traditional Lessons

These two analyses of the IRE/IRF pattern of classroom discourse point to general features of discourse structure (Mehan) and of the relationship of structure to function (Wells). We have already seen that there is not a one-to-one relationship between structure (form) and function. This is true at any level of language. For example, Mehan labeled the first slot in the triadic structure Initiation rather than Question because it was not always filled with an utterance in the form of a syntactic question; sometimes the initiation was a directive (for a nonverbal action, as in Birthplaces, sequence 6) or an informative (a declarative sentence, as in 26 and 27). The function of Initiation was to govern the talk that followed. Then we noted how directives to take certain actions can be understood despite great variation in form, from bald imperatives to very indirect requests or statements. In the Time lessons, Wells extends our consideration of form–function relationships by considering pedagogical functions (planning and review) realized by the form of the IRE/IRF discourse structure as a whole.

At the end of their analysis of a particular teacher's move that they call *revoicing,* one of the discourse variations discussed in Chapter 5, O'Connor and Michaels refer to Wells' article and argue for the potential value of IRE/IRF sequences for particular functional phases of larger activity structures:

> The structure of the sequence allows the teacher to maintain the necessary control over the flow of information and the advancement of the academic content. Both the topic of the Initiation move (the teacher's questions) and the content of the Evaluation move allow the teacher to advance the intended topic of discussion or learning. In addition, they allow her to check the status of knowledge, awareness, and attention of students by calling on individuals and posing particular questions. Wells . . . takes the study of the sequence a step further, observing that very different activities and goals can emerge from the same structural sequence.[18]

The value of such IRF sequences should then be judged for their contributions to student learning.

But some curriculum goals being advocated now require a different kind of talk.

## Nontraditional Lessons

To highlight the differences between traditional lessons and the non-traditional discourse now being developed in many classrooms across the country and across the curriculum, I have selected examples from elementary mathematics. Surprising as it may seem, mathematics is the subject area in which the current movement to change patterns of classroom discourse got its first and, arguably, still most powerful push.

As the first of the professional educational organizations to develop a set of national standards, the National Council of Teachers of Mathematics (NCTM) issued two sets of guidelines—*Curriculum and Evaluation Standards* in 1989 and *Professional Standards for Teaching Mathematics* in 1991.[19] With these documents, teaching objectives extended far beyond computational skills, and classroom discourse received major attention as the medium for achieving them. According to NCTM:

"We need to shift

- toward classrooms as mathematical communities—away from classrooms as simply collections of individuals;
- toward logic and mathematical evidence as verification—away from the teacher as the sole authority for right answers;
- toward mathematical reasoning—away from merely memorizing procedures;
- toward conjecturing, inventing, and problem solving—away from an emphasis on mechanistic answer-finding;
- toward connecting mathematics, its ideas and its applications—away from treating mathematics as a body of isolated concepts and procedures . . .

The teacher of mathematics should promote classroom discourse in which students:

- listen to, respond to, and question the teacher and one another;
- use a variety of tools to reason, make connections, solve problems, and communicate;
- initiate problems and questions;
- make conjectures and present solutions;
- explore examples and counterexamples to investigate a conjecture;
- try to convince themselves and one another of the validity of particular representations, solutions, conjectures, and answers;
- rely on mathematical evidence and argument to determine validity."[20]

With statements such as these, classroom discourse becomes more than the inevitable group context for "teaching for understanding" by each individual student; it becomes also the essential and dynamic medium for accomplishing fundamental communication goals. In short, "[c]lassrooms should be 'mathematical communities' rather than collections of individual learners."[21]

As examples of math lessons designed with these standards in mind, I have selected elementary school lessons simply to make it easier to understand the subject matter being discussed.[22] Three widely cited teacher educators and researchers in elementary mathematics are James Hiebert, Magdalene Lampert and Deborah Ball and their collaborators. All three are based at universities; Lampert and Ball also teach mathematics at a local elementary school on a daily basis. They analyze their own lessons from a videotaped record in order to understand, from both inside and outside perspectives, the challenges that this kind of teaching poses for teachers.

In these lessons, teachers still ask questions, but student responses and subsequent teacher turns do not fit an IRF structure. In presenting the following examples, I have sometimes separated quoted speech from surrounding discussion in the original articles, and numbered turns for easier reference. Significant differences from traditional lessons in the T's role are highlighted at the beginning of each subsection.[23]

### Example One: Finding the Difference in Two Heights

*Accepting alternative student answers and asking for comparisons with supporting reasons.* In what Hiebert and his colleagues call a "reflective inquiry" classroom in an urban school with a large Latino population, Ms. Hudson posed a problem to her second-grade class: "find the difference between the height of two children, Jorge and Paulo, who were 62 inches tall and 37 inches tall, respectively." (Take a minute to remember how you were taught to solve such problems.)

The teacher had deliberately not demonstrated computational procedures, "so the students constructed their own methods, either individually or collectively through peer interactions, using their knowledge of the base-10 number system."[24] After most of the students had worked on a solution for about 10 minutes, some working with base-10 materials such as sticks with 10 dots on them, Ms. Hudson asked for volunteers to share their methods. Figure 3–4 presents the ensuing talk.

In contrast to traditional arithmetic lessons in which the teacher demonstrates computational procedures and children practice them, this discourse sequence has several distinctive features. The teacher did not stop the discussion with Gabriela's first response, even though it was the correct answer; her "OK" (2) expresses acceptance of Gabriela's explanation rather than positive evaluation that ends discussion. Nor did

**Figure 3–4**

Discussion about calculating differences in height

---

1  **Gabriela:** I said, "How much does Paulo have to grow?" So, 37 plus 3 more [*pointing to the three dots*] is 38, 39, 40, and 50 [*pointing to a 10 stick*], 60 [*pointing to another 10 stick*], 61, 62 [*pointing to 2 more dots*]. So, this is 23, 24, 25 more he has to grow.

2  **Ms. Hudson:** OK. Roberto?

3  **Roberto:** I shrunk the big guy down by taking away the little guy from him [*pointing to his drawing of Paulo and Jorge*]. I took 3 10s from the 6 10s and 7 from this 10 [pointing to the fourth stick]. That leaves 3 and these 2 are 5 and 2 10s left is 25.

4  **Ms. Hudson:** OK. Now I am going to ask Jose how he did it.

5  **Jose:** I did it like Gabriela, but I wrote 3 and then my 10 sticks and 2 and then added them to get 25 more the little guy needs.

6  **Maria:** I subtracted Paulo from Jorge like Roberto did, but I used numbers. I took one of the 10s to get enough to take away the 7, so that was 3 and 2 more was 5 1s, and there were 2 10s left, so 25.

7  **Ms. Hudson:** Can someone tell how Roberto's and Maria's methods are alike?

8  **Carlos:** They both took away from the little guy.

9  **Ms. Hudson:** Anything else?

10  **Jazmin:** They both had to open a 10 because there wasn't 7 1s to take away. So Roberto took his 7 from that 10 stick. He took 7 and left 3. And Maria took a 10 from the 6 10s and wrote it with the 1s and then took the 7 to leave 3.

11  **Ms. Hudson:** So, they were both thinking kind of alike but wrote it in different ways?

12  **Students:** Yes.

---

she positively evaluate any one student's computational procedure as the best.

For their part, the students in their answers show that they have internalized two important norms for such discussions: explanations are as important as answers, and listening and referring to what other students have said is expected:

- Jose (5): I did it like Graciela, but . . .
- Maria (6): I subtracted Paulo from Jorge like Roberto did, but . . .
- Carlos (8) and Jazmin (10): They both . . .

Note also that the ratio of teacher talk to student talk is the reverse of most traditional lessons. There, typically teachers talk about two-thirds of the time; here, Ts' turns are short and student answers are expanded.

With T's final comment (11), this lesson comes to a clear and positive end. But that is not always the case in nontraditional lessons. Sometimes the lesson ends without such resolution. In such events, an Australian researcher reports: Teachers, regardless of their theoretical frameworks for learning and teaching, may feel uncomfortable with the notion that there may be no closure at the end of a lesson.[25] Such discomfort is understandable, but shouldn't we admit that even when we make sure to get closure in the form of desired understanding into the classroom air, the same understanding may not exist in each individual student's mind?

### Example Two: An Introductory Lesson on Functions

*Understanding student understanding.* Here Lampert is the teacher in a whole-class discussion with her fifth-grade math class as well as researcher and author.[26] As in the first math example, this discussion occurred after small-group work. Many of the students had found one problem especially hard, so Lampert raised it with the whole class. They were given four sets of paired numbers:

- 8—?  4
- 4—?  2
- 2—?  1
- 0—?  0

The students were then asked to "state the 'rule' for getting from the numbers in the first column to their corresponding 'outputs' in the second column." Lampert et al. present and analyze a long excerpt from the whole-class discussion. Figure 3–5 shows a shortened version of the presentation that highlights the rule suggested by one student, Ellie; the reactions of three of her peers; and Lampert's role. Ellie was the first to speak.

Here, in contrast to the previous math lesson, there is disagreement among the students, expressed by the gasp after Ellie's answer. Lampert avoids evaluating that answer and opens the floor to other ideas. The following is a capsule summary of the discussion that ensues.

- (5) Enoyat agrees with Ellie and explains why.
- (7) Charlotte disagrees with Ellie's formulation but "see[s] what Ellie's doing—she's taking half the number she started with."
- (10) Ellie restates her original answer.

## Figure 3–5
### Stating the rule

---

1 **Ellie:** Um, well, there were a whole bunch of—a whole bunch of rules you could use, use, um, divided by two—And you could do, um, minus one-half.

2 **Lampert:** And eight minus a half is?

3 **Ellie:** Four [*a gasp arose from the class*]

4 **Lampert:** You think that would be four. What does somebody else think? I started raising a question because a number of people have a different idea about that. So let's hear what your different ideas are, and see if you can take Ellie's position into consideration and try to let her know what your position is. Enoyat?

5 **Enoyat:** Well, see, I agree with Ellie because you can have eight minus one half and that's the same as eight divided by two or eight minus four.

6 **Lampert:** [*revoices Enoyat's response and then calls on Charlotte*]

7 **Charlotte:** Um, I think eight minus one half is seven and a half because— [*Lampert: Why?*] Um, one half's a fraction and it's a half of one whole and so when you subtract you aren't even subtracting one whole number. . . . But I see what Ellie's doing, she's taking half the number she started with and getting the answer.

8 **Lampert:** So you would say one half of eight? Is that what you mean? [*Lampert and Charlotte alternate for three turns. Then, Lampert "checks in" with Ellie.*]

9 **Lampert:** Ellie, what do you think?

10 **Ellie:** I still think . . . [*restating her answer in 1 and 3*] [*Lampert alternates with Ellie for four more turns, then with three other students, and calls on Shakroukh.*]

*(continued)*

- (11) Shakroukh qualifies his agreement with Ellie with a significant amendment to her formulation: "if she had said one-half of the amount that you have . . . "

- (12) Lampert summarizes, in more technical language, what Charlotte and Shakroukh have said about fractions, then alternates with two other students, and again turns to Ellie.

- (13) At this point, Ellie agrees with Shakroukh, but disagrees with Charlotte (actually, with Lampert's revoicing of Charlotte in 10)— that is, the rule can't be one-half of eight because: "Not all of the problems are eight."

- (14) Lampert explains the importance of conventions about language in mathematics (an even more "meta"-intervention than she made about fraction in #12).

**Figure 3–5** (*continued*)

11 **Shakroukh:** I would agree with Ellie if she had added something else to her explanation, if she had said one-half of the amount that you have to divide by two.

12 **Lampert:** OK. You guys are on to something really important about fractions, which is that a fraction is a fraction of something. And we have to have some kind of agreement here if it's a fraction of eight or if it's a fraction of a whole. Let's just hear from a couple more people, Ellie, and then I'll come back and hear from you, OK? . . .
[*Lampert alternated with Darota and Anthony and then returned to Ellie.*]

13 **Ellie:** Um, well, I agree with Shakroukh and um, when Charlotte said, um, she thought that, um, it should be one-half of eight, um, instead of just plain one-half. I don't agree with her because not all of them are eight. Not all of the problems are eight.

14 **Lampert:** OK. Let's um, one of the things that is a kind of convention in mathematics is that when we just talk about numbers and we don't associate them with any object or group of objects, that the symbol means half of one whole. So, if, if you were gonna communicate with the rest of the world who uses mathematics, they would take this [*pointing to the expression "8-1/2" on the chalkboard*] to mean eight wholes minus one-half of a whole. OK? Ellie?
[*Ellie and Lampert alternate for a total of nine turns.*]

15 **Lampert:** If, if you had said that the number that comes out is half the number that goes in, it would be easier for you to understand?

16 **Ellie:** That's what I meant, but I just couldn't put it in there, but that's what was in my mind. . .

17 **Lampert:** Okay. But I think you raised a lot of interesting questions by your idea of taking away a half.

- (15) After Ellie's explanation that she had had a hard time saying what she meant, Lampert positively acknowledges the importance of the discussion opened up by Ellie's original answer.

This lesson calls attention to the importance of the teacher's understanding of mathematics beyond what may seem to be required in the students' curriculum. When I first read this transcription, I mentally "gasped" along with Ellie's peers at her assertion that eight "minus a half" is four. But Lampert understood, as I did only slowly after reading what followed in the discussion and in Lampert's analysis, that Ellie might be expressing a beginning understanding that "a number could be both a *quantity* [a half] and an *operator on quantities* [one half of the amount you have] . . . an understanding on the boundary between arithmetic and algebra."[27]

Lampert's understanding is what Lee Shulman has called "peda-gogical content knowledge,"[28] and it is much more important in non-traditional lessons than in a more traditional curriculum. What historian Lawrence Cremin wrote about the Progressive Education movement of the 1930s and 1940s applies even more emphatically today:

> There is a point to be made here, one that [John] Dewey argued for the rest of his career but never fully communicated to some who thought themselves his disciples. A teacher cannot know which opportunities to use, which impulses to encourage, or which social attitudes to cul-tivate without a clear sense of what is to come later . . . with respect to intellect this implies a thorough acquaintance with organized knowledge as represented in the disciplines. To recognize opportuni-ties for early mathematical learning, one must know mathematics.[29]

### *Example Three: Equivalent Fractions*

*Facing the dilemma of honoring child logic and teaching conventional knowledge.* In the Lampert discussion, the disagreement among the participating students is about the way in which a mathematical relation is being ex-pressed. In Deborah Ball's third-grade discussion, the disagreement is about such relations themselves.[30] Three days before the end of the school year, disagreement erupted over whether four-fourths (4/4) and five-fifths (5/5) are "the same." Ball's report does not give a full tran-scription, but from her narrative, we can understand the dilemma she faced as the teacher and re-presents for her readers. Here are four girls' answers to the 4/4 versus 5/5 problem:

**Mei:** Let's say—here, I'll just . . . [*draws two equal-sized rectangles*] You have to use the same shape and—here it doesn't tell you the size of the shape. It tells you to divide this—4/4s tell you to divide this in *four* pieces, and 5/5 tells you to cut this in *five* pieces. . . . They're both the whole square so they're actually the same.

**Cassandra:** Five, 5/5 is not the same because they are different numbers just like three and two are different numbers. So how could they be the same?

**Jeanie:** [*who spoke rarely in a large group discussion, agreed with Mei*]

**Sheena:** [*spoke up on Cassandra's side, but with a different reason*] With 5/5 there is enough to pass out one piece to each of your five friends, but with 4/4 one friend will not get any cookie.

Ball explains her dilemma. On the one hand, she had worked hard throughout the year "to create a classroom culture in which mathe-matical ideas were established with evidence and argument" and to sup-port all children's confidence in their own thinking and speaking about math. On the other hand, she wanted "their next teacher to see them as competent."[31]

Her dilemma was intensified in this instance by the realization that, of the four girls who had been most active in this debate, Mei and Jeannie (whose position that 4/4 and 5/5 are "the same" would be considered correct) were Asian and white, respectively, while Cassandra and Sheena (whose position that they are not "the same" would be considered wrong) were African American.

So, with the school year nearly over, Ball decided to "just tell" them, "something impatient observers sometimes urge me to do," by means of a careful demonstration. Afterward, she asked them to write their conclusions in their notebooks, and found that "their thinking still spanned the alternatives."[32]

To Ball and her social studies colleague Suzanne Wilson, the issues are moral as well as intellectual:

> What is right or good here? Perhaps it is irresponsible to allow Cassandra and Sheena to think—and try to convince others—that 5/5 is more than 4/4. Five-fifths is not, after all, more than 4/4, even if their interpretation of this is sensible. But perhaps it is wrong to invite students to think, only to refute their ideas when they do not match accepted mathematical ones. And how does who they are—and the characteristics one considers as relevant when thinking about individual students—shape what counts as good practice?

Some colleagues who read or hear about this example question the public identification of "correct" and "incorrect" answers with children identified by their ethnicity. Ball has done so, and I have re-presented her identification here, to express her fear that subsequent teachers may infer more global traits of low-academic potential from such answers, especially when given by children of color. The ethnic identification of Cassandra and Sheena explains nothing about what the children said, but it explains something about the teacher's concern.

Through these three nontraditional lessons, we can understand some of the beliefs that underlie current efforts toward reform, about what math education should be:

- Children should problematize mathematical ideas rather than just practice arithmetical operations, explaining their answers and listening to those of their peers. Answers and explanations should be validated by the mathematical community, here the classroom group, rather than by the sole authority of the teacher.

- Teachers for their part need to understand mathematical ideas, such as those embedded in elementary arithmetic, in order to glimpse the potential value of their students' talk, even when not yet clearly expressed.

- Inherently, teachers will finally confront the dilemma of reconciling the goal of respecting children's thinking with the goal of helping them acquire "conventional" knowledge and procedures. This dilemma may be lessened if there is *schoolwide* consensus on the philosophy and practice of curriculum and teaching.

## Traditional and Nontraditional Lessons: Not Either/Or But Both/And

In this chapter, I have deliberately contrasted traditional and nontraditional patterns of lesson discourse in order to highlight some currently influential ideas. But on the ground in classrooms, alternatives never seem as starkly either/or as they can become in rhetoric about practice and policy. And the overall goals of schooling rarely fit an either/or contrast either.

Controversy continues as I write about the benefits (for conceptual understanding and problem solving) and liabilities (for automatic skills) of these NCTM-sponsored reforms in mathematics teaching.[33] Comparable differences in kinds of learnings, and controversies about their relative importance, exist in other curriculum areas. Language arts teachers will see similarities to the recent "whole language versus phonics" debate in early literacy instruction. I would argue that in both curriculum areas we need both/and, not either/or. The arguments for a balanced or integrated curriculum are not to achieve a political compromise. More significantly, the seeming alternatives are cognitively interdependent. In math, according to Israeli math educator Anna Sfard, the so-called basic skills are necessary not only for practical matters but as the objects of deeper reflective understanding. In literacy, automaticity in word analysis and word recognition is necessary to free mental space for thoughtful, even critical, understanding of larger units of text.[34]

In emphasizing what's new and different about nontraditional, standards-based math lessons, this chapter is admittedly guilty of the same unbalanced presentation that Sfard finds in the NCTM standards, and for the same reason. It is the new that most needs describing and defending. The wisest teachers and researchers understand that, and make sure their programs help students learn across the range of desired objectives.

Although this book is not directly about curriculum issues, we have detoured into them because of the crucial link between curriculum purpose and discourse structure.[35] The new importance of discourse in school-improvement efforts comes not from any anticipated substitution of nontraditional for traditional lessons, but from the need for teachers to have a repertoire of lesson structures and teaching styles, and the understanding of when one or another will be most appropriate for an increasingly complex set of educational objectives.

# Notes

1. Upublished edited transcripts for Mehan 1979 on the top; Ball 1991 on the bottom.

2. Mehan 1979 and unpublished transcripts.

3. Cazden 1976, my personal account of this teaching year, includes further discussion of this common phenomenon of social and psychological distance between a teacher and her students.

4. Evidence of dependencies across nonadjacent units within a larger structure became an important argument in cognitive critiques of behaviorist explanations of complex human behavior. *See* Lashley (1961) and Chomsky (1957) for examples from music and language, respectively.

5. The sequential and selectional dimensions are also referred to as syntagmatic and paradigmatic, or horizontal and vertical dimensions (as is more obvious with the rubber stamp for date numbers), respectively.

6. Sinclair and Coulthard 1975.

7. Lemke 1990, 60–61.

8. Griffin and Mehan 1981, 205. In this book, I use the term *structure* to refer to the patterns analyzed by a researcher. Other researchers use the terms *rules, scripts,* and *schemata* to refer, by contrast, to knowledge of those patterns that we assume must be present (in some as yet not-understood form) in the minds of participants.

9. Erickson 1982, 178.

10. The phrase "apprenticeship of observation" is from Lortie, 1975.

11. Wells 1993; this article is richer than I am reporting here. Wells describes more episodes in the time unit; and his theoretical framework draws on Halliday's analysis of language and Leont'ev's analysis of activities. Figures 3–2 and 3–3 come from Wells pp 18–19 and 26–28 respectively.

12. Ibid., 15

13. Ibid., 25.

14. In a book on teaching primary school science, Ogburn et al. (1996, 61) give "fair test" as an example of a "didactic transposition" of one aspect of scientific method to make it intelligible and memorable for young students. This is an example of what British sociologist of education Basil Bernstein 1990 calls the "recontextualizing principle of pedagogic discourse": It appropriates discourse from outside the classroom, here from the world of scientific work, and transforms it for teaching and learning.

15. This is Lemke's 1990 interpretation of the triadic dialogue structure of the high school physics lessons he observed.

16. Wells 1986, 27.

17. Edwards and Mercer 1987.

18. O'Connor and Michaels 1996, 96. In her discussion of this same Wells article, Hicks agrees: "In other words, although the *structure* of the IRF may be consistent across instructional settings, its *functions* may vary widely" (1995, 69).

19. NCTM 1989, 1991; Putnam et al. (1990) give the background for the NCTM work.

20. National Council of Teachers of Mathematics 1991, 3, 45.

21. Lampert et al. 1996, 739. *See also* the 1991 article for teachers by Ball, a leader in the development of the 1991 Standards and the teacher in the bottom example at the beginning of this chapter.

22. The conceptual difficulty of the curriculum material is a problem in understanding Lemke's (1990) otherwise valuable analysis of the language of high schools' physics teaching from which two of the indirect directives here were quoted. Lemke's use of Michael Halliday's functional linguistics (1978) is unusual in U.S. analyses and therefore important; but when the referents of talk are chemical constructs, such as "orbitals," the reader's task is compounded: One can't use known relationships among curriculum referents as clues to relationships in the linguistic analysis or the reverse.

23. In the original articles, directly quoted speech is embedded in explanations rather than presented in sequence as a transcription. While this may be because all four articles are by mathematics educators rather than discourse analysts, it may also be because the new and nontraditional usually needs such explanations more than the traditional. Schifter (1996) includes examples of teacher research on their elementary math lessons.

24. Hiebert et al. (a consortium of colleagues from four universities) 1996.

25. Groves 1997, handout p. 2.

26. Lampert, Rittenhouse and Crumbaugh 1996.

27. Ibid., 734. This example also raises important questions about social relationships among students in these frequently argumentative discussions. Lampert's interview with Ellie is discussed in Chapter 6.

28. Shulman, 1987.

29. Cremin 1961, 138; for discussion by Dewey himself, see (among other places) his *Experience and Education* 1938/1963.

30. Ball and Wilson 1996.

31. In their still important analysis of the dilemmas entailed in British "open" (progressive) education in the 1970s, Berlak and Berlak (1981) discuss several dilemmas that are related to Ball's (personal knowledge versus public knowledge, and knowledge as given versus knowledge as problematical). None fits exactly, because it is the nature of the current math reforms that, for teachers, have so sharply focused the tension between valuing children's understandings and yet somehow inducting them into conventional mathematical knowledge ("spontaneous" versus "scientific" concepts—Vygotsky's terms 1962).

32. Even if Cassandra and Sheena weren't immediately convinced by Ball's "careful demonstration," other interventions can be imagined. One person with whom I was discussing Ball's dilemma suggested the teacher might say: "Try thinking of it this way: Yes, you can give pieces of 5/5 to more of your friends. But if a cake cut into 5/5 costs more than a cake cut into 4/4, would you pay more for it?"

Such a response does not try to shift the child's thinking into the logic of formal number relationships abstracted from the human world. Instead, the teacher enters the child's imagined narrative (as Vivian Paley often does with her younger children) and asks a hypothetical question from within it.

33. *See The Kappan,* March 2000, and the February 1999 issue for discussion of these math reforms, and Sfard (in press) for a detailed analysis, especially manuscript pages 11 to 15. NCTM (2000) published a revised set of standards that seem designed to pay more balanced attention to both computation and problem solving.

34. Saunders, Goldenberg, and Hamann (1992) and Saunders and Goldenberg (1996) report their professional development discussions with California language arts teachers during a shift in state pronouncements on educational philosophy from whole-language to basic skills. In Cazden 1992, the integrated curriculum goal is called "whole language plus." For a more theoretical presentation of the necessarily complex "how" of literacy education (involving situated practice, overt instruction, critical framing, and transformed practice), see the work of the trinational New London Group (1966) and Cope and Kalantzis (2000). I am indebted to all I have learned from my colleagues in this group: Bill Cope, Mary Kalantzis, Carmen Luke, Allan Luke, and Martin Nakata from Australia; Norman Fairclough and Gunther Kress from England; and James Gee and Sarah Michaels from the United States.

35. We need more detailed analyses of lessons with different kinds of learning objectives and how those shift over time. For example, Rex and McEachen (1999) analyze high school English teacher McEachen's teaching over twenty-one days of "how to make a case" and develop an argument about text interpretation. They find more IRE traditional lesson structure in the early days of the sequence during the "how to" phase, but then by Day 16 both teacher and students have shifted roles in discussions of particular cases to patterns more similar to the nontraditional math lessons. Leinhardt (1987) presents a detailed longitudinal analysis of a successful eight-day sequence for teaching "an expert explanation" of subtraction with regrouping in second grade, but she does not present enough speech excerpts to make the discourse structure visible.

# Chapter Four

# Classroom Discourse and Student Learning

Classroom discourse happens *among* students and teacher. But arguably the most important goal of education is change *within* each student that we call learning. How do the words spoken in classrooms affect this learning? How does the observable classroom discourse affect the unobservable thinking of each of the students, and thereby the nature of what they learn? In the words of Douglas Barnes, written twenty-five years ago and quoted in the introduction to this book's first edition, how does speech *unite the cognitive and the social?* In the more recent words of anthropologist Barbara Rogoff, how can we best understand relationships among three "planes of analysis" of any event: individual development, social interaction, and the cultural activities in which both take place? [1]

It is never easy to talk about relationships between individual (silent) thinking processes and the dyadic or group (often noisy) interactions in the classroom. But because that relationship is at the heart of student learning and must therefore be at the heart of teachers' planning, we have to try. To make what follows as understandable as possible, I've tried to select examples in which descriptions of the external and social are easy to follow, and hypotheses about the internal and mental can be imagined. Most of the examples in this chapter come from the language arts.

## Discourse as Scaffold

In a recent report on what is known about *How People Learn* prepared by a committee for the National Research Council, the seventh and last of their "key findings" states:

Adults help children make connections between new situations and familiar ones. Children's curiosity and persistence are supported by adults who direct children's attention, structure experiences, support learning attempts, and regulate the complexity and difficulty levels of information for children.[2]

The metaphorical term *scaffold* is one way of thinking about complex learning environments that provide these kinds of support.[3]

Scaffolds vary in scope. The first set of examples are the simplest to describe: sequences of interaction between an adult and one child, at home and at school (Reading Recovery). Then we'll look at scaffolds constructed by a teacher for small groups (Reciprocal Teaching) that become incorporated into a more complex literacy and science program (Community of Learners). It is not a coincidence that both Reading Recovery and Reciprocal Teaching are programs for students having the hardest time with literacy tasks—those who need the most carefully planned help. But my reason for selecting them goes beyond a concern for such students alone. I hope that, because of their careful design, these examples will help readers infer a principled sense of the kinds of assistance for all learners that *How People Learn* calls for.

The final example extends the scaffolding metaphor beyond interaction to consider curriculum as a sequence of increasingly difficult tasks in which each constitutes a scaffold for the next (Hillocks' "gateway activities" for composition).

## Scaffolds for Young Children at Home

Scaffolded assistance that socializes children into the practices deemed important in their culture can start very early, with infants trying (at least as mothers from some cultures believe) to communicate. Psycholinguist Catherine Snow describes how hard some mothers work to achieve a "conversation" despite the inadequacies of their conversational partners. At first they accept burps, yawns, and coughs as well as laughs and coos—but not arm waving or head movements—as the baby's turn. They fill in for the babies by asking and answering their own questions, and by phrasing questions so that minimal responses can be treated as replies. Then, by about seven months, the babies become considerably more active partners, and the mothers no longer accept all the vocalizations, only speech–sound babbles. As the mother raises the ante, the child's development proceeds.[4]

In Wertsch's analysis of a mother guiding her child through the task of making a copy puzzle just like a model, assistance consists of guidance in directing the child's visual (rather than oral) attention, also important in school learning, as we'll see in the following Reading Recovery example. Here is Wertsch's description of three episodes of interaction between a mother and her two-and-a-half-year-old child as they worked through the pieces of a single puzzle:

> The first two episodes began with the child asking where a piece was to go and the mother responding by directing the child's attention to the model puzzle. In both these episodes, the child's original question led to a response by the mother which, in turn, led to the child's response of consulting the model. All of these "moves" or "turns" were part of the external, interpsychological functioning. The third episode began quite differently. First, the child did not produce a fully expanded question about where a piece should go. Second, and more importantly, her gaze [toward] the model puzzle was not a response to an adult's directive. Rather than relying on an adult to provide a regulative communication, she carried this out independently using egocentric and inner speech. That is, in the case of some of the strategic steps required here, there was a transition from external social functioning to external and internal individual functioning.[5]

This description comes from a research project, but essential features of the parent's guidance occur in naturally occurring puzzle activities at home. I saw many variants as I watched one father assist his son during his puzzle-loving preschool years.

Next are the early language games, such as peekaboo. And similar to peekaboo in its early versions, but open to greater complexity of meaning and language form, are book readings, often at bedtime. Language acquisition researchers Catherine Snow and Beverly Goldfield have analyzed, qualitatively and quantitatively, a sequence of repeated readings in which Nathaniel (age 2–3 years) and his mother read and talked about his favorite pages in Richard Scary's *Storybook Dictionary*. Information the mother supplied during one reading was repeated, in part or whole, by Nathaniel the next day or so later.[6]

There can even be cultural differences in this early socialization. Book-reading can have more than one participant structure depending on the kind of text selected (picture book or collection of nursery rhymes, for example) and the adult's conversational style. Sharon Haselkorn, while a graduate student at Harvard, reported such differences during research in which she read books with various young children. Sharon was used to playing a "What's that?" game appropriate for picture books, but one of her young subjects had learned a "fill-in-the-blank-at-the-end-of-the-line" game that fits nursery rhymes better. As a result, they had a hard time getting their book-reading acts together.

In all these examples, the adult enacts the entire script herself in the beginning, but the child gradually appropriates more and more of what had been the adult role. The adult so structures the game that the child can be a successful participant from the beginning. That's the source of the pleasure of the activity for both child and adult, and it is that pleasure—in the intimate relationship and in the child's growing competence—that sustains their continued engagement. Variations in the game over time are crucial to their success as support for children's learning. As the child's competence grows, the game changes so that there is always something new to be learned, including taking over more and more of what had been the adult's role.

The concept of a shifting zone of competence within which a learner, with help, can accomplish what later can be accomplished alone was what Russian psychologist Vygotsky called the "zone of proximal development"—the distance between the actual developmental level as determined by independent problem solving and the level of potential development through problem solving under adult guidance or in collaboration with peers. In all these home examples, children do come to do independently what they could formerly do only with help.

The metaphorical term *scaffold* has become a common caption for this kind of assistance, and it is a good name if we remember that this is a very special kind of scaffold—one that has to change continuously as the child's competence grows, just as a physical scaffold is raised higher and higher up on a building as construction proceeds. In the strictest definition, the name *scaffold* properly applies only if we have evidence that the learner's competence does indeed grow over time.

## Individual Scaffolds in School

All the previous preschool examples involve dyadic interactions between an adult, usually a parent, and a child, and our first example of scaffolds in school is similarly dyadic. It comes from my analysis of videotapes made in New Zealand as part of the Reading Recovery program for children who have not yet learned to read after one year in school. The program was developed by developmental psychologist Marie Clay in collaboration with experienced primary teachers, and has since been imported into Australia, Canada, the United States and England.[7]

During a segment in each half-hour Reading Recovery tutorial lesson, the child composes a "story" (usually just one sentence) and writes it, with help from the teacher as needed, in an unlined notebook. Then a sentence-strip version of the same story, copied and cut up by the teacher, is given to the child to reassemble immediately and take home to reassemble later "for Mum." On the more macro level of activities that can motivate the hard work of becoming literate, transcribing one's own spoken ideas into writing is a significant task for six-year-olds; on the more micro level of specific learnings essential for literacy, phonemic awareness, sound–letter relationships, and spelling patterns are all practiced in these writing activities.

The Reading Recovery videos show six-year-old Premala's progress in writing down a sentence she has herself composed at three points in

**Figure 4–1**
How Premala's sentence got written down

---

I   (C) A  ①        g        k              a  c t.
    (T)     ittle   irl  is  cuddling          a


II  (C) The  little  red  h e n   m a d e   c

    (T)                                        some cakes.


III (C) I  am  going  swimming  at  school  now.

---

time near the beginning (PI), middle (PII), and end (PIII) of her 12 to 20 week individual half-hour tutorial sessions. Here are the stories Premala orally composed at 6- to 8-week intervals:

- PI. *A little girl is cuddling a cat.* (about a book)
- PII. *The little red hen made a cake.* (about a book)
- PIII. *I am going swimming at school now.* (about a personal experience; the sea is so accessible to New Zealand children that most do have swimming lessons at school)

Figure 4–1 shows how these three sentences got written down. What the child (C) wrote is on the top line; what the teacher (T) wrote is underneath. If the child wrote the letter, but only after some kind of help from the teacher, the letter appears on the child's line with a circle around it. (The "boxes" around the letters in *hen* and *made* in PII are explained below.)

Premala's progress in transcribing her stories can be summarized in the increasing number of letters written correctly by the child, alone or with help, and the corresponding decreasing number that had to be written by the teacher, as shown in Table 4–1.

To achieve this progress, the teacher constructs various kinds of scaffolding help: asking questions, modeling actions, and directing the child's practice.

- Calling attention to the sounds in spoken words:
  - PI. "Do you know how to start writing *little?*"
  - PIII. [*After Premala has written s for swim*] "Let's listen to it [*saying the word slowly*]. What can you hear?"
- Prompting visual memory of previous experience with specific written words:
  - PII. "Something needs to go on the end [*of little*], doesn't it?"

**Table 4–1   Premala's progress in writing
(in number of letters)**

|       | C Alone | C with Help | T   | Total |
|-------|---------|-------------|-----|-------|
| PI    | 5       | 1           | 19  | (25)  |
| PII   | 9       | 10          | 9   | (28)  |
| PIII  | 19      | 8           | 0   | (27)  |

- Drawing boxes to correspond to the sounds (phonemes, not letters) in the word, and showing the child how to push counters into the boxes, left to right, while saying the word slowly: h-e-n, m-a-de. When these boxes are first introduced, the teacher accepts letters in any order, as long as they are in the correct place. Later, the teacher will encourage the child to fill in the letters (4 in *made*) in the correct order and will draw the boxes to correspond to letters rather than sounds (only 3).

- Asking the child to develop and use her visual memory for words:
  - In PII, the teacher asked Premala to write *red* several times, increasing the difficulty of the task each time: first with a model available to copy, then with the model covered; then to walk over and write it on the blackboard from memory, and finally to finish it after the teacher had erased the last two letters.
  - In PIII, there was similar practice for the harder word, *school.*

- Praising strategies (not items), even if the result is only partially correct:
  - PI. "That's a good guess, because *cuddling* sometimes sounds like that [*k*]."
  - PII. "Good thinking. You remembered that" [*e on little*].
  - PII. "I liked the way you checked it all through" [*referring to the child's careful reassembly of her cut-up sentence*].
  - PIII. "You don't need to look [*referring to P now writing* school *from memory*] because you've got it inside your head, haven't you?"

- Introducing new information
  - PIV. "Let's have a look and I'll show you what else *cuddling* can sound like."

- Increasing the difficulty of the task: Because the child composes each sentence about a self-chosen topic, the teacher cannot unilaterally increase the challenge of the overall writing task as she does in selecting a new book for the child to read each day. But she can increase the challenge of the reassembly of the child's sentence from the sentence-strip pieces. Slash lines show how she cut up the sentences for PII and PIII. [*There was no sentence strip in PI.*]

- PII. The / little / r/ed / hen / made some / cakes. [*Note the relationship between her segmentation of red and the writing Premala did at the blackboard.*]
- PIII. I/ a/m/ go/ing/ swi/mm/ing/ a/t/ school/ now. [*Note here the segmenting within as well as between words.*]

Although both sentences have seven words, the teacher increases the number of segments for Premala to reassemble from 8 to 12. In both lessons, Premala succeeds, rereading and checking as she goes. Her success offers another indication of her learning, and of the accuracy of the teacher's inferences about just how much she can achieve by herself at each time.

This writing example from Reading Recovery shows the advantages of the one-to-one teacher–child relationship for both teacher and researcher. For the teacher, it makes it easier to fine-tune both the problems she poses and the help (as little as possible is the general principle) that she gives along the way—fine-tuning that, with careful observation and written records of the child's growing competence, is close to what parents can do from memory of their continuous interactions with their children. For the outside observer, the one-to-one relationship makes the structure and function of the teacher's scaffolding clearer, more "transparent," than if the teacher were teaching a group. Because the child's writing at three points in time provides strong evidence of Premala's learning, we can say with confidence that she was functioning in her "zone of proximal development," doing at first with the teacher's scaffolding help what she could in a few weeks do alone.

## Group Scaffolds in School

All teachers work with individual students some of the time—regularly as in writing conferences, or as needed when students are working alone and the teacher circulates around the room giving help. Fortunately for busy teachers, most children can also learn from well-designed but less individually tuned group instruction. There may even be individual benefits from group scaffolds if the more varied models and feedback available from peers compensate for the impossibility of the teacher's fine-tuning. Many children can benefit, in other words, if a more varied "cafeteria" of resources to learn from—a diversity of expertise—replaces a single, individually tailored "diet."

One well-documented literacy program for older students that works through small-group instruction is called Reciprocal Teaching (RT). It was developed by Anne Marie Palincsar, then a graduate student and experienced special education teacher, and psychologist Ann Brown. Like Reading Recovery, it was developed for struggling students—in this case, middle-school students who were having a hard time with reading comprehension. Also, like Reading Recovery, it was designed for external, interactional help with the internal cognitive actions that expert readers perform.[8]

RT lessons begin with an adult teacher and a group of four to five students taking turns leading a discussion of an expository passage. During the discussion, the teacher guides structured practice in four comprehension strategies:

- *Questioning:* The leader begins by asking a question to get the discussion going—not any question somehow related to the passage but a question that requires understanding the main points, the topic sentence (stated or implied), and the key ideas of the passage as a whole.

- *Clarifying:* Used as needed for any problem in understanding—for example, asking about and explaining unfamiliar vocabulary and vague references (by less experienced readers) and more complex inferential reasoning (by the more experienced).

- *Summarizing:* The leader ends by establishing what they've learned in preparation for moving on to a new piece of text.

- *Predicting:* Where appropriate, the leader also provides, or asks for, a prediction about what information may be expected to follow.

As Brown explains:

> These four activities—questioning, clarifying, summarizing, and predicting—were selected to bolster the discussion because they are excellent comprehension-monitoring devices; for example, if one cannot summarize what one has read, this is an indication that understanding is not proceeding smoothly and remedial action is called for. The strategies also provide the repeatable structure necessary to get a discussion going, a structure that can be faded out when students are experienced in the discourse mode.[9]

RT thus has two simultaneous purposes: a probing discussion of text meanings for the group, and enhanced self-monitoring of text comprehension for each individual. Scaffolding the four strategies is a temporary means to both ends.[10]

As Brown explained retrospectively, the role of RT in a larger curriculum design has evolved over years of classroom research. Initially, it was conceived as a series of small-group reading lessons to provide practice in the four comprehension strategies, using texts from the students' regular reading lessons. But the sequence of unconnected texts read over a series of RT discussions did not permit the students to build up background knowledge on a topic (as Nathaniel did in a more simplified way in his repeated book-readings with his mother), which is so essential for reading comprehension.

Later Brown and her colleagues embedded RT in several phases of a complex literacy and science program they called "Community of Learners" (COL) — one of the best-documented examples of challenging, discourse intensive, curriculum and teaching. Briefly, a class of middle-school students become researchers of a key principle of biology such as "interdependence." They are divided into research teams, each team becoming expert in their group-selected aspect of the topic. They work together, in RT discussions of relevant (book and electronic) texts, and group planning and revising of team reports. Periodically, the students regroup into "Jigsaw" groups[11] that consist of one member from each research team. Here, students teach the rest of the group what their research team has learned, calling on shared RT experience when needed in reading both published and student-authored texts. "Let's RT it" becomes a familiar suggestion among the students themselves. Over the school year, Brown and her teachers report that as these RT interludes become more student-led, they also become more flexible in discussion structure, attending less to the four focal strategies and more to what the text can contribute substantively to the class project.[12]

Without some larger curriculum purpose for RT such as a science project, students can be reluctant to engage in the work. Researcher Sarah Michaels and teacher Richard Sohmer encountered this reaction from Worcester, Massachusetts, middle-school students in an after-school science and literacy program called the Investigators' Club (I-Club). As a free-standing activity, RT seemed to those students too remedial, too much like regular school (from which they were alienated). But when RT was embedded in a larger project of becoming "experts" so that they could teach what they were learning to younger students, the I-Club members not only accepted RT but initiated it themselves.

In his book on *Communities of Practice: Learning, Meaning and Identity* Wenger has a vivid metaphor for this important contrast: "This brings to mind the story about the two stonecutters who are asked what they are doing." One responds: "I am cutting this stone in a perfectly square shape." The other responds: "I am building a cathedral." Sohmer's I-Club students wanted to "build a cathedral." As Wenger goes on to say, these contrasting responses reflect different relations to the world, and different self-identities.[13]

From transcripts of RT sessions with the same students over time, their learning of the four focal strategies can be tracked. But the ultimate goals of both general reading-comprehension strategies and specific substantive knowledge, in this case about science, can't be inferred from that evidence alone. So the COL program also includes other kinds of assessments: tests of knowledge co-constructed by the teacher and the student "experts"; more standardized reading-comprehension tests (although these can be problematical if they include primarily narrative texts, which require different comprehension strategies); and locally devised forms of "dynamic assessments" that measure how much help students need to answer particular kinds of questions.[14]

Even with all this evidence, however, it is not clear how Reciprocal Teaching works. How does overt group focus on four specific strategies generalize into more powerful silent individual reading comprehension? Early in RT's development, Resnick acknowledged the evidence of its success but pointed out that "the automatic nature of many reading-comprehension processes, the speed at which reading proceeds, and its sequential nature make it implausible that in the normal course of skilled reading people actually pose questions or create summaries for themselves."[15] In a review of research on social interaction and reading comprehension, Kucan and Beck suggest that RT's success could be due either to instruction in specific strategies or to the time RT discussions require readers to reflect on what they're reading, monitor their understanding, and learn from other people's thinking aloud about the kinds of thinking that reading comprehension involves.[16]

### Curriculum as Scaffolds

In a book on classroom discourse, we have to pay most attention to activities that take place over a short enough time frame to be analyzable in relatively short transcriptions of talk. But by themselves, these examples from Reading Recovery and Reciprocal Teaching give a falsely limiting picture of the potential scope of the scaffolding metaphor. As Palincsar writes in a 1998 special journal issue devoted to revisiting the metaphor for its value in programs for children with learning disabilities, we need to consider the ways in which "contexts and activities— and not just individuals—scaffold learning."[17]

*Curriculum* is another name for a coherent set of "contexts and activities" carefully sequenced over days or weeks to build students' competencies toward a valued goal. Brown's COL, with its complex integration of science and literacy experiences, is one example. I hope one additional example will suffice to suggest possibilities for thinking about curriculum, as well as interaction, as scaffold.

An explicit discussion of this philosophy of curriculum planning in the teaching of secondary school writing is given by George Hillocks, professor of English education at the University of Chicago. Hillocks calls curriculum activities "episodes."

> to emphasize the sense in which teaching constructs an ongoing narrative made up of episodes through which characters move in pursuit of some goal. (In successful teaching, the characters, including the teacher, share comparable goals.) If we think of chunks of teaching in

this way, we are almost forced to consider not only their content, but also their sequence and coherence.[18]

When "one episode prepares or seems to prepare students for work they will be engaged with in the next," Hillocks speaks of a series of "gateway activities" (as I would speak of a series of scaffolds). They "open up new journeys," and the teacher's task is to "invent the activities that will engage students in using, and therefore learning, the strategies essential to certain writing tasks."[19]

From the teaching that his university students, who are learning to be English teachers, have done with him for more than fifteen years in a Chicago public junior high school, Hillocks gives examples of sequences of gateway activities for various genres of writing, such as personal narratives and arguments. Here is one especially detailed sequence designed for seventh-grade students whose initial writing showed almost none of the features of effective personal narratives. As Hillocks points out, personal narratives are important not only for self-discovery but as frequent components of complex genres such as essays and arguments. This sequence is planned for a fifty-two-minute period for twenty-two school days.

1. *Initial writing sample.* Write about an experience that is important to you for some reason. . . .

2. *Examples of personal narrative.* Students read and talk about examples by professionals and other students. . . .

3. *Idea sheets.* After receiving a sample from the teacher, students work individually, writing a few sentences about their own experiences [*that they might write about*]. . . .

4. *Introduction to using specific detail.* Describing shells in teacher-led lesson, small groups, and individually, with feedback episodes [*and revision demonstrated and tried*].

5. *Details about people and places.* Teacher-led talk about an interesting drawing or photograph, small-group work then read aloud, workshop with individuals working on character from scenario on idea sheets, read aloud, feedback, revision.

6. *Describing sounds.* Teacher-led talk about recording of various sounds.

7. *Writing about bodily sensations.* Various in-class exercises followed by writing about a strenuous activity from one's own experience.

8. *Writing about the "dumpster scenario."* Students asked to make an imaginative leap into a teacher-given scenario, write individually, with teacher coaching as useful. Read in small groups, feedback, revision.

9. *Pantomine of characters in emotional states.* Volunteer acts out teacher-given pantomine. Then in small groups with student acting and others writing details for an audience who did not see the actor.

10. *Invention of dialogue.* Read and discuss examples as in #2. Teacher-led development of dialogue (in play form) based on one scenario, followed by small-group work on another scenario. Students presented with feedback.

11. *Individual work on dialog from idea sheet scenario.* Read aloud, feedback, and revision.

12. *Punctuation of dialogue.* Teacher demonstrates; groups punctuate dialogue already written out. If successful, individuals convert dialogue from #11 to prose form and edit each other's punctuation.

13. *Workshop.* Students select an incident from idea sheets. Drafting, periodic reading in small groups for feedback; revision, using a checklist to prompt ideas for revision.

14. *Class publication.* Students choose which to include, with all students represented if possible.

15. *Final writing sample* comparable to #1.[20]

I have given this list in full because it is such a detailed example of curriculum sequencing in one area—the teaching of writing. Many of the separate episodes constitute scaffolds in themselves, with the teacher demonstrating, followed by students' first try in small groups, then by read alouds and feedback, and only then writing alone. In #4 revision itself is demonstrated and then followed by practice in many of the subsequent episodes. Some of the episodes parallel each other, assisting students in moving toward a different dimension of the same goal, as for details (4–7) and dialog (10–12). Throughout, the teacher assumes that if she teaches well and monitors their progress, the students can learn to write well. To do that, like the math teachers in Chapter 3, T needs pedagogical content knowledge, here what good writing in each genre involves.

## Discourse as Reconceptualization

The metaphor of discourse as scaffold applies easiest to adult assistance with mental actions—in our examples, mental actions necessary for literacy, such as transcribing spoken language into writing and understanding increasingly complex texts. Teachers also have to assist their students with related but more substantive kinds of learnings. They need to induct them into new perspectives and new ways of thinking about, reconceptualizing, or recontextualizing whatever phenomena (referents) are being discussed. Like scaffolds, assistance in the form of reconceptualizations is given both at home and at school.[21]

## Reconceptualizations at Home

We can consider as reconceptualizations the "expansions" with which some adult caregivers respond to their young children, repeating what they assume the child meant but rephrasing that meaning in their own culturally mature terms:

| Child | Mother |
| --- | --- |
| Mommy eggnog | Mommy had her eggnog. |
| Eve lunch | Eve is having lunch. |
| Mommy sandwich | Mommy'll have a sandwich. |

In the three instances, the adult is putting into words what the child omitted: the action connecting the two noun phrases that in English must express the temporal relationship between the narrated event and the conversational present.

Such expansions have been documented in the speech of many caregivers, and sometimes have been interpreted as contributing only to the child's acquisition of the syntax of their native language. But in the first article calling attention to expansions, developmental psycholinguists Roger Brown and Ursula Bellugi wrote: "It seems to us that a mother in expanding speech may be teaching more than grammar; she may be teaching something like a worldview."[22] In these early conversations, children are learning not only *how* to express their meanings, but *what* to mean as well.[23]

## Reconceptualizations at School

A great deal of education is devoted to teaching students to see phenomena in a new way. A teacher's response, like a caregiver's, can offer "something like a worldview." Remember the new ways of thinking and talking about mathematics Lampert explained to her fifth graders in Chapter 3, in both cases building on, while reconceptualizing, their previously expressed ideas:

- First about fractions (12): "You guys are on to something really important about fractions, which is that a fraction is a fraction of something. And we have to have some kind of agreement here if it's a fraction of eight or if it's a fraction of a whole."

- Then about conventions of mathematical expression (14): "[O]ne of the things that is a kind of convention in mathematics is that when we just talk about numbers and we don't associate them with any object or group of objects, that the symbol means half of one whole. So, it you were gonna communicate with the rest of the world who uses mathematics, they would take this [*pointing to the expression "8 − 1/2" on the chalkboard*] to mean eight wholes minus one half of a whole. OK, Ellie?"

In a second-grade classroom observed by Cobb, it is the computational procedure of adding two-digit numbers that becomes reconceptualized in the teacher's revoicing of what her children had said. They had been working in pairs on the problem of adding three twelves and were now reporting to the class how they did it. Here is a sequence that, in Mehan's terms, would be a Topically Related Set (TRS).

1 **T:** Jason and Brenda, how did you do it?

2 **Jason:** I added up—Well if—one plus one plus one. Well, one plus two, one more equals three.

3 **T:** Uh huh.

4 **Jason:** Two plus two equals four and two more equals six. Takes it up to thirty-six.

5 **T:** How about you, Brenda?

6 **B:** Well, I got thirty-three [thirty-six?]. I just counted. First, I counted by two's.

7 **T:** All right [*meaning "I understand what you're doing"*]

8 **Brenda:** Two, four, six.

9 **T:** Two, four, six.

10 **Brenda:** And then ones, and I came up with thirty-six.

11 **T:** All right. So what they did. They split up their twelves into tens and twos. They added up their twos and added up their tens and then they combined that number. I'll bet that's what a lot of you did.[24]

Just from what's said here, it seems as if Jason added the columns, left to right (2, 4), and Brenda added them right to left (6, 8, 10). But, in her feedback to the whole class about "what *they* did," T describes Jason and Brenda's actions: "They added up their twos and added up their tens . . . " (11) as if both children were acting from a conceptual understanding of underlying place value. Cobb et al. learned from many other observations in this class and from talking with the teacher that she knew Brenda had such understanding while Jason did not. Nevertheless, her description of their actions in these terms may reinforce that understanding for everyone. According to the researchers, "Her attempts to facilitate the institutionalization of this intellectual practice by the classroom community proved successful as the school year progressed."[25]

These examples, from home and school, show how responses by parents and teachers can enrich the meaning of a previous child's comment. Three Vygotskian psychologists—Newman, Griffin, and Cole—point out a crucial difference between useful enrichment for researchers and for teachers:

> In psychology, such overinterpretations can be dangerously misleading. . . . In education such assumptions may be a useful way of importing the [teacher's] goal into the teacher–child interaction and from there into the child's independent activity.[26]

Young children's learning about verb tenses doesn't happen after one parental expansion, and learning about our base-10 number system won't happen after one teacher reconceptualization either. In school, assistance to such new understandings takes many forms across the curriculum. But these adult verbalizations, contingent as they are on what students are likely to be attending to at the moment, may be especially helpful. Just remember that we still have to track children's progress to see if, in Newman, Griffin, and Cole's terms, the teacher's goal is indeed imported into the children's independent activity and thereby appropriated into their own understandings.

At the beginning of this section on discourse as reconceptualization, I included as a synonym the related term, *recontextualization,* in order to suggest a contrast with the more common description of school tasks as *de*contextualized. Perhaps too often, that term fits. Remember the I-Club students' reaction to RT alone (more decontextualized) versus when it was instrumental to their cross-age teaching (more contextualized).

The difference is cognitive as well as motivational. Psychological experiments offer examples of more and less decontextualized tasks. For example, in two Russian experiments, preschool children were able to stand still longer when asked to "be a guard" (contextualized instruction) than when simply asked to "stand still" (decontextualized instruction), and were better able to remember a list of objects when playing store (contextualized task) than when asked simply to remember a list (decontextualized task).[27]

When school language use is called *decontextualized*, it is generally because talk refers less often than it does at home to one kind of context: the physically present situation to which exophoric (pointing) reference can be made. But the learning difficulties inherent in classroom discourse are due less to that loss, and more to the many implied, but often unstated, references to another kind of context: the words of other oral and written texts (especially in language arts and social studies) and to systems of related meanings in math (as we have seen) and science. The successful learner is continuously reconstructing such "contexts in the mind," and in "communities of learners" teachers actively foster the build-up of increasingly rich stores of such "common knowledge."[28]

## Internalization, Appropriation, and Constructivism

John Bruer, a foundation executive who has funded research on applications of cognitive theory in the classroom, offers five hypotheses about why discourse-intensive reform programs "work":

- [S]ocial interaction . . . allow[s] skilled thinkers to demonstrate expert strategies to the naïve. . . . [It] makes hidden thought processes public and shared. . . .

- [C]ommunal interactions allow students to share and distribute the cognitive burdens of thinking. A group provides a more informationally rich context for learning. . . . [T]here are greater varieties of cues to trigger recall of information from individual memories. . . .

- [D]ialog requires both language comprehension and language production. [Because] production is cognitively more demanding, dialog might then result in deeper processing of information.

- [S]ocial settings send the message that thinking and intelligence are socially valued.

- Thought, learning, and knowledge are not just influenced by social factors, but are irreducibly social phenomena. Discourse doesn't make thought visible, rather thought is internalized discourse.[29]

Bruer attributes his first three hypotheses to the theoretical framework of information-processing psychology, the fourth to social psychology, and the last to Russian theorists Vygotsky, Leont'ev, and Bakhtin.

Vygotsky referred to the processes through which individuals learn from social interaction by the metaphoric term *internalization,* and I adopted that term in the first edition of this book. Since then, it has become more controversial. One reason is that "internalization" connotes too passive a process, and what is "acquired" is too easily considered a mere copy of the meanings circulating on the social stage. Such copies, as in memorizing poems or play scripts, have their own value, but they cannot account for the development of flexible, adaptive expertise for which much of schooling should be designed. Vygotsky certainly did not intend such passive copying.

In the words of his Russian colleague Leont'ev: "The process of internalization is not *transferral* of all external activity to a preexisting internal 'plane of consciousness'; it is the process in which this internal

plane is *formed.*" [30] Remember what Resnick said about the difference between what RT teaches and what good comprehenders do. Mental
transformations of some kind must be taking place.

The writings of Vygotsky's contemporary Bakhtin offer another
way of thinking about such transformations.[31] In one of his rare references to schools, he contrasts "two basic modes for the appropriation
and transmission—simultaneously—of another's words (a text, a rule,
a model): "reciting by heart" and "telling in one's own words." In his
more formal terms, the contrast is between "authoritative discourse"
and "internally persuasive discourse," respectively. *Authoritative discourse* "demands that we acknowledge it, that we make it our own; it
binds us, quite independent of any power it might have to presuade us
internally; we encounter it with its authority already fused to it." But
when we transform the authoritative discourse of others into our own
words, it may start to lose its authority and become more open. We can
test it, consider it in dialog—private or public—with other ideas, and
"reaccentuate" it (Bakhtin's term) in our own ways.[32]

To make clearer the distinction between passive transferral and active transformation of knowledge, Leont'ev and Bakhtin's metaphorical word *appropriation* is now often used instead of internalization. Its
use eliminates another problem as well. *Internalization* implies a unidi-
rectional process: Only students are expected to internalize what they
hear and see and read. Appropriation, by contrast, can be reciprocal.
Parents and teachers can be said to appropriate children's utterances in
order to revoice more culturally mature formulations, which the children then will gradually—we hope—appropriate into their own mental knowledge systems. It also makes it possible to extend the metaphor
by speaking of mutual appropriation among students, as Brown and her
colleagues do in descriptions of COL, and as Gallas does in her description of sharing time.[33]

Note that substituting "appropriation" for "internalization" still says
nothing about the internal mechanisms. It only helps to emphasize
their active constructive (as opposed to passive copying) origin. The
crucial importance of the learner's active construction, even if out-of-
consciousness to the learner, as well as invisible and inaudible to the
teacher, has led to the most common name for the now-dominant theory of individual learning: *constructivism.*

Consider again part of the writing sequence from Reading Recovery. Premala copied the action of moving the counters slowly into the
boxes drawn by the teacher, simultaneously elongating her pronunciation of the word and thereby coordinating her fingers and speech. But
that is all still just external behavior. Beyond, or behind, those visible
and audible external actions, out of the teacher's sight and hearing, the
child's all-important mental task remains to be accomplished, for which
these external behaviors are only the self-generated "mediational

means." Premala's mental task is learning to use her own slowed speech to attend more easily to the sounds she has spoken (phonemic awareness) and then remember what letters represent those sounds.

A long paragraph to describe something that seems so simple and that must eventually happen so rapidly! My purpose in writing it all out is to emphasize that what can be internalized, or appropriated, from other people still requires significant mental work on the part of the learner. That mental work is what "constructivism" refers to. Variations on this term combine it with references to origins of the externally provided assistance—the external building materials, so to speak. *Social constructivism* highlights the source of such assistance in other people, from patterns of discourse to human-made artifacts like computers; *sociocultural* and *sociohistorical* call our attention to the origins of social resources in a particular culture with a particular history.[34]

*How People Learn* emphasizes that "constructivist theories of knowing" are about how people learn, not how other people should teach:

> A common misconception . . . is that teachers should never tell students anything directly but, instead should always allow them to construct knowledge for themselves. This perspective confuses a theory of pedagogy (teaching) with a theory of knowing. Constructivists assume that all knowledge is constructed from previous knowledge, irrespective of how one is taught—even listening to a lecture involves active attempts to construct new knowledge.[35]

Lampert describes the multiple teaching roles that are embedded in her classroom discourse:

> Sometimes, I straightforward told students. . . . At other times, I modeled the roles that I wanted them to be able to take. . . . And at other times, I did mathematics with them, just as a dance instructor dances with a learner so that the learner will know what it feels like. . . . [36]

She is thinking about assistance to student constructivism in math learning, but the same principles apply across the curriculum.

## Learning as Affective as Well as Cognitive

In both the scaffolding and reconceptualization sections of this chapter, the first examples were of talk by parents. In the course of his extensive research on first language acquisition, Roger Brown concluded that parents' two underlying intentions must be to communicate clearly and to express affection.

Consider again parental expansions and the difference between them and (teacher?) corrections. The formal difference may be only in intonation and an optional initial Yes or No. But that difference may matter a lot to the child. Suppose that while looking at a picture, a young child says, "Fall down." Say to yourself the following alternative responses, stressing the underlined words:

- Expansion: (Yes) he fell *down*.
- Correction: (No) he *fell* down.

The intonation of the expansion expresses satisfaction, even delight, in how much the child has already achieved on the way to learning the family's language. The intonation of the correction, by contrast, expresses dissatisfaction, even annoyance, over what the child still has to learn.

In classrooms, noncognitive aspects of underlying interpersonal relationships—*affective* aspects—are no less important for children's learning. Yet in descriptions of even nontraditional classrooms, where interactions are deemed so important, mention of affective qualities of the learning environment are hard to find.

The three editors of one important book that reports on neo-Vygotskian research in education lay some of the blame on Vygotsky himself for not saying more about cognitive/affective connections.[37] In his chapter, editor Addison Stone calls the quality of interpersonal relationships one of the missing ingredients of the scaffolding metaphor. The affective quality that perhaps best expresses what both teachers and students need is what Stone calls "mutual trust"—trust by teachers and students in each other. Parents don't have to worry so much about establishing trust—it is inherent in the parent–child relationship; but teachers can't assume it. Trusting relationships undoubtedly take many forms, including the shared enjoyment of humor, depending on both individual and cultural histories and preferences.

We need more descriptions of alternative forms of such relationships that are functionally equivalent in engaging and supporting student learning.[38] To put the problem bluntly, changing the name of a classroom of students from a "group of conscripted workers" to a "community of learners" doesn't make it happen.[39]

# Notes

1. Rogoff 1995, 141.

2. Bransford, Brown, and Cocking 1999.

3. The term *scaffold* was first used in this metaphorical way in D. Wood, J. S. Bruner, and G. Ross (1976). Cazden 1979a, written after a professional trip to the then Soviet Union with colleagues Ann Brown and Michael Cole, may have suggested the first connection between their analysis of tutoring and Vygotsky's (1962, 1978) construct of a child's "zone of proximal development."

4. Snow 1977.

5. Wertsch 1984, 10; Wertsch and Stone 1985, 175–76.

6. Snow and Goldfield 1981; Snow and Goldfield 1983.

7. This account of Premala's writing is adapted from Clay and Cazden (1990). The tapes were made in about 1983, the year when plans began for importing Reading Recovery from New Zealand into the United States. For a comprehensive history and international perspectives on the Reading Recovery program, *see* Clay 1997.

8. Among the many articles by Brown and her colleagues are (chronologically) Palincsar 1986, Brown and Palincsar 1989, Brown et al. 1993, Brown and Campione 1994, and Brown 1994. Writing about this work only months after Ann Brown's death from an illness, I want to honor her not only as a preeminent scholar but as a warm and generous friend.

9. Brown et al. 1993 [pp 7–8 in ms.].

10. For a helpful description of RT for teachers, *see* Schoenbach et al. 1999, 79–98.

11. Aronson 1978. Also www.jigsaw.org.

12. Personal communications with Brown during the 1990s.

13 Michaels and Sohmer personal communication 1998; Wenger 1999, 176.

14. *See* Brown et al. (1993) for a discussion of "dynamic assessment" in COL. Briefly, an adult poses a problem and then carefully keeps track of how much graduated assistance, from most general to most specific, the novice needs in order to solve it. Cazden (1979a) reports a trip to Moscow when Brown and I saw such assessments demonstrated at the Institute of Defectology (*sic*), founded by Vygotsky, that was then still working with his ideas.

15. Resnick 1985, 177.

16. Kucan and Beck 1997.

17. Palincsar 1998.

18. Hillocks 1995, 171.

19. Ibid., p. 149.

20. Shortened with some paraphrasing from Hillocks 1995, 178–79.

21. For the sake of separate descriptions of scaffolds and reconceptualizations in this chapter, I have probably overdrawn the contrast between learning to do and learning to know, learning how and learning that. In an analysis of how physical therapists learn their trade (and treat him!), Mike Rose (1999) has wise words on the dangers of this dichotomy.

22. Brown and Bellugi 1964, 143.

23. In the research literature on second language learning, the structural equivalents of expansions—when the teacher confirms what the learner has just said by reexpressing the meaning in the mature target language—are called "recasts," and research continues on how helpful that response strategy may be. Some researchers have suggested that expansions like those of Eve's mother are

only frequent in mainstream middle-class families. So I was surprised when Alaskan Native elder Eliza Jones (Koyukon Athabaskan) spoke about her childhood (Fairbanks, Alaska June 2000). When her father told stories in the evening, she was expected to retell them as a way of learning. If she made a mistake, "he would say back to me the way I should say it." Thus, adult responses similar in form are part of different larger cultural patterns.

24. Cobb, Wood, and Yackel 1993, 108–109.

25. Cobb et al. 1993, 110–11.

26. Newman, Griffin, and Cole 1989.

27. Manuilenko 1975; Istomina 1975.

28. Edwards and Mercer 1987.

29. Summarized from Bruer (1994, 286–89).

30. Leont'ev 1981, 57 (emphasis in the original); *see also* Wertsch and Stone 1985.

31. Although Vygotsky and Bakhtin were born in the same year, Vygotsky died in his thirties while Bakhtin lived into his seventies. There seems to be no evidence that the two ever met, so the compatibilities among their ideas must come from a shared intellectual milieu. As an example of Bakhtin's growing influence, compare Wertsch 1985 and 1991. British researchers Barnes and Todd (1995) have added an excellent discussion of Bakhtin's ideas in the final chapter of their revised interpretation of a 1977 experimental study of peer discussion groups with thirteen-year-olds in various curriculum areas.

32. Bakhtin 1981, 341, 342. I have been influenced by Morson and Emerson's (1990) book about his ideas, especially on this authoritative/internally persuasive contrast.

33. Some social constructivists avoid the issue of "internalization" entirely by speaking of learning as "the transformation of participation" (e.g., Rogoff 1995, 389). I continue to prefer to consider learning as *facilitated by,* and *enacted in* the transformation of participation.

34. From the many recent writings on constructivism, here are some of my favorites: Airasian and Walsh 1997, Bereiter 1994, Cobb 1994, Driver et al. 1994, O'Connor 1998, Sfard 1998.

35. Bransford et al., 1999, 11.

36. Lampert 1990, 42.

37. Forman, Minick, and Stone 1993; Stone 1993; *see also* Goodnow in the same volume.

38. Cazden (1976, 1992) is a personal report of my efforts as a primary teacher, with references to some other classroom descriptions. Teacher research on the role of shared humor in building a community of learners is badly needed.

39. "[C]onscripted workers" is Lortie's phrase. We shouldn't lose sight of the nonvoluntary presence of school learners. For a teacher's exploration of resistance to learning, *see* Herb Kohl, *I Won't Learn From You* (1994).

# Chapter Five

# Variations in Discourse Features

Chapter 3 ended with the need for teachers "to have a repertoire of lesson structures and teaching styles for an increasingly complex set of educational objectives," all in support of student learning discussed in Chapter 4.

As an aid to teachers' development of such repertoires, this chapter focuses on specific features of classroom discourse that teachers and researchers can select for attention and possible change. The intent is not to argue for or against any particular alternative, including traditional lessons, but rather to heighten awareness of possibilities. My hope is that such awareness will aid conscious local decisions about how classroom talk can be more effective.

No change has value for its own sake. In considering these possibilities, keep two points in mind. First, educational purpose and equitable opportunities to learn remain the most important design principles. Both teachers and researchers need to monitor who participates and how, and who doesn't and why. In the lessons presented in Chapter 3, often the reader cannot tell who is participating—students of color as well as white students and/or girls as often as boys? Deborah Ball's report about her own teaching was a welcome exception.

Second, as we saw with Reciprocal Teaching (RT) and Hillocks' "gateway activities," the more micro actions, which are the main focus in this chapter, are embedded in classroom activities; these, in turn, are part of larger curriculum units. I hope teachers will find it heuristically useful to consider component actions in planning how their classroom discourse might be changed, but researchers should not expect to be able to isolate and track the effect of any one such micro-change on learning outcomes. As Ann Brown puts it simply in reflecting on her evolving design for a Community of Learners (COLs), "the whole really is more than the sum of its parts." [1]

## Speaking Rights and Listening Responsibilities

In traditional classrooms, the most important asymmetry in the rights and obligations of teachers and students is over control of the right to speak. To describe the difference in the bluntest terms, teachers have the role-given right to speak at any time and to any person; they can fill any silence or interrupt any speaker; they can speak to a student anywhere in the room and in any volume or tone of voice. No one has the right to object. But not all teachers assume such rights and few live by such rules all the time. [2] Given teachers' rights inherent in their institutional role, *speaking rights* here refers to the ways by which students get the right to talk—to be legitimate speakers—during teacher-led group activities.

### Getting a Turn

Frequently, the teacher chooses to direct verbal traffic by asking students to raise hands and then selecting someone to speak. In the nine traditional lessons Mehan analyzed in the Birthplaces classroom, the teacher nominated student speakers 88 percent of the time. The rest of the time (57 out of 480 times), students spoke out-of-turn, without being called on, despite the supposed "rule" about raising hands. More interestingly, those students were only reprimanded half of the time; in the other half of the cases, student turns were accepted, even welcomed. Here are two examples in the Birthplaces transcript (Figure 3–1):

**Carolyn:**  Where's that at? (about Baltimore) (21)

**Wallace:**  That's ten times farther than . . . (31)

Both students' utterances extended, via student-initiated question (Carolyn) or comment (Wallace), the specific activity of locating family birthplaces, and contributed to the more general curriculum purpose of helping children understand how maps represent geographic space. It's probably not accidental that both contributions came, in this multigrade group, from the oldest third graders (both African Americans). They had had a chance to learn when they might speak out (note the Comments column in Figure 3–1) and what kind of things to say. [3]

Teachers may decide during some activities not to exercise their power to select student speakers. Instead of preallocation of turns by the teacher, there is then more local management of turn-taking by in-dividual students at the moment of speaking. With this shift, classroom talk becomes more like informal conversation—not the same as con-versation, because there is still the large group of potential speakers and the educational necessity to stick to an agenda, but closer to it.[4]

Here's one example from Vivian Paley's kindergarten classroom, in-troduced and reported by the teacher: "Lisa is telling us the story of 'Tico and the Golden Wings' by Leo Lionni. The children and I do not agree about Tico: I applaud him as a nonconformist while they see him as a threat to the community."

1 **T:** I don't think it's fair that Tico has to give up his golden wings.

2 **Lisa:** It is fair. See, he was nicer when he didn't have any wings. They didn't like him when he had gold.

3 **Wally:** He thinks he's better if he has golden wings.

4 **Eddie:** He is better.

5 **Jill:** But he's not supposed to be better. The wishing bird was wrong to give him those wings.

6 **Deanna:** She has to give him his wish. He's the one who shouldn't have asked for golden wings.

7 **Wally:** He could put back black wings on top of the golden wings and try to trick them.

8 **Deanna:** They'd just sneak up and see the gold. He should just give every bird one golden feather and keep one for himself.

9 **T:** Why can't he decide for himself what kind of wings he wants?

10 **Wally:** He has to decide to have black wings.

Instead of the teacher regaining the floor after each student turn, as is usual in traditional lessons, the sequence of turns here is: T–S–S–S–S–S–S–S–T–S–. When T does take a turn, she first offers an opinion of her own (1) and later asks a question, but one directed to the group as a whole (9), not just to the previous speaker. Paley's topic—fairness in possessions and relationships—may have contributed to the eagerness and fluency with which her young children spoke up.[5]

Allowing such self-selection of student speakers can be considered a way of "deregulating" classroom discourse, and like deregulation in other domains of social life, it can lead to new forms of inequality. For some years, when Paley's children acted out the stories they had dic-tated to her, she allowed authors to select their own casts. When she realized the exclusivity and rejection that happened all too often, she changed the rules so that she picked the actors in order of their seating around the circle. The change did not come easily.

Even though "You can't say you can't play" had been accepted in other activities, when acting out the stories the children seemed to feel that "the author owns all production rights." As the change came to be accepted, gender casting issues emerged. If a boy was next for a girl's part, the children decided that the author had to change the gender in the story or add a character. Finally, to Paley's delight: "They dare to take on implausible roles [of the opposite gender, when necessary], shyly at the start, but after a while with great aplomb, as if accepting the challenge to eliminate their own stereotyped behavior." [6]

With older students, achieving more equitable speaking rights can be more difficult. At the request of a sixth-grade teacher she was observing, sociolinguist Penny Eckert brought in a bar graph "displaying the students' rates of participation in three subject areas"—each student on a separate bar but with no names attached. The teacher led the lively ensuing discussion, making it clear at the beginning that no bars would be individually identified.

> Why is it that the girls who participate regularly tend to participate in all subject areas, whereas the boys tend to specialize? Why do some people, particularly some boys, not participate at all? How can we make it easier for shy people to participate? Do people who participate in class learn more than those who do not? [7]

High school teacher Sara Allen engaged in more direct intervention. When she first turned more control over to her students for discussions of literature, some of the boys dominated: "Classes were lively, students were engaged, but too many people felt excluded." [8] As part of a teacher/researcher project, Allen videotaped discussions, showed them to the students themselves, and involved them in considering desirable changes. Then, when collective reflection about the videotaped evidence was not enough to achieve what can be called more "affirmative interaction," Allen re-intervened more directly. She spoke to some of the students privately; she suggested that students not sit in the same seats every day; and at least once, she asked three boys not to speak at all for twenty minutes.

Teachers who are trying to make self-selection work with older students often find that well-learned habits, especially those literally embodied, as in handraising, are hard to set aside. I remember a small seminar at Harvard that had been meeting for several months discussing Marxist writings on education. Even though I was officially responsible for the seminar and the only faculty member in the group, I played a relatively minor role, intellectually as well as managerially; student self-selection was the norm. But once, when I did take a turn to speak, the next student momentarily lost his sense of this particular discussion context and, much to everyone else's amusement, started to raise his hand.

Teacher nomination and student self-selection are not the only ways to structure speaking rights. The possibilities are many, and I have selected a few to describe here, not as models to be imitated but to stimulate readers' imagination about purposeful alternatives.

In the Investigators' Club (I-Club), an after-school junior high science program, teacher Richard Sohmer invoked various turn-taking practices, depending on shifting purposes. Sometimes he encouraged "handing-off," by which each student called on the next speaker. When necessary, he added a gender rule whereby students had to call on someone of the opposite gender. At other times, when students were developing hypotheses to explain their predictions about an observed air pressure phenomenon (the topic of the I-Club for one year), he asked every student, one by one, not only to predict but to restate their reasons in their own words.[9]

In Juneau, Alaska, third-fourth grade teacher Sue Baxter used a "talking stick" to regulate turns. During a daily class meeting, the stick was passed around the circle of children seated on the floor. On the two days I was visiting, Baxter set different speaking guidelines each morning. The first day, the time was used for personal sharing. When the stick came to each of them, children could take their turn or silently pass the stick to the next person. Because of time pressures that morning, Baxter said there would be no time for the usual questions or comments after each turn.

The next day, a class disaster preempted meeting time. This was in October and the class had been seriously collecting data at several sites outside school on "brown down"—when and where particular leaves fell. Overnight, some of the sites had been disturbed! After an opening discussion, almost funereal in tone, in which it was clear how seriously everyone took this destruction of their data, Baxter started the talking stick around. This time, "Everybody needs to share. Everyone needs to say what you feel about our study sites being disturbed. You can say, 'I agree with so-and-so.' But everyone needs to speak." And everyone did. Whereas personal sharing was optional in her class, taking a position on an ethical public issue was required.[10]

In these turn-taking variations, junior high teacher Sohmer and elementary teacher Baxter had created clear and familiar structures for children to speak within, while leaving room for adaptations to the day-to-day needs of the classroom community. My interpretation of the difference in the demands Baxter and Sohmer placed on their students relates more to those needs than to differences in their students' ages. Baxter wanted each student simply to take a public moral position. Sohmer wanted each student to use the appropriate discourse of scientific explanations as well as to learn the content of particular scientific knowledge. So, it was not enough to say which theory one believed; one had to try actually explaining it. To repeat, or take from, what another student had said was OK, but all students had to re-articulate the explanations for themselves.

What I've said about speaking rights thus far seems to assume that all students are eagerly waiting for the chance to speak. Teachers know that's not always true, and that they then have to decide what to do, if anything, about students who choose to be silent. If a silent student is otherwise doing well academically, as shown by written work, should relative silence be ignored? Or is speaking up and explaining ideas, and listening and collaborating verbally with peers, a valued outcome of school in its own right—especially now when "communicative skills" appear on lists of abilities needed for high-paying jobs?

Parents of young children just learning their first language and researchers who document that learning often report children who stay silent for what can seem to a parent an agonizingly long time, and then start speaking in surprisingly mature sentences. Inaudibly, seemingly miraculous processes had been at work in the child's mind, somehow analyzing the conversation contextualized in the child's experience, until finally something prompts a spoken response. In a similar way, teachers report the occasional student who, after silence and seeming inattention in lesson after lesson, one day speaks up in a way that shows that, after all, previous discussions had been taken in. Like parents, teachers have to decide when to wait and see, and when to try somehow to help. Because girls as a group do as well or better than boys in K–12 school grades, opportunities to become fluent and confident in speaking in public may be the most important aspect of gender equity in classrooms.

Teachers and researchers need to be careful not to interpret silence or one-word answers as lack of knowledge. Many years ago, psychologists Eleanor Heider, Roger Brown, and I conducted an experiment with 11-year-old white boys that turned up social class differences in how they answered questions about information they had all been exposed to. Contrary to our hypothesis, we found no differences in what the boys had learned. But there were striking differences, which we had not expected, in the number of requests for further information that the interviewers had to make to elicit that information: an average of only 3.56 requests for each middle-class boy, but an average of 6.11 requests for each working-class boy.[11] Students will always vary both in what they know and in the situations in which they are most apt to perform well. The trick, for teachers and researchers, is not to get the two mixed up.

Sometimes the teacher's problem is not silence but the opposite—too many students talking at the same time. Then, it becomes important to try to understand when overlapping speech is an interruption and when it expresses peer solidarity and support. In her doctoral research,

Lowry Hemphill studied social class differences in speaking styles. Separate groups of working-class inner-city and middle-class suburban high school girls, all white, were asked to discuss two controversial topics: whether women should register for the draft (informal peer-conducted discussion) and whether the drinking or driving age should be raised (formal teacher-led discussion).

In the informal discussions, unregulated by an adult, when the middle-class girls commented while a peer was speaking, it functioned as a bid for the next turn and predicted who would speak next. When the working-class girls made the seemingly same move, it was unrelated to who took the next turn and seemed to function as support for the speaker.[12] Sociolinguist Deborah Tannen calls such patterns "interruption" and "cooperative overlap," respectively.[13] Hemphill's analysis reminds us of the importance of analyzing qualitatively any speech–act categories, such as overlapping speech, before starting to count.

It is easier to find analysis of problems in the distribution of student participation—whether too few speakers or too many—than of successful attempts to change them. This is an important area for teacher research.

## Getting the Floor

So far, we have talked as if *speaking rights* refers only to the chance to get one's words into the conversational air. As speakers, we know how unsatisfactory that can feel if one speaks but no one else seems to listen, if subsequent topic development closes around what one has said like tissue around a scar, if in an important way one never really "got the floor" at all.

To monitor speaking rights in this less procedural and more substantive sense, we have to look beyond the sequence of speakers to the sequence of ideas. Consider again the excerpt from Paley's kindergarten classroom (see p. 83) and follow the sequence of ideas about fairness through all ten turns: Lisa disagrees directly with the teacher, substituting "he" for Tico; Wally expands on Lisa's last sentence; Eddie agrees with Wally, maybe adding emphasis (depending on his intonation); Jill disagrees with Eddie; and so on. Each speaker has been "heard."

Sometimes students even address each other directly, in first person. This happened often in a class of fifteen-year-olds in a London comprehensive school—perhaps not only because teacher John Hardcastle encouraged it, but also because he taught an integrated English and social studies course to the same group of students for five years, so they came to know each other well. The school was in Hackney Downs, then one of the poorest districts in London. The class included students from Africa and the Caribbean as well as from white working-class families. Alex McLeod recorded one discussion on the place of Afro-Caribbean culture in the school curriculum.

Hardcastle started with a provocative question: "Really what I'm working around to is asking a big question; that is, is all this business about racism something that's only of interest to black people, or is it something that's got to be important for everybody?" At one point, discussion goes back and forth between David (whose family came from Trinidad) and Ricky (who is white).

1 **David:** It goes back to the days of slavery.
2 **Ricky:** David, how can white people accept the full of what their ancestors done?
3 **David:** They can recognize that it's not them.
4 **Ricky:** Don't you reckon that black people know that? Don't you think that black people are using that as an excuse, sort of, to ask for more sympathy?
5 **David:** Don't you think that some white people don't even know about the history of black people? [14]

Note the use of *you* and the addressee's first name in turns 2, 4, and 5. In many classrooms, such direct address among students is rare.

## Seating Arrangements and Gaze

Teachers who want to change the structure of speaking rights need to consider two physical matters: seating arrangements and their own patterns of gaze. Discussion like that in Paley's or Hardcastle's classroom is harder—for everyone, not just students—when seats are in rows. Not evident in transcripts, and often hard to determine even on videotape, is eye gaze, especially of student speakers. Typically, students look at the teacher while speaking, signifying that they consider her the only official addressee. One primary teacher who valued discussion in which she did not have to call on children, told me she tried to avoid looking at the child who was speaking. Rude as this may seem, she felt it encouraged the speaker to make eye contact with peers, thereby making it more likely that another child would self-select to be the next speaker.

## Listening Responsibilities

The importance of listening is not news to teachers. But too often it brings to mind only the importance of students listening to teachers, especially when they are giving directions. To maximize the kinds of learning described in the last chapter requires more and more complex listening by all members of the classroom community. Students can only "get the floor" if someone listens and responds. Teachers are also learning to listen to their students in new and more complex ways.

Deborah Schifter, an applied mathematician and staff developer, describes how the teachers she works with are "developing a new ear." She quotes their memories of previous listening habits:

> I listened for right answers, confirmation that students understood what they had been taught.

> It is almost as if I heard them previously, but had my next statements already planned. I attempted to adjust their thinking to what I planned to say next, instead of analyzing what they said to determine what I should ask, say, or do next.

She quotes also their reflections on how those habits are changing:

> I'm [becoming] able to see how individual kids are thinking and see what concepts are troublesome for kids to make sense of. . . . I feel like I'm getting more skilled at finding out what kids do "get" rather than just thinking "they don't get it." [15]

Being able to *hear* students' ideas, to understand the sense they are making, is not as easy as it may sound. In challenging curriculum areas, like math and science, hearing will be affected by the teacher's own understanding of the subject. Remember from Chapter 3 how Lampert could "hear" the potential value of Ellie's surprising assertion that "eight minus a half is four."

But even in seemingly unproblematical activities like sharing time, we have seen the miscommunication that happens when child and adult are in conflict about the newsworthiness of particular aspects of some event, or the teacher becomes impatient with episodic narratives. The goal is not for teachers to abdicate their responsibility for teaching new ideas and clearer ways of expressing them, but to realize that those new ideas will grow best—in the words we quoted in Chapter 4 from the National Research Council's report on *How People Learn*—if "[a]dults help children make connections between new situations and familiar ones."

In a community of learners, students have to listen to and learn from each other as well as the teacher. That's the only way for them to learn during the time spent solving problems in a group rather than just working alone at more traditional seat work. Beyond careful listening herself, the teacher's responsibility is to help peer listening happen.

Such help can take many forms. One teacher discouraged students from raising their hands while another student was speaking on the principle that eagerness for the next turn made listening to the present speaker less likely. When a student made a comment that seemed off-topic, another teacher realized that the seeming irrelevance might be due to the omission of an expressed connection, and would ask: "How do you see that related to [the preceding comment or general discussion topic]?"

Several researchers have identified another listening/teaching strategy that they call "revoicing." [16] One detailed analysis by two applied linguists, Catherine O'Connor and Sarah Michaels, is of group discussions led by two Cambridge, Massachusetts, teachers (identified by their real names)—Judy Richards (third–fourth-grade science) and Lynne Godfrey (sixth-grade math).[17] Here's an excerpt from Richards' classroom while the class is discussing whether a balance beam will balance with one weight on the 2 point on the left and two weights on the 1 point to the right. Richards' revoicings are in bold type.

1 **Allen:** um / well / I think that / it will / um / tip to the right / like what Dorian said / because / um / it's just getting a little bit / like / when it's farther out it's heavier //

2 [*another student*]

3 **Richards: 'kay so it'll still be / still to the right but less so //**

4 **Allen:** well it's still / right but Yeah //

5, 6 [*another student and Allen*]

7 **Jane:** I sa - / I th- / I think it's a / a little bit like um / Dorian and Allen but um / it's a little different . . . cuz / even though these are more / these are heavier / they / double the amount / but / but / since this is further out / it / would be / in / the um weigh more /

8 **Richards: okay / so you're suggesting since this is farther out /**

9 **Allen:** wait //
you know what I discovered? / that it's double the / I think it might balance because / it's / um / double as far as that is / and that's double it's weight // so I—that's why I might change my vote to balance /

10–14 [*many students agree*]

15 **Richards: kay so you're gonna predict it balances / lemme see if I got / right / what your theory is //**
**Jane says / it's not—it's gonna tip / a little bit to the left / because this is further out //**

16 **Jane:** but it'll sorta balance /

17 **Richards: but /**

18 **Richards: sort of**

19 **Richards: not— / sort of / but a little bit to the left //**
**and you're [*referring to Allen*] thinking / that it's going to exactly balance / because since this is / twice the dist— / this is twice the weight / but this is twice the distance //**

20 **Allen:** yeah /[18]

O'Connor and Michaels point out how Richards' revoicing moves serve two functions. First, with respect to the curriculum content, they repeat a student's contribution and rebroadcast it back to the group—often reformulating it in the process—to "give it a bigger voice" (in Richards' words). In revoicings 3 and 8, the teacher extracts the essential core of previous student utterances that are hard to hear because of the disfluencies typical of exploratory talk when speakers are thinking out ideas as they speak, and repeats them otherwise unchanged.

In 15, she expresses her interpretation of student ideas in the more technical terms of what scientists do—make predictions on the basis of a theory. In 19, she reformulates Allen's idea into a succinct statement of the key relationship between weight and distance. In these examples, revoicings become what I called in Chapter 4 *reconceptualizations*—"a fusing of the teacher's words, register, or knowledge with the original intent of the student" and "conferring on (or attributing to) that student a stance with respect to the topic under discussion, a stance the student may only dimly be aware of."[19]

O'Connor and Michaels also point out how the teacher's—"So . . . lemme see . . ."—positions herself in relation to the student very differently from the Evaluation/Feedback slot in a more traditional lesson. In the latter, she is the validating authority; in revoicing thus expressed, she maintains the originating students as a continuing negotiator about their ideas and gives back to them "the right to evaluate the correctness of the teacher's inference."[20]

The second purpose of revoicing positions students not only in relationship to curriculum content but in relationship to each other. This requires the teacher to be listening not just to individual students, one by one, but to relationship among ideas being voiced by students as a group. In 15 and 19, which are parts of a single response to Allen, the teacher is contrasting the predictions and theories of Jane (7) and Allen (9). Note that even though he is not explicitly named in 19, Allen recognizes it as a restatement of what he had said in 9 and ratifies that the teacher got it right. In this respect, the teacher

> has inducted them into public versions of key intellectual roles. These roles—theorizer, predictor, hypothesizer—must be stated in terms of other participants in the ongoing activity and in terms of the actual propositional content under discussion. Here the teacher has created a dramatic landscape for this event, featuring two protagonists. This provides an opportunity for other children (perhaps silently, perhaps vocally) to place themselves in relation to the balance experiment themselves, through Jane and Allen as proxies.[21]

In these ways, teachers' revoicings can be one strategy for building both an ever-increasing stock of common knowledge and an ever-more-powerful community of learners.

## Teacher Questions

Teachers ask lots of questions. At their best, teacher questions can both assist and assess student learning. Piagetian Eleanor Duckworth describes one kind of question that does both:

> To the extent that one carries on a conversation with a child as a way of trying to understand a child's understanding, the child's understanding increases "in the very process." The questions the interlocutor asks in an attempt to clarify for him/herself what the child is thinking oblige the child to think a little further also. . . . What do you mean? How did you do that? Why do you say that? How does that fit with what was just said? I don't really get that; could you explain it another way? Could you give me an example? How did you figure that out? In every case, those questions are primarily a way for the interlocutor to try to understand what the other is understanding. Yet in every case, also, they engage the other's thoughts and take them a step further.[22]

Duckworth's examples can be called *process,* or more technically *metacognitive,* questions; they call the learners' attention to their own thinking and their own knowledge. In nontraditional lessons, teachers are encouraged to ask more of such questions, often addressed in a group as part of encouraging students to explain their own thinking and reflect on what others have said.

For teachers and researchers alike, a lot of variation in cognitive impact is not caught by frequency counts of isolated question types. For the teacher, that variation includes the importance of optimal placement of particular questions, and the difficulties in continuing the discussion with a single student in a group lesson. For the observer, there is the analytical problem of trying to decide the import (to the student) and the intent (of the teacher) of any question considered in isolation. The context in the mind of the student responder at the moment of answering will affect the amount of work any answer requires. And the real intent of the teacher's question is often clear only from her subsequent evaluation of student answers. That ambiguity causes problems for anyone who has to make a decision about the answer immediately after hearing the question: for the student trying to answer and for the observer–researcher as well.

British researchers Edwards and Furlong reflect on the difficulty of making even the seemingly simple two-value distinction between open and closed questions:

> Talk is not one distinct item after another. It involves what has been called "conditional relevance": the meaning of an utterance arises partly from something else which has been (or will be) said, perhaps some distance away in the interaction. . . . This point, of great importance for our analysis of classroom talk, can be illustrated by considering a problem facing many systematic researchers, that of distin-

guishing between closed and open questions. . . . Many questions which appear to be open are closed because of the context in which they are asked (perhaps the teacher has recently provided "the" answer), or because the teacher has clear criteria of relevance or adequacy or correctness of expression to which he refers in evaluating the answers. The narrowness of the question only appears in what happens next.[23]

Barnes, another British researcher, calls questions that are open in form but demonstrably closed in function "pseudo-open" questions. One of his examples is: "What can you tell me about a Bunsen burner, Alan?" This sounds completely open; anything Alan knows about a Bunsen burner should suffice. But, as the lesson ensues, it becomes clear that from all possible answers, the teacher is seeking a particular statement about the conditions for luminous and nonluminous flames.[24]

With respect to all questions, there is a crucial difference between helping a child somehow get a particular answer and helping that child gain some conceptual understanding from which answers to similar questions can be constructed at a future time. Consider the following teacher–student sequence:

**T:** What's four times three?

**S:** Eigh—

**T:** What is two times four? [Note the shift from *what's* to *what is,* as if for emphasis.]

**S:** Eight.

**T:** Mm [*yes*], three times four?

**S:** Nine, ten, eleven, twelve.

**T:** So what's three times four?

**S:** Twelve.

T may hope that, from such a sequence, students will learn something about the relationship of addition to multiplication. But they may only be responding to a verbal sequence in which the connector *so* introduces a question that has the same answer as the preceding one. This pattern gets the right answer into the air. But as Swedish researcher Lundgren points out: "The language used establishes a pattern of communication which gives [only] the illusion that learning is actually occurring."[25]

## Pace and Sequence

One important source of variation in classroom discourse is the temporal relationship between a student utterance and the teacher's prior question and subsequent feedback. Here we'll consider two aspects of that relation. The first and more micro relation (a matter of seconds) is what has come to be called *wait time*. The second and more macro relation (a matter of minutes or even a day) is between assistance that is more immediate and assistance that is either further in advance or delayed.

## Wait Time

Most observations of talk in classrooms are not done with stopwatches, and attention is not usually given to the absence of talk or to the placement, duration, and effect of silence.

The late science educator, Mary Budd Rowe, made this a major focus of her research. In a summary of this work—in classrooms from elementary school to college, from special education teachers to museum guides—Rowe confirmed her earlier findings that "when teachers ask questions of students, they typically wait one second or less for the students to start a reply; after the student stops speaking, they begin their reaction or proffer the next question in less than one second." By contrast, she confirmed that when teachers wait for three seconds or more, especially after a student's response, "there are pronounced changes in student use of language and logic as well as in student and teacher attitudes and expectations."[26]

Rowe describes the following "pronounced changes" as a result of increased wait time:

- Teachers' responses exhibit greater flexibility, indicated by the occurrence of fewer discourse errors and great continuity in the development of ideas.

- Teachers ask fewer questions, and more of them are cognitively complex.

- Teachers become more adept at using student responses—possibly because they too are benefiting from the opportunity afforded by the increased time to listen to what students say.

- Expectations for the performances of certain students seem to improve, and some previously invisible people become visible.

- Students are no longer restricted to responding to teacher questions and get to practice all four of the moves. (Rowe adds "structuring" to the three-part sequence of soliciting, responding, and reacting.)

So many significant changes from a seemingly small change in pace that may seem like a change only in surface behavior. But that change seems to enable a different social and cognitive relation to knowledge.

High school physics teacher James Minstrell, knowing about Rowe's research, recounts his experience in a classroom discussion of force. Here is an excerpt from his account, with wait-times, and his comments on the significance of this slower pace:

**T:** Is the falling rock moving at a constant speed, or is it speeding up or slowing down? How do you know?

[*T should allow several seconds to pass before calling on students or allowing them to answer so everyone has an opportunity to develop an answer.*]

**Student:** The same speed all the way because I saw a film where some guy said that all things fall at the same speed.

[*T pauses here for 3 to 5 seconds before commenting or calling on another student so the first student can evaluate her answer.*]

**Student:** No wait, that's if two things fall, they both fall equally fast. I don't know.

[*More wait time.*]

**Student:** I think the rock speeds up.

**T:** What evidence do you have that makes you think it accelerates?

**Student:** The higher you drop it from, the harder it hits the ground or whatever.

[*The teacher allows more wait time here too.*]

"Even if students' answers are consistent with the scientist's views, give them time to evaluate their own ideas to decide their validity. The sources of validity should be experience, both informal and experimental, and logical, rational argument, but not the authority of a teacher or a text."[27]

Waiting out the silence before a student answers can be difficult, and it probably won't always work. One practice adopted by Elisa, a Latina teacher in a transitional class for Latino students who had been in bilingual classes through third grade, might be a solution to this problem for other teachers:

Elisa asked specific students questions, but, when they failed to respond after a sufficient period of time, she often included the comment, "Should I call on someone else?" She made this option available to students whenever they hesitated or seemed reticent to answer one of her questions, and they seemed to appreciate it.[28]

### Teacher Assistance: Alternate Timings

Adult assistance to learners' understanding can be separated analytically into three contrasting temporal relations to the learners' verbal or nonverbal actions. For examples of each, consider again the scaffolds constructed by the teacher during Reading Recovery and Reciprocal Teaching.

Some scaffolds are immediately contingent on the learner's actions, close together in time. Premala's teacher helped her write down her oral sentences in this way: word by word, even letter by letter, as needed.

Other scaffolds are built in advance—*front-loaded*—we can say. Here the time elapsing between adult provision of help and child use of that help is somewhat longer, though not too long to remain in the child's mind. This happens when the Reading Recovery teacher introduces a new book. She constructs the scaffold ahead of time by talking the child through the book: reading the title; looking at pictures; asking about possible relevant personal experiences; and most important, using orally certain words and phrases from the book that she predicts may be difficult for the child to read. In these ways, T gets not only the gist of the book as a whole but also specific words and phrases into the air and, she hopes, readily available in the child's mind as he or she reads the book for the first time.[29]

While these two temporal relations can be contrasted analytically, they are often combined in good teaching. In the more contingent writing segment of Reading Recovery, the sentences that the child orally composes are more likely to be more complex and varied if that oral composition is preceded by a scaffolding conversation in which the teacher draws out the child's ideas about the books they've read together, or about events in the regular classroom or at home, sometimes reformulating what the child says in more expanded form. Then that language will also be in the air for the child's subsequent appropriation into his or her own composition. Conversely, in the more front-loaded book orientation, the teacher can also call attention to text features again as the child reads. Thus, in both writing and reading, an initial scaffold can be followed by more contingent help as needed.

Reciprocal Teaching is generally described as if adult help with the four comprehension strategies were only given contingently, in the course of the group dialogue. But in a review of research on RT, Rosenshine appends a generalized script developed by Palincsar that illustrates explicit teaching of one strategy, questioning, prior to the group discussion.[30] So, potentially, RT also includes both kinds of temporal relations.

When the contingent "just-in-time" kind of help can be given quickly, the main focus and flow of the lesson is not disrupted. But if that help needs to be developed into an embedded mini-lesson, the teacher faces an on-the-spot decision as to whether to do the mini-lesson now or delay it until later.

In a study of conversations in an adult English as a Second Language (ESL) classroom, Polly Ulichny formatted a transcription that shows these alternatives. As shown on Figure 5–1, the sequence of talk zigzags vertically, line by line, down the page.[31] Talk transcribed in the left column is the main road of "conversation" about the students' volunteer experiences; talk transcribed in the middle column constitutes brief inserted "corrections/conversational replays." Sequences of talk transcribed in the right column, especially in Part II, form longer instructional detours.

In line 4, T corrects the student's "I go" to "I'LL [*elongated and louder*] go." In 34, she makes a more complex correction, from the student's "should" to "was SUPPOSED to." Then, seeming to decide that this phrase merits time for practice ("that's a good one"), she leads the students in rhythmic repetitions. As Ulichny points out, the correction is directed to one student, whereas the instructional sequence is for the whole class. At the end of this episode, in 54 and 55, T has to deliberately refocus the group's attention and conversation on the main topic—at this point, the student's sick baby who is keeping her from her volunteer job.

In all language arts teaching, teachers face such decisions because of the necessary dual attention to meaning and form. Teachers are sometimes urged to contextualize and embed all their explicit teaching about language forms in activities designed around meaningful content. But can such immediately contextualized instruction be detailed enough to be effective without going on a long formal detour that means getting back onto the main meaning road is awkward or has to be given up? How long should you stop a child's, or group's, reading for instruction in some frequent spelling pattern rather than just help with the specific word? How much teaching about punctuation or paragraphing should you try to insert into writing conferences? How much contingent, just-in-time teaching of a second language or second dialect should be inserted into ongoing discussions designed for communicative teaching?[32] In all such teaching, when is it necessary, in addition to help on the spot, to note problems and needs and address them in a more carefully planned way at another time?

A comparison of the first and second editions of middle school writing teacher Nancie Atwell's book, *In the Middle,* turns up an interesting contrast on just this choice. In pointing out the changes between the two books (from 1986 to 1998), she lists as one of the earlier edition's "orthodoxies" that she has now revised: "Conferences with individuals [which enable more immediate feedback] are more important than minilessons [necessarily more delayed] to the group." The second edition explains why she has changed toward more minilessons.[33]

CD-Roms offer new and more flexible solutions to this temporal relationship problem. John Bransford's Cognition and Technology Group has developed CDs with dynamic science problem scenarios that include "teaching tool" presentations that are either embedded in the scenarios or, when too many such embeddings get in the way of the story line, included separately in hypertext form to be accessed as needed.[34]

**Figure 5–1**

Transcript of interaction in an ESL classroom

K: Katherine      A: members of the class and Ms. Towers
T: Ms. Towers      C+: members of the class participating chorally
S: Suki      C−: a few members of the class, not functioning in unison

| | Conversation | Correction/Conversational Replay | Instruction |
|---|---|---|---|
| **Part 1** | | | |
| | **T:** [*Not recorded on tape*] (How was your volunteer work at the hospital?) | | |
| 1 | **K:** well I I don- don- I don't | | |
| 2 | think that I go back / /. | | |
| 3 | **T:** why not [*high tone*] / /. | | |
| 4 | | I don't think I. 'LL go back / / | |
| 5 | | why not / / | tell us WHAT happened, why |
| 6 | | | don't wanna go back, / but we / / |
| 7 | | | all the students can learn from your |
| 8 | | | experience too / / huh= |
| 9 | **K:** =uh* | | |
| 10 | **T:** | | *even if it's a bad experience |
| 11 | | | it's ok / / you still learn / / |
| 12 | | | [*laughs*] |

13 **K:** no no it's not a bad experience

14 or anything / / I just uhm mm / / in

15 the moment the baby's sick and

16 she's crying all the day / / and

17 uh the family really need *me

18 **T:** *oh / /

19                                        at the present time you mean / /

20 *uh-huh / / aoh=              now the baby's sick / /

21 **K:** *yah / yah

22 =and the family really need me

23 (but I don't have the time?) / /

24 maybe I go there another

25 time/ /.

26 **T:** aah/ / so you can start again / / (..?)

27 **K:** yah / /

### Part II

28 **T:** you were delivering mail to the

29 patients? / /

30 **K:** yah / /

31 **T:** how many times did you go / / =

32 **K:** =no no/ / the I should go but I

33 didn't go / /

(continued)

**Figure 5–1**
Transcript of interaction in an ESL classroom (*continued*)

| | Conversation | Correction/Conversational Replay | Instruction |
|---|---|---|---|
| 34 **T:** | | I was SUPPOSED to go / / | that's a good one / / . I was |
| 35 | | | SUPPOSED to go [*taps table* |
| 36 | | | *rhythmically while repeating*] / / |
| 37 | | | everyone / / |
| 38 | | | |
| 39 **A:** | | | I was SUPPOSED to go / / |
| 40 **T:** | | | but I couldn't / / . but I couldn't= |
| 41 **C+:** | | | =but I couldn't / / |
| 42 **T:** | | | (ev-?) again / / |
| 43 **C−:** | | | =but I couldn't / / |
| 44 **T:** | | | I was supposed to go but I |
| 45 **A:** | | | couldn't / / again / / |
| 46 **T:** | | | I was supposed to go but I |
| 47 | | | couldn't / / |
| 48 **C+:** | | | I was supposed to go but I DIDN'T |
| 49 | | | you can also say but I DIDN'T |
| 50 **T:** | | | |
| 51 | | | |
| 52 | | uh-huh [*rising intonation*] / / because | |
| 53 | | the baby's sick / / | |
| 54 | aah/ / is the baby still very | | |
| 55 | sick? / / what's the matter? | | |

# The Influence of Larger Curriculum Activities: Routines and Tests

Although this is not a book about curriculum, we have to shift again from our zoom lens on discourse features to a more panoramic view of larger activities that influence discourse—as we did in Chapter 4 in moving from analyzing scaffolds in the moment-to-moment dyadic interaction of Reading Recovery to Hillocks' gateway activities in composition. One positive influence of such larger activities comes from well-established classroom routines. A more negative influence too often comes from the pressures of high-stakes tests.

### *Classroom Routines*

One benefit of a clear and consistent activity structure is that it allows participants to attend to content rather than procedure. The children's TV program, *Sesame Street,* offers a clear and simple example. Often, at least during the years I watched the program, the shows included a categorization game—"one of these things is not like the other." It was always played on the same visual format (a two-by-two matrix) and was introduced by the same music. The visual and audible "contextualization cues" told frequent listeners quickly and without further introduction what game was going to be played and what mental task would need to be performed. Then, once the format was familiar to viewers, a wide variety of content—categorizations by color, shape, number, species, function, and so on—could be inserted into the game without further directions.

So too in the classroom. If students can be socialized into a set of activity structures that become familiar and predictable, yet flexibly open for improvisations at the moment and for evolution over time, management problems and transition times can be minimized; then, both teacher and students can give their attention less to choreographing the activity and more to the academic content. As psychologist William James put it a century ago in his "Talks to Teachers" in Cambridge, Massachusetts: "The more the details of our daily life we can hand over to the effortless custodian of automatism, the more our higher powers of mind will be set free for their own proper work."[35]

In the description of Reciprocal Teaching in Chapter 4, we saw how it had become a part of the complex Community of Learners (COL) literacy/science program developed by Ann Brown and colleagues. RT was only one of a variety of discourse structures in that program. If the literacy and science goals were to be realized, all of the structures had to become routine, familiar, and predictable to the students.

Martha Rutherford, the first COL classroom teacher, has described the routines in her sixth-grade class in East Oakland, California.[36] Her class of 30 students included only four monolingual speakers of English. The following sections contain paraphrases of her descriptions of the COL routines she used.

**Benchmarks.** These are whole-class discussions, led by the teacher, about the large topic within which the student teams select subtopics for their research. The opening benchmark draws out the students' initial ideas in the new area of study. Later benchmarks introduce students to more sophisticated understandings (reconceptualizations). "For example, the students will need to understand the function of a food chain if they are to understand the impact of animals becoming endangered."

**Research rotations.** Once small research teams were established, during research days, the class was divided into thirds, each group then rotating through three activities:

- Two groups worked at the computers—finding resources, writing papers, and communicating with each other and outside experts via electronic mail.
- Three groups worked independently on research tasks such as finding resources, reading, note-taking, and so on.
- One group engaged in RT with the teacher, reading the scientific texts they needed for their research, and sometimes "RTing" the sections of the group report each student had written. These discussions with the teacher enabled her to clarify students' understanding of English vocabulary along the way—for example, that "fewer" in the sentence, "There have been fewer and fewer hungry chicks," means "not as many," not smaller in size as Robbie (trilingual in Thai, Laotian, and English) had said.

**Jigsaw.** Periodically, as the research teams are becoming experts on their subtopic, a child from each team meets with a group of students representing all the teams and teaches peers the results of their work-in-progress, perhaps including moments of RT or reading from the "teacher's" draft research report. This teaching not only validates each student expert as teacher, but also enables all students to see connections among their subtopics, and to think about peer questions that still need to be answered.

**Writing a team research paper.** This too was routinized in ways somewhat different from some process writing models. Here students always wrote at the computers, and always worked in pairs, with varying divisions of responsibility, such as dictator and typist. The writing continued over the life of the unit and included conferences with the teacher, also at the computer, so that text could be edited on-line.

In the year described by Rutherford, only four of her thirty sixth graders were monolingual speakers of English. In her teacher research, she follows the development of four bilingual girls who were members of the same research team, and shows how these activity routines provided multiple opportunities for them to learn both the science ideas and their expression in speech and writing through their changing participation in each of the routine contexts. For example, in four sequential RT sessions, Robbie's volunteered contributions increased from 5, 8, 22, to finally 37 times. Rutherford concludes:

> The multiple group configuration and the ritualistic [routinized] function of the activities aided language learning. . . . The predictable structures, like RT, enabled children to anticipate what was expected, thereby giving the students more choice of how and when they would enter into the discourse community. Moreover, anticipation of events allowed the children to prepare for those times that were forthcoming. Preparation diminished anxiety, particularly for these language learners.[37]

Rutherford's Community of Learners' routines are described in some detail here, along with her evidence of their benefits, not to suggest that anyone should try to imitate these specific activities. Rather, they are presented to suggest the value of planning some recurring activities that will structure academic discourse (in addition to managerial routines, like getting papers passed out).

Barnes and Todd warn about the danger of what they aptly call the "fossilization" of routines, specifically Reciprocal Teaching and Jigsaw. At least as used by its designers, Palincsar and Brown, RT is intended to evolve into more locally managed discussions about texts. In my personal experience, Jigsaw is flexible too. At a professional development workshop I attended, the topic was portfolios. We were divided into groups of four, each group counted off one, two, three, four, while the leaders passed out to each group a set of four short articles on portfolios that were also numbered one to four: "You have ten minutes to read your article, and twenty minutes to Jigsaw." No further directions were needed, and we immediately became a room of 100 silent readers. But the subsequent discussion was ours to conduct.

### *The Discourse of Testing Versus the Discourse of Teaching*

Just as this is not a book about curriculum, so it is not a book about assessment. But we need to consider the influence of formal tests on the discourse of teaching and learning—especially the high-stakes tests now so common.

Deborah Poole did an unusual January to May longitudinal study of such influence in three social studies classes in a California junior high school with predominantly Latino students. Her focus was on how

## Figure 5–2
### Seventh graders discuss braceros before and after tests

---

**A. Lesson**

1 **T:** r'member what they did to the Mexicans who came up here to work on the farms right? The braceros ( . . ) shipped 'em back to Mexico when Americans couldn't find jobs ( . . )

   [*later in the same class period*]

2 **S:** [*reading from book*] In many regions of the Southwest, Mexican immigrants faced prejudice and segregation. However, their work was important to the growth of the Southwest. In the 1920s, they began to have better job opportunities.

3 **T:** *maybe.* (1.2) you know when they didn't kick 'em back out to Mexico.

**B. Pretest review (TR-4)**

1 **T:** [*writes "bracero"*] You know what a *bracero* is?

2 **Ss:** Farmer!

3 **Ss:** [*silence*]

4 **S:** They pay 'em a little bit

5 **S:** Yeah

6 **T:** 'n then they send 'em back ( . . ) but ( . . ) all right ( . . ) *bracero* is a farmer from Mexico who works up here for a little bit and then goes back.

**C. Written Test**

    10. Identify *two* of the following:

        Charles Lindbergh    Prohibition

        Bracero    Pasadena Freeway

**D. Posttest review (TR-5)**

1 **T:** bracero is:

2 **Da:** a farmer from Mexico (that comes over here) to work for a while and then goes back.

3 **T:** and then goes back.

---

the forms of classroom discourse changed from a lesson for teaching and learning to a review before and after a mandated unit test. Figure 5–2 gives a typical contrast exemplified in the way the term *bracero* is discussed in Mr. Chavez's seventh-grade geography class during a lesson (5-2-**A**), a pretest review (5-2-**B**), the test (5-2-**C**), and a posttest review (5-2-**D**).[38]

    Poole points out several contrasts between the language of sequence **A** (the lesson) versus **B, C,** and **D** (test and reviews):

- Whereas the lesson includes expression of politically charged issues about what "they" did to the Mexicans, who are the objects of being "shipped back" "when the Americans couldn't find jobs" (**A**1), talk in the test reviews makes the Mexican braceros (farmers) themselves the agent of that action ("goes backs" in **B**6 and **D**2).

- The presence in the lesson of the teacher's evidential marker, *maybe* (**A**3), expressing T's uncertain attitude toward the sentence a student has just read, contrasts with bald, unqualified, assertions in the reviews ("bracero is" in **B**1, **D**1).

- Not shown in these brief excerpts is a contrast in the source of topic sequence. In the lesson, sequence comes from substantive relationships within the topic as discussion unfolds, while in the posttest review sequence, the sequence is based only on the numbering of the test items.

Poole describes her study as an investigation of the influence of pretest reviews on how "knowledge is constructed in teacher–student discourse."[39]

To the extent that threats of tests, particularly multiple-choice tests, hang over teachers, creating high stakes for them as for their students, it also will be harder to make time to try out the discourse variations suggested in this chapter. Only if assessments become more open-ended performances can we expect classroom discourse to vary in principled ways, from more traditional IRE to less and from one activity setting to another, depending on the purpose of the moment.

# Notes

1. Brown 1992, 166.

2. As I have read references to the first edition of this book in the writings of colleagues, I have been struck by how often these sentences are cited. I considered omitting them here, but teachers' interactional power, which they describe, still inheres in classroom life because of the moral and legal responsibility of teachers for safety and security. Beyond that necessary bottom line, this blunt portrayal may also highlight the importance of considering alternative patterns of speaking rights.

3. Parenthetically, I want to make it clear that, as the teacher in that lesson, I was completely unaware of the nomination patterns that Mehan (1979) found on his videotapes, and of those twenty-nine anomalous cases. But afterward, I appreciated his analysis of those cases most of all. In metaphorical terms, "school" is always a performance that must be constituted through the collaborative work of a group of actors: the teacher who assumes the dual role of stage director and principal player, and the students who are relative novices yet essential to the enactment of a culturally defined activity. With such a cast, the

unexpected is inevitable and then teacher and students have to improvise. Even Mehan's names for the improvisational strategies he identified ring true, especially "getting through." For the teacher, that's the bottom line—whatever else happens, one somehow has to "get through."

4. The still-classic study of turn-taking in conversation is Sacks, Schegloff, and Jefferson (1974). *See also* Irvine's (1979) discussion of dimensions of formality in communicative events.

5. Paley 1981, 25–26. Lionni's power as an author to engage children's moral imagination became the curriculum theme for a whole year in Paley's last year of teaching sixteen years later—reported in Paley 1997. Readers of Paley's many books have commented on her transcriptions of classroom talk and wondered why they read more smoothly than many others. Paley explained:

> In editing a child's speech, my aim is to preserve meaning, cadence, and inflection, and to avoid distractions for the reader. It is, I believe, the way we hear one another in the classroom. . . . For example, Deepak, speaking of his toy snake, says, "His name is Snaky, um, and everybody calls him by his . . . um . . . not Snake, um, Tommy, um . . . and I had another . . . that other . . . um . . . it was a little bear . . . it was called Tommy . . . and the snake is . . . uh . . . Tommy the snake . . . I mean Tommy the snake is Tommy's the bear's friend."
>
> Edited, the sentence might read: "his name is Snaky and everyone calls him Tommy. And I had another . . . a little bear . . . and it was called Tommy. And Tommy the snake is Tommy the bear's friend" (personal communication, March 1987).

I'm sure Paley is right that sensitive teachers, like normal conversationalists, hear children in this way. But making a transcript as an analyst is different from hearing speech as a participant and requires decisions contingent on purpose and focus. Paley's editing is right for her books. But for other purposes, the disfluencies themselves are informative. As we saw in Chapter 2, Sharing Time, they may indicate a speaker's increased cognitive load, as in telling episodic stories, and may also be a possible explanation for differential listener response.

6. Paley 1992, 122–30 (quotes are on 124, 127).

7. Eckert 1998, 148–49.

8. Allen 1992. Erickson (1996) describes the student "turn-sharks" who are ready and waiting to grab the floor.

9. Sarah Michaels and Richard Sohmer, personal communication, 1998.

10. Personal observation, October 1998. Talking sticks, or speaking staffs, are a part of many Native American traditions. According to an exhibit in the Museum of the Plains Indians (Browning, MT, August 1999): "[talking sticks] were used to keep order. If used during a meeting, the leader would pick up the stick which was placed in the center of the circle. He would begin the meeting, then pass the stick on. It was honored, so that no one was interrupted while holding the stick. The person holding the meeting would use their stick which

had symbols or designs that represented themselves or their stories." In the Tlingit (Alaska Native) tradition, the speaking staffs of two clans, Raven and Crow, have different designs. In an evening gathering for sharing family stories in the same Juneau, Alaska, elementary school, two traditional speaking staffs were available. Native children and adults, knowing their clan identities, took the appropriate staff when speaking, and seemed especially empowered by the added cultural meaning. Non-Native children and adults were welcome to take either one (Nancy Douglas, personal communication, February 2000).

11. Heider, Cazden, and Brown 1968.

12. Hemphill 1986. Her hypothesis for this research was that the social class differences in teenagers' syntax found by British sociologist Basil Bernstein (which he called codes 1971) and the subject of much subsequent controversy, are mediated by, or have as their intervening variable, different conversational styles. Hemphill's research is further discussed in Cazden 1994. In a study of peer literature discussions in a public library after-school program, Alvermann and colleagues found that the adolescents "thought it was fine to talk all at once" and noted that others had found this happening in adult book club discussions as well (1999, 248).

13. Tannen 1984.

14. This class has been discussed by McLeod (1986, 42–43), from which this excerpt is taken, and by Hardcastle (1985). In his study of high school physics classes, Lemke (1990) calls such sequences "cross-discussion."

15. Schifter 1997, 16.

16. Twenty-five years ago, sociologist Erving Goffman pointed out that the dual categories of speaker and listener(s) are inadequate for analyzing the multiple roles that people can assume in relation to ideas and to each other. In a simple case of speaking for oneself, a person both authors (composes) an utterance and speaks it aloud. But one can also re-speak—*animate* in Goffman's terms—the utterance of another, sometimes altering it in some way for the animator's own purpose (Goffman 1974, 516–23; or 1981, 144–46). *Revoicing* is another name for Goffman's animation. *See* Hoyle and Adger's edited book about *Kids Talk* for other applications of Goffman's ideas (1998). McCreddy's chapter in that book gives examples of students as animators when they are asked to fill-in-the-blanks, individually or chorally, in utterances that the teacher has authored.

17. O'Connor and Michaels (1996).

18. Ibid., 73–74.

19. Ibid., 81, 76, and fn. 10.

20. Ibid., 82.

21. Ibid., 78.

22. Duckworth 1981, 51–52. It is too easy to contrast questions that *assist* from those that *assess* as if any question will be only one or the other, in intent and effect. Duckworth's hypothetical examples show how this is not always the case.

23. Edwards and Furlong 1978, 41. Levinson (1979) discusses the general problem of coding utterances for their function (as speech act analyzes require) with examples of question sequences from classrooms and elsewhere.

24. Barnes et al. 1969, 24.

25. Lundgren (1977, 202), from which the example is adapted. Beck et al. (1998) give helpful discussions of questioning strategies.

26. Rowe 1986, 43. Tobin (1986) reports research on wait time in other curriculum areas.

27. Minstrell 1989, 135–36.

28. Jimenez and Gersten 1999, 290. These authors interpret Elisa's practice as a combination of high expectations and "respect" for her students.

29. Clay describes this book orientation in Clay and Cazden 1990.

30. Rosenshine and Meister 1994, 524–27.

31. Ulichny 1996, 746–47.

32. Wolfram, Adger, and Christian discuss such embedding in their excellent book on dialect differences and teaching (1999, Ch. 5, especially 125).

33. Atwell 1998, 17, 24.

34. Cognition and Technology Group at Vanderbilt 1997.

35. James (1900, 1958, 62). In Reading Recovery lessons, not only the set of activity structures is predictable, but the sequence as well: from reading two or more familiar books at the beginning to reading the day's new book for the first time at the end. Richard Anderson calls them "instructional frames" and points out their benefits to *teachers:* "When so many decisions about how to assist learning have to be made, it's helpful to have some givens" (1999, vii). In British sociologist of education Basil Bernstein's terms (1990), "regulative discourse" (which would include setting up, monitoring, and changing routines) is crucial to the success of the "instructional discourse" (about curriculum content) that is embedded (his term) within it.

36. In her 1992 manuscript, Rutherford uses the term *ritual.* I prefer the term *routine* not because it is more secular, but because it seems to connote more possible flexibility. My descriptions of her routines are shortened and paraphrased from that manuscript. *See also* Brown, Ellery, and Campione (1998) for another set of descriptions of these same routines.

37. Ibid., ms. 31. Rutherford doesn't describe how she established these routines. That important work has been described by an observer/teacher pair, de la Cruz and Brandt (1995) for writer's workshop in Brandt's first-grade class.

38. Poole 1994, 138–39.

39. Ibid., 126. *See also* Poole (1990) for a detailed analysis of the IRE sequences in a test review in another one of the classes. Chafe (1986) lays out the rich set of evidential devices that are available for expressing attitudes toward knowledge in spoken and written English.

# Chapter Six

# Talk with Peers and Computers

If you think about the meaning of the vague preposition *with* in this chapter title, you'll realize that it refers to different kinds of assistance. *With* peers means "together with peers," whereas *with* computers means "by means of computers," like eating *with* a spoon. Computers don't actively collaborate with us as peers can do, and we don't expect peers to let themselves be used solely in our service, as we wish computers would always do. Despite these differences, working with peers and computers often go together. When the number of available computers is limited, collaborative work among students is not only theoretically advocated but practically necessary. Student computer expertise can supplement the limited availability of the teacher. Moreover, an inherent feature of the technology is that work in progress on the screen is public in a way that paper on a student's desk is not.

In general, differences between learning in teacher-led lessons and learning in peer groups are becoming less marked. Teachers do not always maintain the stance and voice of authority, and there are often more student–student exchanges, even when the teacher leads the discussion—preceding chapters have presented examples. In Gallas' nontraditional sharing time and Lampert's nontraditional lessons, students are expected to respond to what has been said by peers as well as by the teacher. In other discourse variations, some teachers deliberately "revoice" one student's contribution to a discussion in order to position students to speak directly to each other. In Reciprocal Teaching (RT), teachers start out leading text discussions with the intention of gradually turning that responsibility over to the students. Brown's Community of Learners (COL) classrooms have multiple participation frameworks with opportunities for varied speaking roles—some including the teacher and some without. This fluidity, rather than a sharp contrast between talk with the teacher and talk with peers, characterizes many of the current innovations in classroom organization and participation structures.

Shifts between interacting with the teacher and with peers can even happen over a very short span of time. One striking example occurred in a second grade I was observing toward the end of the school year. During shared reading time with the whole class, controversy erupted between two interpretations of a short story the teacher was reading aloud. To make discourse space for more children to participate in the controversy, the teacher said simply, "Turn and talk," twirling her fore-finger in the air as she was speaking. Children immediately turned to their neighbor and talked excitedly. A few minutes later, the teacher asked for new interpretations, took a vote on alternative predictions, and returned to the text to read on. "Turn and talk" had obviously be-come a familiar routine in this classroom, and by May the teacher's twirling forefinger might have been a sufficient cue by itself. (A teacher in Anchorage, Alaska called the same brief activity "buddy-buzz.") But even with such increased opportunities for student talk within teacher-led lessons, there are still reasons to arrange times for students to work together, in pairs or small groups.

The discussion of "internalization" or "appropriation" as an essen-tial learning process (Chapter 4) included Bakhtin's contrast between two modes of appropriation: "reciting by heart" and "telling in one's own words." More formally, Bakhtin contrasts "authoritative discourse" with "internally persuasive discourse."[1] If we encounter the ideas of others as authoritative discourse—the words "of a father, of adults, and of teachers":

> [It] demands that we acknowledge it, that we make [that authorita-tive discourse] our own; it binds us, quite independent of any power it might have to persuade us internally; we encounter it with author-ity already fused to it.

This is the way students often hear the words of their teacher, even the way teachers may want to be heard.

Authoritative discourse can be learned by heart, to be repeated in the future, on demand. But until it becomes detached from that au-thority, it is not "one's own word"; it is not yet "internally persuasive." Again, in Bakhtin's words:

> Internally persuasive discourse—as opposed to one that is authorita-tive—is, as it is affirmed through assimilation, tightly woven with "one's own word." In the everyday rounds of our consciousness, the internally persuasive word is half ours and half someone else's. Its cre-ativity and productiveness consists precisely in the fact that such a

word awakens new and independent words, that it organizes masses
of our words from within, and does not remain in an isolated and static condition. . . . The semantic structure of the internally persuasive
discourse is not *finite*, it is *open;* in each of the new contexts that dialo-
gize it, this discourse is able to reveal ever new ways to mean.

Theoretically, it seems possible that students will be more apt to actively
struggle with new ideas—rephrasing them, arguing with them, con-
ceptually trying them out and verbally trying them on—when they are
spoken by (less authoritative) peers than by the (more authoritative)
teacher.

From this perspective, we look at examples of activities in which
peers talk together without computers and then ones in which they in-
teract in various ways with them. At the end, we consider the relationship between discourse quality and students' social relationships with
each other.

## Talking with Peers

In pair and small-group activities, students can take on various intellectual roles vis-à-vis each other. Four such roles are spontaneously
helping one another, tutoring another student when assigned by the
teacher, reciprocally providing "critique" of each other's work (as in
peer writing conferences), and collaborating as presumably equal status learners on assigned tasks.

### *Spontaneous Helping*

Students of all ages regularly ask for help and give it to each other—
regularly, that is, unless such help is outlawed as "cheating." [2] One such
helping interaction occurred in a fifth grade in a central Los Angeles
school in which 90 percent of the students are Latino and helping others is encouraged. Earlier grades in this school are taught bilingually,
but the fifth grade is taught mostly in English.

The class had taken a trip to the desert, and now back in the classroom they were asked to record words and illustrations that describe
the desert. Students sitting together at one table are Alvaro and Desiree
(of Mexican descent) and Bonita and Carlos (of Fijian descent). Bonita
asks for help in remembering a word. In Figure 6–1, Schegel has numbered lines of speech rather than turns, and analyzes how the children
"use each other's memories as word search resources, in addition to
their textbook and their teacher." [3]

Bonita describes what she is trying to name, simultaneously adding
gestures that reinforce her "rolling" image (1–4, 8). From their shared

**Figure 6–1**
Spontaneous helping

---

1  **Bonita:**  [*Bonita gazes straight ahead*] uh, What are those rolly things? [*Bonita holding a marker, begins twirling her hands as she say "rolly." Alvaro turns his gaze to Bonita as she twirls her hands.*]

2  They be rolling on the ground . . .

3  (.3) You know on cartoons or the commercials sometimes?

4  Ib //

5  **Alvaro:**  // From movies? [*Bonita looks at Alvaro.*]

6  (.3) Like the one // with Pee Wee Herman? [*leans back and points index finger as he says "one"*]

7  **Bonita:**  [*leans back as Alvaro leans back*] // Ye: ah.

8  [*twirls her hands as she speaks*] And then // you start ro: lling

9  **Alvaro:**  [*twirls his finger, then his hand*]

10  **Bonita:**  Yeah tho=iye. [*drops marker*]

   **Alvaro:**  [*places his hand on his mouth: thought position*]

11  I remember that.

12  Let me tell the teacher. [*leaves the group and goes to the teacher*]

\*   \*   \*

19  **Teacher:**  → [*off camera*] Tumbleweed? [*Desiree looks toward Alvaro and the teacher.*]

20  **Alvaro:**  [*off camera*] (.4) Tumble?

21  **Carlos:**  (.3) What is that?

22  **Bonita:**  (.7) What?

23  **Carlos:**  (.3) That, [*Carlos points at the picture.*]

24  **Alvaro:**  → tumblewe // ed [*uttered as he walks back to the table*]

25  **Bonita:**  // It's just be

26  **Desiree:**  → (1.0) [*to group*] tumble // we:ed.

27  **Bonita:**  [*looks up and out, possibly at the teacher*]
        → // oh yeah tumblewe:ed.

28  **Alvaro:**  → (2.4) [*sits*] It's tumblewe:ed.

---

experience on the class trip, her peers can help. In addition, "group members can rely on their shared experiences . . . as children who participate in and have knowledge of popular culture meaningful to them"— namely, cartoons and commercials (3, 5–6). Bonita's clues work for Alvaro, who joins in her gesture (9) and leaves to "tell" the teacher (out of hearing of the tape recorder) what they together have described. The teacher offers a candidate name, "Tumbleweed?" (19). Alvaro relays her suggestion back to the group (24). It is eventually ratified by Bonita, and the word search is successfully completed with a word whose first morpheme, *tumble,* is a lower-frequency synonym for Bonita's initial verb, *roll.*

In his analysis of this "socially shared cognition," Schegel emphasizes the importance of the children's body positionings and gestures accompanying their speech that serve to encode and communicate the image of rolling or tumbling. When synchronized by two children, as when leaning back in 6 and 7 and twirling fingers in 8 and 9, these movements also serve to reinforce social bonding.[4]

Note also how Bonita's success depended on the recently shared in-school resource of the field trip, especially by contrast with another word search in the same classroom. When a small group of Mexican-descent children are asked to write about anything they see in a surrealist painting by Marc Chagall, Hector sees something he cannot name and asks peers and teacher for help. He tries many gestures, and the teacher offers several candidate names. But it takes longer than for "tumbleweed" before someone off-camera suggests the subsequently ratified "plow." Hector later explains "he was recalling a photograph of his grandfather as a young farmer working a plow in Mexico,"[5] a personal image that was not shared knowledge and could not be easily communicated in words or gestures to peers or teacher.

### Assigned Teaching or Tutoring

In the fall of 1999, two teachers—Frank McCarthy (English) and John Sullivan (Social Studies)—at Cambridge Rindge and Latin High School in Massachusetts organized a "millennium project." Their tenth-grade students worked in pairs to investigate the most important events and the most infamous persons of one of the last twenty centuries and then presented their findings to their peers. Fourteen-year-old Siobhan O'Sullivan comments on the whole project:

> The best part was that we learned from our friends. When they got up to present the research on the events and people of their century, we understood it more because the information was being given in a way we could understand.[6]

This project is similar to the Jigsaw participant structure that is a recurring activity in the Community of Learners program described in Chapter 5. Each participant is responsible not only for learning a part of the whole curriculum unit themselves, but also for teaching that part to their peers. What Brown found in California is undoubtedly also true in Massachusetts: Knowing from the beginning their later responsibility for teaching makes the students especially serious about their own initial learning.

In *Children of Promise: Literate Activity in Linguistically and Culturally Diverse Classrooms*, Heath and Mangiola recommend that students' resistance to formal schooling can be overcome when they find new dignity and identity in becoming an "expert" in some activity. As one example, they describe cross-age tutoring, in which "at-risk" non-native English-speaking fifth graders become reading tutors for first graders in Redwood City, California. The teachers worked with the tutors before their tutoring began, and met with them in small groups as it proceeded.

The goal of these discussions was to help the tutors see themselves as becoming "experts" about the processes of reading, writing, and talking . . . and to see themselves as sources of knowledge that matters to someone other than a distant adult.[7]

Heath and Mangiola found that the tutoring benefited both tutors and their tutees in several ways:

- Students could read and tutor in either Spanish or English; many tutors started out in Spanish but then began to read and discuss in English, demonstrating their ability to transfer knowledge about literacy across languages.

- Tutors increasingly asked their tutees to retell stories with puppets and to write stories, thereby helping the tutees' comprehension and enjoyment.

- Tutors were encouraged to write about their tutoring. In letters to their tutees and to the tutees' teachers at the end of the year, the tutors expressed appreciation of the literate development of the tutees, perhaps thereby gaining new awareness of the value of literacy for themselves too.

Moreover, while literacy was the main school goal for the cross-age tutoring program, the tutors' classroom teachers noticed "a growth in their [students']willingness to speak out in class and to take leadership roles."[8]

For research on interaction in the San Diego multigrade classroom where the Chapter 3's Birthplaces lesson took place, Mehan and I set up what we called "instructional chains" in which the teacher taught a language arts task to one student and then asked that student to teach one or more peers. In two of the chains, third-grader Greg taught first-grader Everett (both African American) and first-grader Veronica taught first-grader Alberto (both Mexican American). In both pairs, the tutors engaged in remarkable style-shifting for their speech in the "expert" role. These shifts have been summarized from the San Diego tapes by Zina

Steinberg for her research with another instructional chain in a school for emotionally disturbed middle school children:

> Greg was often in trouble with both teachers and principal, both for not doing his work and for getting into fights. On the morning when he was to be tutor, he was wandering around the room alone, hidden in a paper-bag mask, singing to himself and making "jive" movements with his body. Yet once he was involved in learning the task and then teaching it, he did an excellent job. Moreover, his casual, even slurred black dialect shifted to a careful, crisp, even exaggerated pronunciation as he read sentences to his younger tutee. When the job was done, he poignantly asked one of the teachers, "Why am I so special today?" and explained that he meant by that "teaching" and "them fun things."
>
> Veronica could not give an adequate description to the adult teacher of what she was going to tell her tutee to do; yet in the course of repeating the directions in response to his noncompliance, her directions became more and more elaborated and complete. . . . Like Greg, Veronica's pronunciation of the English words for her tutee to spell was crisp and precise; but in her case this is all the more remarkable because she was still going to daily lessons in English as a Second Language (ESL) and gave her instructions to her tutee in Spanish, except for these words.[9]

For the student in the teaching role, the tutoring relationship provides an opportunity to engage in speaking actions usually reserved for the teacher. Remember the role reversals that developed over repeated occasions of language games played with parents at home, like peek-a-boo and picture-book reading (see Chapter 4). In school, such reversals in speaking roles would be unusual in interactions with the classroom teacher. The best situation for students to give directions (instead of just following them) and to ask questions (instead of just answering them) is with peers.

Beyond the benefits to the students, Steinberg suggests how much teachers can learn about their students' competencies by observing and listening to activities and interactions in which students take on an authoritative role:

> Teachers know that they don't see all aspects of a child's individual and interactional competence in that portion of behavior displayed within eyeshot and earshot of the teacher herself. But teachers may not realize how much of a child's "best behavior" they miss—best in the sense of closest to the goals of education itself—until they have the chance to eavesdrop on them in situations like the ones we have described here.[10]

When such eavesdropping expands teachers' awareness of their students' competencies, it can lead to heightened teacher expectations for the very students who need it most.

## *Reciprocal Critique*

In discussing "social constructivism" as a theory of human learning, I called attention to two meanings of *social*. Resources for learning, at home and at school, are most obviously and immediately available in the social interactions, the discourse that we engage in with others. But there are also the less obvious social origins, even if distant in time and place, of all the processes and products we encounter in our activities, from the math materials in Kate and Ryan's classroom below to computers and their software.

There is a third meaning of *social* as well, what Bakhtin calls the "addressivity" of any utterance—the quality of turning mentally to someone and anticipating, hoping for, humanly needing, a response.[11] When speaking, response can be immediate. But when writing (or painting or creating a video), response often comes too late to be helpful during the formative creative process. So, we can benefit from feedback given by someone else who can take on that audience role while change in still possible.

One general name for the enactment of this audience role is *critique*. Critique differs in important ways from criticism that we read in reviews of films or books:

- Criticism is about finished work; critique is about work still in progress.

- Criticism is often given by persons who do it as their primary job, (such as film critics for a newspaper); critique is a temporary role offered by one artist to another.

- Criticism is one-way, from critic to creator and potential audience; critique is a two-way, reciprocal relationship.

Like "portfolio," the term *critique* comes to us from the arts. In addition to comments from the prospective of audience, it can include comments on more aesthetic (formal) and functional (use) criteria.[12]

One familiar critique activity is peer writing conferences. One second-grade conference was observed by Barbara Kamler, an Australian writing teacher, when she was visiting Donald Graves' research team in the United States. The teacher, Egan, held regular writing conferences with individual children. In addition, she encouraged the children to hold peer conferences with each other. Here is Kamler's account of conferences between two students, Jill and Debbie:[13]

> On March 11, Jill was one of six children scheduled for a writing conference. . . . At Egan's direction, Jill and the other conferees went to the language table. Egan had requested that Jill first spend time with seven-year-old Debbie, going over the book to be sure it was ready for a conference. . . .

Jill began by reading each page aloud to Debbie. . . . As Jill listened to her own words, she made changes on page 1, 2, and 3 without any prompting or comment from Debbie, and on pages 4, 5, and 8 in direct response to questions Debbie asked. . . .

At the conclusion of this half-hour conference, Jill had made six content changes which affected the overall meaning of the piece. She had deleted information which made no sense or which she could not support; she added information to clarify or explain. Debbie's presence forced Jill to reread the book for the first time since composing; Debbie seemed to make the concept of audience visible for Jill. Jill also needs an active reader to ask questions. . . .

[Later] Debbie claimed her time: "OK, Jill, you help me now!" They reversed roles, returned to the language table to work on Debbie's book, *Ice Follies,* until Mrs. Egan was ready to see Jill twenty minutes later.

Kamler suggests that each child author benefits in two ways. More obviously, the peer asks questions, and some of Jill's changes were in direct response to Debbie's questions. Less obviously, the peer silently, but no less effectively, represents the needs of an audience and makes "the concept of audience visible."

Youth worker Elizabeth Soep described a writing conference between two teen-agers that took place in an arts-based summer program, which culminated in a Final Day Performance for families, friends, and mentors. As the writers prepared for their Final Day readings, they turned to peers for "honest feedback and thoughtful guidance." Here is Soep's description of one conference, also between two girls, Maya and Amy.[14]

### Amy's Critique for Maya

In the writing studio, Maya pulled her friend Amy away from the computer, saying, "Come on, we need to workshop." Grabbing copies of several poems in progress, the two retreated to a quiet area away from the tap-tapping of fingers on keyboards. Maya and Amy knew that I was conducting research on out-of-school arts education, so they agreed to let me listen to their critique session. Maya handed each of us a printout of her piece, "I Dreamed of a Bed," and proceeded to read it aloud. Shoulders back and chin up, she shifted into a dramatic vocal delivery that gave the poem lyrical cadence. As soon as she finished, her tone and posture settled back to normal and she observed tentatively, "I don't know. It's so-so—you know?" Amy took another moment to read over the printout of the poem before editing basics like spelling and grammatical errors. Then she tackled the more substantive matters:

"What does *devised* mean?" asked Amy, referring to a line in the poem about how Maya had *devised* her own world: "I knew this place / I knew it well / I had constructed it / I had devised it / These four walls." But Amy was not requesting a simple definition. She was pushing Maya to express the deeper meaning behind the term: "What are you

saying about your world?" Amy probed. "What have you done to it exactly?" "Okay," Maya said, getting the point. "I made it up. *Devised*—I
created it in my head."

They worked their way through the entire piece like this, line by
line, sometimes word by word.

### Maya's Critique for Amy

When the two moved on to Amy's piece, called "My People Love Too
Much," the critique process proceeded in a similar fashion. Amy read
her poem aloud and then encouraged Maya to "go for it. Cut it up."
Amy wondered, "Are there enough images to know exactly what I'm
saying?" and Maya replied. "I mean. I can see like, flashes of it, but you
have to read it twice to understand some of those things, you know
what I mean? Even though I know that's the image you're trying to
portray, but just to make it straighter for the reader." Maya went
through each image and suggested elaboration or clarification where
she deemed necessary. With every comment Amy urged Maya to
"write it, write it! Before I forget!" Maya complied but pointed out,
"See, you don't have to use these words: You can use whatever words
you want."

In contrast to Egan's second graders, these two older students help
each other with their poems in more individualized ways. When Maya
expresses only a general (perhaps formulaic) dissatisfaction with her
piece—"I don't know. It's so-so—you know?"—Amy starts with editing and then initiates a deeper discussion. She follows up her specific
question—"What does *devised* mean?"—with a more unusual invitation
to deeper reconsideration, "What are you saying about your world?"
When roles are reversed, Amy asks Maya for help with her images.
Then, when Maya had made suggestions about each image, even writing them out as Amy requested, she warns Amy, "See, you don't have
to use these words; you can use whatever words you want." She seems
to understand that suggestions from peers can, like those of a teacher,
be taken too authoritatively, while the deeper benefit to learning and
to imaginative creation will come from transforming the suggestions of
another into internally persuasive words of one's own.

Both these conferences can be deemed successful, and teachers
know that making peer conferences happen like that takes a lot of work.
Soep found wide variations in kinds of adult assistance across the programs she observed. "Some programs lay out specific rules for critique—for example, lead with something positive. In other programs,
young people learn how to critique by picking up the communicative
strategies modeled by their instructors and more experienced peers."[15]

In the second edition of *In the Middle: New Understandings About Writing, Reading, and Learning*, teacher researcher Nancie Atwell describes a
complex year-long apprenticeship in conferencing with her seventh

and eighth graders. Her apprenticeship neither scripts their interactions nor simply expects them to learn from their conferences with her. She gives a series of procedural minilessons specifically on conferencing, role-plays effective and ineffective conferences, and periodically calls the attention of the whole class to what she hears in their conferences during writing workshop.[16]

### Collaborative Problem Solving

Two common small-group activities in which students are expected to work together as equal-status collaborators are problem-solving groups in math and "book talk" groups in language arts/English.

Mathematics educator Paul Cobb and his colleagues conducted a year-long study of math teaching and learning in one second grade in which small-group work was a regular activity. The nontraditional "inquiry" curriculum focused on multidigit addition and subtraction, and instructional activities were designed to promote both conceptual and computational development.

The teacher worked hard to establish social norms for learning in her classroom, including explicit expectations for working with a peer partner. According to Cobb, these included:

- explaining one's mathematical thinking to the partner,
- listening to and attempting to make sense of the partner's explanations,
- challenging explanations that do not seem reasonable, justifying interpretations and solutions in response to challenges, and
- agreeing on an answer and, ideally, a solution method. . . .

> It should be stressed that the teacher did not simply list these norms as rules or principles to be followed; instead she capitalized on specific incidents in which students' activity either instantiated or transgressed a social norm by using them as occasions to discuss her expectations.[17]

(Note the similarities between Atwell's and this teacher's complex mix of teaching strategies across differences of grade level and curriculum area.)

In by far the longest chapter in the book on this research, Cobb presents four case studies, analyzed from video tapes, of pairs of students who worked together over ten weeks. Near the beginning of their work together, Katy and Ryan were working with "multilinks" of different lengths to solve their math problem. Figure 6–2 gives sixteen consecutive turns.[18]

While Ryan starts immediately to lay out the multilinks (1), Katy solves the problem by counting on her fingers (2). But when she answers his question (3), whether addressed to her or to himself, she

## Figure 6–2
### Solving a math problem using multilinks

The children were asked to solve, "How many do you add to III::: [36] to make IIIII:. [53]?"

1 **Ryan:** [*Starts to put out bars of multilinks*]

2 **Katy:** [*Counts from 36 to 53 on her fingers*] 17.

3 **Ryan:** Look, 36 [*points to 3 ten-bars and 2 three-bars*]. And how many do we have on that? [*points to the picture of 53 on the activity sheet*]

4 **Katy:** 53. So you add 2 more tens.

5 **Ryan:** 2 more tens and take away one of these [*points to three-bar*].

6 **Katy:** Come here, come here, I think you're not getting this right. All right, you have this many numbers [*points to the picture of 36*] and that makes 36, and that makes 37, 38, 39, 40 . . .

7 **Ryan:** [*Interrupts*] Look, look . . .

8 **Katy:** [*Ignores him and completes her count*] . . . 50, 51, 52, 53.

9 **Ryan:** Well this is 36 [*points to the activity sheet*], and we have to take away one of these things [*a strip of three squares in the picture of 36*].

10 **Katy:** Oh no you don't.

11 **Ryan:** [*Ignores her*] and then we add 2 of these things [*two strips of 10*].

12 **Katy:** Here, I'll explain it to you how I got the number.

13 **Ryan:** [*Ignores her*] and then we add 12 of these things [*two strips of 10*].

14 **Katy:** Here, you have that many numbers, 36, and you add 10 more, makes 46 [*holds up both hands with all 10 fingers extended*], 47, 48, . . . 53 [*puts up 7 fingers as she counts*].

15 **Ryan:** Katy, look, you have to take away a 10 [*remainder of his statement is inaudible*].

16 **Katy:** I'll show you how I got my number. See, you have 36, and add 10 more makes 46 [*holds up both hands with all 10 fingers extended*], 47, 48, . . . 53 [*puts up 7 fingers as she counts*]. Do you agree with 17?

speaks of adding "two more tens" (4). Then ten turns later, after arguing back and forth, she explains her whole process as adding ten and then counting on her fingers only the remaining 7 (14 and 16). In making this strategic shift away from thinking only in ones, Katy may well have been influenced by Ryan's actions with the ten-bars.

Meanwhile, Ryan solves the problem in two ways, both different from Katy's: first, adding 2 tens and then taking away a 3-bar (5); and later, taking away a 3-bar first and then adding 2 tens (9 and 11). We cannot tell from this excerpt what either Katy or Ryan understood about the equivalency of their three solutions; but Katy is at least going to make sure they agree about the answer at the end (16).

In Cobb's analysis, which is more complex than mine and draws on what he knows from his longitudinal observations of the children's work and his conversations with the teacher, he calls their interactions, "multivocal" by contrast with the "univocal" dominance of a single perspective: "Multivocal interactions are constituted when both children attempt to advance their perspectives by explicating their own thinking and challenging that of their partner." [19]

While Cobb does not question how gender may have influenced the interaction between Katy and Ryan, the influence of such potential aspects of classroom status is one focus of Cynthia Lewis's study of peer literature discussions in a combined fifth–sixth grade. In this class of predominantly European American children, age (or grade), gender, and ability, as perceived by the teacher, turn out to be significant. The teacher, Julia, has high standards for her students' interpretive competence, expecting them to refer to the text for supporting claims, and high standards for their social competence, expecting them to be responsible to the classroom community and value learning from others. In analyzes of peer discussions and interviews with focal students, Lewis finds complex peer relationships enacted through the discussions.

One discussion among eight students of "Number the Stars," about the Nazi occupation of Denmark, began with Jason reading from his journal (see Figure 6–3).[20]

When Nikki questions Jason's connection between sadness over Lise's death and her impending marriage (2), Jason does not support his statement from the text, although he could have done so, and withdraws from the discussion. Nikki repeats her disagreement (6), and later escalates it by adding, "I mean, marriage isn't that big of a deal" (10).

From interviews with the students, Lewis offers more interpretation of their interactions than can be inferred from this excerpt. Jason (a fifth grader of medium to low ability, according to the teacher) told her "he didn't like discussing big issues because it was too hard and too slow" and preferred an optional all-male group of fifth-grade boys like himself. In Lewis's observations, this was a group "where the boys focused on plot and action rather than on character relationships." Nikki (a high-ability fifth grader) "was considered an oppositional thinker by her peers and her teacher . . . [who] often read against the grain of the text" in both peer and teacher-led discussions. While Kate (9) seems to dismiss Nikki's ideas as just typical Nikki, David (a high-ability sixth grader) is more positive. Although his position vis-à-vis Jason and Nikki is not clear (7), he told Lewis in a final interview that among his classmates Nikki's comments "particularly stand out for him," and recounted another example:

**Figure 6–3**
Excerpt from a peer literature discussion

---

1 **Jason:** [*reading from his journal*] Lise died when she was just a few days from marriage which was pretty sad since she was so close to getting married. There was also a king named Christian and then her little story was over.

2 **Nikki:** I have a question. Why is it so sad that she got—died just before she got married?

3 **Jason:** Well 'cause /

4 **Lisa:** Because she was getting married and then all of a sudden she died.

5 **Kate:** *Duh.*

6 **Nikki:** But I don't get why that means sad because like it'd be sad if she just got married and died, I think.

7 **David:** It'd be sad*der*. It's always sad when someone *dies.*

8 [*laughter*]

9 **Kate:** Not to Nikki. It's like, oh great a person's *gone. Yes!*

10 **Nikki:** What's it matter if she died before she got married. [*Others are talking over her, teasing her.*] I mean, marriage isn't that big of a deal.

11 **Several Students:** OOOOH!

---

She always thinks like, for some of the books that are from an American point of view, like "April Morning," she'll try and think of what the, what the British soldiers are thinking, you know. And that's exactly what I was thinking, so she says a lot of the same things as me.

Through her interviews Lewis discovered that low-ability Jason was not the only student sometimes reluctant to participate with his peers. High-ability Mackenzie, often asked by the teacher to lead literature groups, expressed trouble of a different kind, sometimes feeling freer to speak her mind when the teacher was present. While other students had told Lewis that "the teacher would sometimes recast their ideas in ways they didn't understand or felt alienated from," Mackenzie considered it easy to disagree with the teacher: "What you need is confidence enough to be able to say, 'No, that's not what I was thinking. I was thinking this.'" But for Mackenzie, that confidence didn't transfer to discussions with peers. She recounted to Lewis a discussion about whether it was right for a character to plot revenge:

Mackenzie felt that she had to say she thought it was right to plot revenge because everyone else in the group thought so, many of whom were her friends. But when Julia asked her what she thought, she found herself saying that it was wrong because, "That's really what I thought." I asked her if having Mrs. Davis there had anything to do with her decision to say what she believed: "Probably, I mean, knowing that Mrs. Davis was definitely gonna, I knew before she said it that she was gonna agree with me."[21]

Lewis's analysis raises many important questions about the dynamics of peer discussions and the influences on whether they promote their goals of enhanced participation and both academic and social learnings. There is no single answer to how to make peer group activities successful for all students. The contextual influences are too varied and too influential. In a review of research on "group processes in the classroom," Webb and Palincsar present the evidence for thirteen possible influences, including ability and gender (discussed by Lewis) and the teacher's role (emphasized by Cobb). At the end, they conclude, "[T]he long list of group and classroom features provides a menu of possible ways to enhance the quality of collaboration in the classroom."[22] Each is thus a candidate for research by teachers in their own classrooms.

## Talk With, At, Through, and In Relation to Computers

Because learning with all forms of electronic technology is such a fast-growing and changing field, this chapter does not attempt a thorough analysis. Instead what follows is more of a conceptual map of the territory and some suggestions about where to pay attention to matters of discourse along the various paths within it.

The ways computers enter into, and influence, classroom talk can be expressed in four prepositional phrases:

- *With* computers refers to interaction between a student and computer software.
- *At* computers refers to interactions between two or more students as they sit at the computer keyboard.
- *Through* computers refers to interactions among students at a distance, via telecommunication.
- *In relation to* computers refers to classroom interaction not at the keyboard but incorporating work done there.[23]

More about each in turn in the following sections.

### Talk with Computers

One of the first uses of computers in education was "computer-assisted instruction" (CAI), in which a solitary student interacts with some kind of computer software. (When more than one student is present at the keyboard, then there is talk *at* the computer, not just *with* it.) Usually fitting the barest IRE/IRF model of interaction, such computer use has been widely criticized as merely an electronic workbook, a high-tech form for a low-tech function.

Because the student–software interactions are completely dependent on the computer software, and those programs vary so widely, little can be said here in detail. Two general points are, however, worth keeping in mind. First, it may be tempting to consider such software as a potential scaffold, helping a learner attain proficiency in some skill—for example, an online tutorial program for a new software program itself. In a book edited by British researchers, *Computers and Talk in the Primary Classroom*, Mercer and Fisher warn against that assumption:

> [B]ecause any educational software that we have observed in use offers, at best, a very limited set of "feedback" responses to children's input, and since such responses are often a poor match for the problems actually encountered by children in the classroom, we do not feel that the use of the term "scaffolding" is appropriate. Moreover, we have observed that (a) pupils often get into difficulties in spite of information or guidance offered by the program, and (b) it is precisely at such times that a teacher's supportive intervention is sought and received.[24]

More positively, we have to admit that when the computer software does give feedback (F) to a student's keyboard response (R), it does so depending entirely on the nature of that response. Unlike a teacher, the computer never sees skin color, never hears dialect or accent, and never knows anything about the student's living conditions (at one extreme, homelessness) or educational status of family members (at another extreme, two professional parents). Because teachers, consciously or not, often do take such factors into account, for better or worse, some advocates for poor and minority students have stressed the potential benefits of computerized instruction.

### Talk at Computers

When two or more students sit together at a terminal, interaction changes in qualitatively significant ways. Discussion can take place between the computer's initiation and students' response:

- I: Initiation by the computer
- D: Discussion between the children
- R: Response by the children acting together
- F: Follow-up move by the computer[25]

IRF discourse is transformed into IDRF in a way that would not be likely in noncomputer interactions. (The second-grade teacher's request to the students, "turn and talk," before predicting the next story event is close.)

**Figure 6–4**

Talk at the computer during a computer game

---

1  **Simon:** Dig [*evidently a possible keyboard response*]

2  **Roger:** What can we do? What can we do?

3  **Simon:** To see if the grass is not that again [*pointing*].

4  **Roger:** What can we do?

5  **Simon:** Just then we can see um um dig to see if the grass is that hard.

6  **Roger:** No, that's too hard, remember.

7  **Simon:** Yeah, but I know but that path is hard but we are going to be on the grass. I (2) look, if we go there we need to get on the grass. If we if we walk in there we'll be on the grass, right? So, we'll press Dig to see if the /

8  **Roger:** Dig.

9  **Simon:** And then we'll see if the grounds ( . . . ) now press Dig.

10 **Roger:** [*presses key*] No it won't work.[26]

---

Figure 6–4 contains a brief snapshot of talk as two boys, Simon and Roger, play Concept Kate, an adventure game. They have met an obstacle, a blocked path ahead, and have to decide how to get through. In this transcription, a pause of less than a second is marked with a slash (/), while longer pauses are indicated by number of seconds in parentheses; ( . . .) indicates unintelligible speech.

Such talk can be analyzed in the same ways as other peer collaboration. In these moments, Simon is speaking in *exploratory talk* in two senses: exploratory in the sense of first draft, with pauses and repetitions (5, 7) and in the sense of hypothetical if–then suggestions (5, 7, 9). Roger takes a secondary role, offering one short-reasoned objection (6, seemingly referring to something they had previously encountered and should "remember") and following Simon's direction about which response to enter.

One difference between interacting at the computer and interacting at a table with other materials, such as the math multilinks that Kate and Ryan used, is that one division of labor is more definite: one participant—here, Roger—will be sitting in front of the keyboard and become the one to physically enter responses. During collaborative composition with word processing software, one person will be the primary typist. Tracking how students collaborate at the keyboard—for example, in suggesting and evaluating candidate sentences when composing—is another context in which to monitor the quality and quantity of speaking rights and listening responsibilities that were discussed in Chapter 5.

More complex software may include what Wegerif and teacher Lynn Dawes call a "talk support module." For example, in a simulation of plant growth "embedded in an overall narrative frame in which students 'role-played' scientists trying to find the formula to help a friend win the local flower show," the program not only explicitly directs the students to discuss predictions, but provides a cumulative visual record of their previous predictions and how they turned out. The assumption behind the provision of such modules is that they will support increasingly complex collaborative thinking and talking.

Without computers, this kind of support can be approximated by the teacher at the blackboard or overhead projector, or by students themselves on paper as they work. But computerized support is potentially both quicker and richer.

## Talk Through Computers

Telecommunication makes possible communication among students at a distance. In the words of technology teacher Philip Sittnick in the Laguna Middle School in New Mexico: "[T]echnology is a bridge between worlds."[27] Electronic bridges are not built easily, requiring accessibility to telephone connections as well as computers. Reports of telecommunication projects, mostly by the teachers involved, describe problems of inadequate planning as well as inadequate hardware, and the benefits for student learnings when the problems are solved.

Many of the telecommunication projects available in published reports are by middle and high school teacher researchers. Some communicate through BreadNet, the electronic network for the Bread Loaf School of English that was established in 1993 especially to connect otherwise isolated rural schools. BreadNet now includes about 500 teachers who are or have been summer school students at Bread Loaf.[28] Typically, their telecommunication projects involve two or three teachers who plan together to coordinate projects in their respective classes and regularly exchange student writing about them.

One important quality of these exchanges is that they are not communication between pen pals. Some personal writings will be exchanged, especially when students introduce themselves to their new audience, often distant in culture as well as geography, but the emphasis is always on substantive curriculum content. In the English teachers' classrooms, this is usually literature all the participating students have read.

In one unusually large exchange, Scott Christian, then a teacher in rural Alaska, participated in a BreadNet exchange with eight other teachers in Alaska, Mississippi, Vermont, and New Mexico. In all classes, students read *Anne Frank: Diary of a Young Girl* and exchanged writings, comments, and questions prompted by the book. Christian subsequently wrote a book about this "Anne Frank Conference," analyzing the growth in student writing that it stimulated.

Sometimes, the curriculum focus is a replication in each classroom of an agreed-on local inquiry. Two teachers in the Southwest each described their exchange about "raptors" (birds of prey like eagles). Sittnick was teaching in the Laguna Pueblo, and Vicki Hunt was team teaching with a biology teacher outside Tucson—her students were from Mexico, Vietnam, and Korea.[29] The study of raptors at each site, and the writings exchanged, included comments and questions about raptors as an endangered species ("Do you believe in shooting raptors or saving them?"); mythology and folklore about raptors from their respective cultures (the Laguna Eagle Dance and the eagle legend on the Mexican flag); and imaginative writing.

In a separate report, Hunt includes a few examples of student writing sent to Laguna. Here's one student's self-introduction, followed by another student's poem:

> Hi my name is Edgar E. Esparza and I'm an 11th grader at Peoria High School. I'm from Monterey, Nuevo Leon, Mexico. I have lived in United States of America for 4 years in Peoria, Arizona. Today 3/31/95 is my birthday.

### Pride

> The hawks hang around in the dark.
> As for the eagles they soar high through the wind
> And they talk with the gods above.
> No other is stronger than the eagles.
> He has a special kind of talent.
>
> —Cheryl Silva

While the primary purpose of these telecommunication projects is to enlarge the audience for student writing, they bring implications for oral discourse as well. Some of the writings—personal introductions, like Edgar's, and brief comments and questions—are the kind of oral/written hybrid that has become familiar to many of us on e-mail. The projects also bring enhanced opportunities for talk "around" computers in each classroom that we'll return to below.

Classroom exchange projects are not restricted to the English language. Teacher/researcher Dennis Sayers has been working since 1985 with De Orilla a Orilla (From Shore to Shore), a network for encouraging exchanges across languages as well as cultures to encourage bilingualism and positive cross-language attitudes. One of the first projects involved an exchange between a class in Puerto Rico and a bilingual class in Connecticut that included recent immigrants from Puerto Rico as well as English-speaking children from Puerto Rican-background families. In the course of producing a bilingual newspaper, the bilingual children in Connecticut became valued experts, and their English-dominant peers' attitudes toward Spanish became more positive.[30]

More unusual is the use of an electronic network in the larger social project of revitalizing an endangered indigenous language. The Leoki bulletin board system was developed at the University of Hawaii at Hilo as one component of its support for the Hawaiian immersion schools in which a seriously endangered "heritage" language is the medium of instruction for initially English-speaking students.[31] As of 1997, there were nine Hawaiian-medium preschools and fourteen elementary and secondary immersion schools throughout the islands. For these students, there is still little opportunity to hear, speak, read, or write the language outside of school. So, being able to exchange writing in Hawaiian among the schools can enlarge their audience significantly. Hopefully, such exchanges will someday include native speakers on the special privately owned small island of Niyihau.

Moreover, because computers symbolize the world of the future, they change students' perception of the "heritage" language they are now learning. "In order for Hawaiian to feel like a real living language like English, it needs to be seen, heard, and utilized everywhere, and that includes the use of computers."[32] Sittnick titles his report of the Laguna computer projects that were conducted in English, "A school at the crossroads of the ancient and the contemporary." That title would be even more apt for Leoki exchanges.

These exchange projects could obviously be carried on in a low-tech fashion by means of regular mail. Cummins and Sayers detail the origin of "global learning networks" in the postal exchanges initiated by Celeste Frenet, a teacher in a one-room rural school in the French Maritime Alps in the 1920s.[33] But all the telecommunicating teachers today agree that computers make a qualitative difference. Speed alone is a benefit when students are waiting for a response and the momentum in each classroom can't be allowed to drop. Beyond speed are positive student attitudes toward learning about computers and about what learning through computers makes possible.

A different use of telecommunication, more common in postsecondary education, is when a class is taught partially or wholly via computers. One semester, Mehan taught a college class (on classroom interaction) via two media: to one group of students in a regular classroom setting and to another group electronically. Some differences were predictable, such as longer lag time between Initiations and Responses via computer. More interestingly, Mehan and his colleagues also found qualitative differences in the discourse. Topically, in contrast to the regular classroom, the electronic discussions pursued "multiple threads" rather than only one at a time. In other words, the criterion of relevance for any comment shifted to the class material as a whole; that is, it was not limited to the immediately preceding talk.

Structurally, the three-part IRF sequence was also changed: Students gave longer, and more thoughtful, answers to questions; teacher evaluations were almost totally absent; and students received more comments from their peers.[34] This classroom–telecommunication comparison is important not only because it offers a glimpse of what may become a more common medium of instruction, but also because it highlights contrasting features of the more familiar classroom.

### Talk in Relation to Computers

In the telecommunications exchange projects described here, there is much talk away from, but *in relation to,* computers simply because each of the projects is central to the class curriculum for a limited period of time. So there is extensive talk both before anyone touches the keyboard to send any writing and after partners' writing is received.

One three-way BreadNet exchange between an Inupiat village on the Alaskan shores of the Bering Sea, a private international school in Kuwait, and a white middle-class suburban school in greater Salt Lake City collected and exchanged oral histories of their communities. In each classroom, students planned and conducted interviews with elder members of their community and participated in deciding what to send to their partner classes. Citrino and Gentry describe some of the talk that ensued:

> We didn't feel obligated to send everything students wrote. Instead, we tried to select what was best or most representative of the whole, and students participated in making these choices. This selection process helped students to analyze the elements of good writing, and the power of narrative in their own writing, and their attention to these concepts was greater than when we simply pointed them out in anthologized literature.[35]

At schools where computer experiences are not so central to the class curriculum, Crook warns against "the danger of their dislocation from a main stream of educational discourse."[36] Whether computers are in a corner of the classroom or isolated in a lab, computer use is too often marginalized from the rest of the curriculum. "The nature of computer-based tasks readily *encourages* this marginalization . . . given that the opportunity for children to use the technology independently is seen as something positive . . . [and] because of the opportunity they can provide to release a teacher's time and attention."[37]

Crook argues that the "dislocation" is less physical than conceptual, involving two kinds of learning loss. One loss is what he calls "lateral loss"—the loss of transfer across learning contexts. Citrino and Gentry's description of the classroom discussions about which writings to forward electronically suggests such positive transfer between the telecommunications' project and the students' own future writing.

A second kind of loss Crook calls "longitudinal loss"—the gradual loss of a build-up of what he calls "intersubjectivity," what Edwards and Mercer call "common knowledge," and what I call shared "contexts in the mind." [38] Individual experiences automatically become part of that individual's private mental context for future experiences. But a common mental context that is shared among members of a classroom community—a shared resource for future learnings—takes deliberate teacher work.

Crook summarizes Edwards and Mercer's analysis of the discourse devices that teachers use to this end:

- "organized recapping that allow[s] the creation of a shared memory of what happened . . .

- "cued elicitation that serves to solicit an agreed [-on] account of what was currently happening . . .

- "summarizing, challenging, questioning, and so on, in ways that both check current positions and update the evolving shared context . . .

"This common knowledge is generative," Crook concludes; "becomes the platform for new understandings and new connections to be made." [39]

We saw an example of such common knowledge construction in Wells' analysis of the IRF discourse in the lesson about "a fair test" in Chapter 3. The unrecorded conversations around these telecommunication projects can contribute to the same end.

To teachers, Crook stresses its importance in planning all computer use in classrooms where learning about something other than computers is the goal. To researchers, he stresses the importance of longitudinal research through which such continuity in learning for a class as a whole can be understood: "The consequent achievements only become visible if we research beyond the moment-to-moment level of conversation; if we concentrate on more protracted structures of social exchange." [40]

The importance of such longitudinal continuity for learning is in no way tied to computer use. Crook stresses it in a book about how technology can enhance learning because computer experiences are particularly vulnerable to isolation. I follow him in stressing it here for that same reason, and also because thinking about optimal computer use highlights more general features of optimum talking and learning environments.

## Social Relationships Among Students

Amidst current arguments for creating a community of learners, it is important not to idealize the notion of "community" and to consider realistically the relationships among students that such learning environments assume. All of the emerging changes in classroom participant structures, and the kinds of discourse that we hope will happen within them, combine to raise the importance of these social relationships.

In more traditional classrooms, social relationships are extracurricular, potential noise in the instructional system and interference with "real" schoolwork. What counts are relationships between the teacher and each student as an individual, both in whole-class lessons and in individual seat-work assignments. In nontraditional classrooms, the situation has fundamentally changed. Now each student becomes a significant part of the official learning environment for all the others, and teachers depend on students' contributions to other students' learning, both in discussions and for the diffusion of individual expertise through the class.

### Social Relationships in Discussions

Researcher O'Connor reminds us of the parallel between the importance of the interpersonal context for teacher–student scaffolding (stressed by Addison Stone and quoted in Chapter 4) and the importance of the interpersonal context for all group discussions. Her blunt statement of the problem applies as much to groups of peers as to talk led by the teacher.

> In recent work on classroom group discussion and its role in learning, an idealized view of classroom discourse frequently appears. In this idealization, content-related meaning is continually negotiated and created in the moment by peers who respect each other's views. . . . Unfortunately, the idealization itself, however heartening, may do a disservice to teachers and students alike, in that it encourages us to avoid serious examination of the complexities posed by classroom group discussion and group learning. . . . Put less elegantly, social relationships of various kinds can work against the desiderata of "group sense-making" and "negotiation of meaning." . . . In short, implementing the classroom discourse practices intended to create a "community of learners" or a "discourse community" or a "thinking curriculum" is not for the faint-hearted.[41]

One way of gaining more information on how these relationships may be affecting patterns of discourse is to supplement analysis of talk with student interviews. Reports of such interviews, whether done by researchers or teachers, are not easy to find. In Cynthia Lewis' research on group literature discussions, we saw how Jason and Mackenzie felt about their participation. Also in language arts, Alvermann heard from interviews with three gifted eighth graders (two girls and one boy) "a continuing concern about the argumentative nature of their small-group discussions."

In math discussions, the option of accepting alternative answers does not remain as viable because students know that in the end some are going to be "right" and others "wrong." So disagreements have a sharper edge. In one thoughtful analysis, Lampert and two colleagues interviewed a group of Lampert's fifth-grade math students about their feelings about public disagreements. One of them was Ellie, whose idea that "eight minus a half is four" was a focal point of the excerpt from Lampert's classroom in Chapter 3.

In quoting what Ellie said to them, the authors' comments have been separated from Ellie's by using square brackets and italic type.

**Ellie:** I don't like reasoning because whenever you have a wrong answer people try so hard to prove you're wrong. [*Her friend Saundra agreed with her . . .*] Um, when, when you do realize that you have the answer wrong they still want to prove it to you that it's wrong . . . and you just want to crawl under your desk. [*But Ellie had an intellectual concern as well. She was worried about her own capacity to hold on to her thinking in the face of disagreement.*] Um, sometimes I don't like discussions because when you're trying to prove something it just turns into something else and you don't get to say what you think. [*After she said this, several students in the class muttered agreement.*] [42]

Lampert and her colleagues conclude that "the teacher's role goes beyond the connection of students' work with the big ideas in the disciplines. . . . Teacher intervention is also significant on the social front." [43]

### Social Relationships in the Diffusion of Individual Expertise

Being able to use technology assumes a set of literacy skills that are special in several ways. Initially unevenly distributed across the classroom due to differences in home computer use (from lots to none), basic computer literacy requires supplementing for each software program. For such tutoring, teacher time will be limited, and some students may quickly become more expert than the teacher. So student-to-student transmission of expertise becomes necessary.

Effective diffusion of expertise through a classroom can involve a mix of assigned tutoring and spontaneous helping. In Brown's Community of Learners project, the teacher would teach a new computer skill to only one research group and then give those students the responsibility for teaching the rest of the class[44] and presumably also for giving subsequent help as needed. In such situations, it is vital that social relationships among students support rather than impede that diffusion.

In a comparative study of two sixth grades in which computers and word processing software had been introduced, Sarah Michaels discovered some of the influential factors. In an end-of-the-year, on-screen performance test of students' individual editing skills, she found large differences between the two classes. In Classroom B, fourteen out of seventeen students completed the editing tasks; twelve students used technical vocabulary, such as *cursor* and *Control C,* in explaining what they were doing; and there were no obvious gender differences in these results. In Classsooom A, however, only one student completed the tasks (Richie, whom the teacher had taught and then relied on to teach others), only two students used any technical vocabulary, and not a single girl showed that she knew how to insert or delete text.

From field notes written throughout the year, Michaels was able to figure out some of the reasons for this extreme disparity.

> [I]n Classroom B, the single most important factor is that the students often worked in pairs at the computer (at least 30 percent of the time). Partners were assigned on the basis of the order in which first drafts were completed and edited by the teacher; hence, a certain unpredictability was introduced. Mixed sex and mixed computer ability pairings were common. . . .
>
> In Classroom A, there was no official partner policy. . . . As a rule, groupings at the computer divided along sex lines (as did groupings in the lunchroom and on the playground). . . . Not surprisingly then, on the computer quiz, the only two other students to demonstrate some knowledge of the QUILL commands were boys who were close friends of Richie.[45]

This study offers a particularly clear picture of how information, once introduced, spreads, or doesn't, through two classrooms and some aspects of the participation structures that supported or constrained that spread. In other classrooms, other aspects will be influential. But in all classrooms, the quality of the classroom "community" is at stake.

"Interventions . . . on the social front," which Lampert calls for, are necessary both for the discussions that are her concern and for diffusion of student expertise that is Michaels' focus. Beyond their importance to academic learning, such interventions are also essential for student's development toward active citizenship in a pluralistic democratic society. It makes no sense, and it seems almost dishonest to "mainstream" students across some dimensions of diversity and "integrate"

them across others unless the social organizations of classrooms promote the habits of speaking and listening from which positive interpersonal relationships across those differences can grow.

# Notes

1. Bakhtin quotes are taken from 1981, 342–346 (italics in the original).

2. In May 2000, six members of an audience of teachers in Haifa, Israel,
joined me in reading aloud the math lesson from Chapter 3 studied by Hiebert
(Figure 3–4) as a play script; each person read the part of one child, as the rest
of the audience followed our reading on an overhead. The man who read (played)
Roberto inserted an additional comment after Maria's answer (6): "She stole that
from me! That was my idea!" The audience laughed appreciatively as an important commentary about attitudes toward "cheating" was implicitly expressed.

3. Schlegel 1998, 187, 190–92.

4. Gestures deserve more attention by teachers and researchers alike, especially of children who are only recent learners of the classroom language.
Schlegel refers to psycholinguist David McNeill's 1992 pioneering study of *Hand
and mind: What gestures reveal about thought.* Bonita's gestures and words encode
the same *rolling* meaning, but McNeill shows on his videotapes how gestures
sometimes encode complementary aspects of meaning not caught by words
alone. He argues, in contrast to Vygotsky, that verbal language often does not
fully express the thoughts and images in the speaker's mind. Erickson 1996 analyzes the importance of body positionings.

5. Schlegel op cit., 198.

6. Franklin 11/14/99, 5.

7. Heath and Mangiola 1991, 21, 23.

8. Ibid., 23. An appendix gives suggestions for initiating such a program.

9. Steinberg and Cazden 1979, 263. The full analysis of Greg's tutoring is
in Cazden et al. (1979), and of Veronica's in Carrasco et al. 1981. Anyone who
tries to audio- or videotape peer speech in the classroom will probably encounter problems in getting good sound. Wireless microphones that children
take turns wearing are one solution. Surprising as it may seem, children (at least
young children) quickly forget about them, even after thorough "informed con-
sent" discussions.

10. Steinberg and Cazden op cit., 264. Another kind of helping—spontaneous or requested, in public or private—happens when bilingual students use
their valuable expertise in translating for a new immigrant peer. Common as this
undoubtedly is in many classrooms today, descriptive research is hard to find.

11. Bakhtin 1986, 99.

12. Grubb (1999) includes critiques in a little-studied educational setting:
vocational classes in a community college. I know of no such descriptions of
comparable research in vocational high school classes.

13. Kamler 1980, 683–85.

14. Soep 1996, 43–44. *See also* Heath and Smyth 1999 about Arts programs based in out-of-school youth organizations that have been the subject of decade-long research by Heath and Milbrey McLaughlin. Soep was a researcher on this project.

15. Soep op cit., 43.

16. Atwell 1998, 148–49. Atwell and Paley are probably the most widely known teacher researchers and most influential through their books. In both, the significance of their research for changes in their own teaching practice is most evident when reading across their books written some years apart. Paley's rethinking about the problem of equity in speaking rights was discussed in Chapter 5; Atwell's rethinking from the first edition to this revision includes the all-important role of the teacher.

17. Cobb and Bauersfeld 1995, 104, 22 (with bulleted format added). Cobb and Whitenack (1996) explain in more detail their methodology for the longitudinal analysis of video recordings and transcripts. Their analysis categorizes the pair discussions by four themes: social relationships, mathematical meanings, learning opportunities, and mathematical learnings.

18. Cobb and Bauersfeld 1995, 48–49.

19. Ibid., 42.

20. Lewis 1997, 193; quotes following the excerpt are from 193–94.

21. Ibid., 186.

22. Webb and Palincsar 1996, 867.

23. This typology is adapted from Crook 1994. This book and Wegerif and Scrimshaw (1997) are excellent discussions of discourse aspects of using computers for learning. Crook is especially fine on collaboration for learning generally; Wegerif and Scrimshaw present more observations of classroom computer talk, especially from the *at* computer category, as we'll see later.

24. Mercer and Fisher 1997, 202.

25. Wegerif and Mercer 1996, 56.

26. Wegerif and Scrimshaw 1997, 106.

27. Sittnick 1999 (in Howard and Benson 1999, ch. 12).

28. For example, Edgar and Wood 1996, Christian 1997, Howard and Benson 1999. Because I have taught at the Bread Loaf School of English for many summers, I am more familiar with exchanges by these teachers than by others.

29. Sittnick 1999; Hunt 1996 (in Edgar and Wood 1996, ch. 11).

30. Sayers 1994; Cummins and Sayers 1997/2000.

31. Warschauer, Donaghy, and Kuamoyo 1997; Warschauer 1999.

32. Warschauer, Donaghy, and Kuamoyo 1997, 353.

33. Cummins and Sayers op cit., ch. 4.

34. Quinn et al. 1983; Black et al. 1983.

35. Citrino and Gentry 1999, 127.

36. Crook op cit., 106. *See* his entire Chapter 5, "Collaborative interactions *in relation to* computers."

37. Ibid., 109.

38. Edwards and Mercer 1987; Crook op cit.; Cazden (1992) discusses individual "contexts in the mind" in several places (*see* index), but doesn't sufficiently emphasize the value of them becoming shared within a classroom community.

39. Crook op cit., 114.

40. Ibid., 111. On this same page, Crook criticizes Schegloff, and thereby implicitly the methodology of conversation analysis, for attending only to contexts created in the moment of talk. Wells' presentation of the IRF discourse in the lesson about "a fair test" in Chapter 3 is one example of such common knowledge construction and the way it creates a shared mental context for future teaching and learning.

41. O'Connor 1996 and 1998. (Both discuss this important point, although I fail to find these exact words—CBC.)

42. Lampert et al. 1996, 742.

43. Ibid., 760.

44. Brown et al. 1993.

45. Michaels 1985a.

# Chapter Seven

# Differential Treatment
# and Cultural Differences

"Differential treatment" and "cultural differences" refer to different perspectives on the single problem of achieving greater equity in opportunities to learn. As frequently used, the terms refer to perspectives that contrast with each other. The *differential treatment* perspective usually refers critically to *over*differentiation, to the ways in which schools and classrooms give some students more and better opportunities, thereby reinforcing, even increasing, inequalities of knowledge and skill present when students start school. The *cultural differences* perspective, in contrast, usually refers critically to *under*differentiation and asserts that some students would be better served if qualitative differences among students were taken into account more rather than less.

Continuing research and practice contribute to a more complex picture of both. Differential treatment can be helpful as well as harmful, and a focus on generalized cultural differences can detract from the close observation of individual learners and from attention to the perception, attitudes, and expectations of the dominant group of students and teachers.

## Differential Treatment: Helpful or Harmful?

In this book, we have already discussed examples of helpful and harmful differential treatment. In Chapter 4 on learning, Reading Recovery was described as an example of beneficial scaffolded instruction for individual children having the hardest time learning to read. New Zealander Marie Clay, the original designer of Reading Recovery, explains the justification for such extra help:

> Most people want to give children time to come to literacy learning,
> and they resist the call for early intervention. Reading Recovery's op-
> posite view is that once teachers are helping competent children to
> race ahead with reading and writing, schools have an immediate re-
> sponsibility to give extra learning opportunities to children who are
> showing clearly that they cannot make sense of what is going on in
> the classroom.
>
> There is a strong bias toward "an even playing field." People would
> rather spend educational resources evenly on all groups, despite vast
> differences in prior opportunities to learn. Consequently, teachers plan
> for all children to have the same amount of exposure to each activity,
> though actually individual learners need differential exposure.[1]

Clay's justification for differential opportunities applies to more
than Reading Recovery. In many early literacy programs, small reading
groups homogeneous according to reading level are now being recommended again as one part of a total "balanced" program.[2] As with Reading Recovery, there is research evidence that such temporary and par-
tial differential treatment can improve the learning and relative
achievement status of initially low-achieving children.[3]

In Chapter 5, on variations in patterns of classroom interaction, the
longest section was devoted to ways of reducing harmful differential
treatment affecting students' opportunities for participation and for response. Unfortunately, there are more documented cases of differential
treatment harming rather than helping. As the folk saying puts it, "The
rich get richer and the poor get poorer." This happens at many levels of
educational action, both before and after children walk through their
classroom doors. Linda Darling-Hammond synthesizes this research in
her chapter, "Inequality and access to knowledge" in the *Handbook of
Research on Multicultural Education.*[4]

Outside the classroom, but affecting what happens inside it, are inequalities in school financing, among states and among districts within
them, even after taking into account differences in the cost of living. In
study after study of school financing, Darling-Hammond shows how
the students who get fewer and lower-quality resources are dispropor-
tionately from poor and minority families. One recent observational
study of twenty first grades in the Boston area, divided between schools
in high- and low-social class areas, gives a more detailed picture of the
differences Darling-Hammond summarizes. Reading educator Nell Duke
found differences in the amount, type and uses of print. In the lower-
social class area, there were fewer reading materials, less frequent reading of extended texts (instead of workbooks), and fewer opportunities
for children to develop "agency as a print user" by reading and writing
for audiences beyond the teacher.[5]

Within schools, tracking is widespread, especially in middle and
high schools, from Advanced Placement (AP) and Honors classes on

down. Under the heading of "Tracking and the Rationing of Curriculum," Darling-Hammond summarizes the national picture:

> Tracking endures in the face of growing evidence that it does not substantially benefit high achievers and tends to put low achievers at a serious disadvantage . . . in part because good teaching is a scarce resource, and thus must be allocated. Scarce resources tend to get allocated to the students whose parents, advocates, or representatives have the most political clout. This results . . . not entirely but disproportionately—in the most qualified teachers teaching the most enriched curriculum to the most advantaged students.[6]

In elementary schools, students are often tracked within classrooms, especially into small homogeneous reading groups.

Darling-Hammond's national picture provides a context for more detailed research reports of what goes on in higher and lower tracks that include differences in the quality of talk, and of what it takes (harder to find) to make heterogeneous grouping work.

### Tracking Within Middle and High Schools

A large study by Nystrand and his colleagues of four lessons in each of fifty-eight eighth-grade and fifty-four ninth-grade language arts and English classes in eight Midwestern communities reports the effects of within-school tracking in one curriculum area. Even after controlling for differences in student knowledge at the beginning of the school year, and for gender, race/ethnicity, and social class, they found significantly higher learning gains in the higher-track classes. They also found differences in the discourse.

Overall, "The near-universal preference for 'recitable information' afflicted low-track classes even more than regular- and high-track classes."[7] More specifically, teachers' authentic questions (those for which they did not know the answer) and their "uptake of" (reference to) student responses in their follow-up comments occurred at similar rates across the tracks. But when the researchers shifted from coding and statistical analysis to a qualitative look at what those questions were about, they found a substantive difference. In the higher tracks, the content of teacher questions, and classroom discourse in general, was more of the time about literature.

### Tracking Within Primary Classrooms

Here we come to the homogeneous grouping of students according to diagnosed reading level that has been traditional in primary grades and is advocated again in newly designed "balanced" reading programs. Older studies of the potentially negative effects of such grouping can therefore serve as a warning of patterns of inequality to be avoided.

## Table 7–1
Group Differences in Twenty Primary Classrooms

|  | Lowest Reading Group | Highest Reading Group |
|---|---|---|
| Percentage of teacher correction of all student errors | | |
| Immediately, at error | 66 | 22 |
| Later | 8 | 9 |
| Total | 74 | 31 |
| Percentage of teacher correction of semantically appropriate errors | 55 | 11 |
| Percentage of teacher correction of semantically inappropriate errors | 79 | 48 |
| Percentage of various types of cues supplied by teacher (totaling 100 percent within each group) | | |
| Graphic/phonic | 28 | 18 |
| Semantic/syntactic | 8 | 32 |
| Teacher pronounces | 50 | 38 |
| Other | 14 | 12 |

*Note:* From Allington 1980 (Tables 2–4 and personal communication, 1982), with group norms translated into percentages. Copyright © 1980 by the American Psychological Association. Adapted by permission of the publisher and author.

The studies include both survey research, in which teacher and student behavior is coded and counted in a number of classrooms (like the Nystrand high school research), and more detailed qualitative case studies of instruction in one or a few classrooms. Fortunately, for this research summary, though unfortunately for the lower-group children, the findings across studies are so consistent that summarizing presents few problems.

Consider first-reading educator Richard Allington's survey of teacher responses to children's oral reading in twenty primary classrooms in three school districts in New York. Table 7–1 summarizes his findings about three differences between the groups.[8]

- First, there were differences in timing of the corrections of reading errors: Teachers were far more likely to interrupt poor readers immediately at the point of error (66 percent versus 22 percent) rather than waiting for the next phrase or clause boundary.

- Second, there were differences in the rate at which different kinds of errors—semantically appropriate (*house* for *home)* versus semantically inappropriate (*want* for *with*)—were corrected: While more of the inappropriate errors were corrected in both groups (79 percent versus 55 percent, and 48 percent versus 11 percent), the 55 percent rate of correction of semantically appropriate errors for the lowest group children is five times the 11 percent rate for the highest group.

- Third, there were differences in the kinds of cues (or clues) teachers provided to help the children read the right word: For the poor readers, the cues were more apt to be graphemic or phonemic (related to spelling patterns or sounds), whereas for the good readers, the cues were more apt to be semantic or syntactic (related to the meaning of words or sentences).

It might be argued that all such differences in instruction between low- and high-reading groups constitute pedagogically appropriate differentiation, the kind Clay recommends, and that low-group children would receive the high-group kind of help at a later time. To confirm or disconfirm this possibility, we would need longitudinal studies following both the instruction and the progress of low-group children.

In one such small study, linguist James Collins analyzed segments of lessons in which low-group children were reading stories comparable in difficulty to those the high-group children had read earlier in the year.[9] In one of his comparisons, the two groups were taped while reading different parts of the very same story. A child in the high group read the following text:

"John, I have your boat—" said Liza.

"And I have a fly for your frog too."

"But you can't have your boat or the fly if I can't come in!"

John looked at his frog, and he looked at Liza.

Then he said, "Come in, Liza. Come in."

Later the same year, a child in the low group read the following passage from the same story:

He ran out of the house with his things.

And then he threw his boat into the garbage can.

Liza was there. And she saw what John did.

Figure 7–1 contains excerpts from Collins' transcription of the taped lessons (with intonation marks deleted).

As Collins points out, the teacher helps the two readers in very different ways. With the high-group child, she interpolates one comprehension question (4), and she corrects the intonation necessary for indicating a clause boundary (2) and for separating spoken messages from addressee (14, 16, and 18). By contrast, with the low-group child, she

**Figure 7–1**
High and Low Group Reading Lessons

**High Group**

1  **C:** John I have your boat / said Liza and
2  **T:**                                        and
3  **C:** And I have a fly for your frog too / /
4  **T:** What's she mean by that
5  **C:** For the frog to eat / /
6  **T:** Okay / /
7  **L:** but . . . I . . . but
8  **T:** wait a minute till she gets through
9  **L:** but          but
10 **T:**       watch your books      watch your books
11 **C:** But you can't . . . have your boat / or the fly / If I can't come in/ /
12 John looked at his frog / and he looked at Liza / . . .
13 Then he said come in Liza
14 **T:** What did he say / /
15 **C:** Come in
16 **T:** How'd he say it / /
17 **C:** Come in Li—
18 **T:**              Did he say come in Liza come in / / Or did he say . . .
19 **C:** Come in              Liza/ come in/ /
20 **T:**           Come in / Liza

*(continued)*

gives not only more help but qualitatively different kinds of help: directions to use phonic cues (6 and 21), and a protracted attempt to correct the reader's pronunciation of one word *garbage* (9–15 and 28), after which even the teacher has lost her place in the story. Overall, the contrast is between help toward meaning for the high group and help toward correct word-calling for the low group.

Teacher emphasis in reading lessons on correct word pronunciation is a special danger for children who speak a nonstandard dialect or English with a foreign accent. In a later article, Collins compared a teacher's correction in high- versus low-reading groups of words recognized correctly but mispronounced. Although not all such errors were corrected in any group, there were more corrections in lower-reading groups (e.g., insisting on *thud* instead of *tud)*.[10]

**Figure 7–1** (*continued*)

### Low Group

1 **M:** Here    he / . . . ran / . . . out / . . . of / . . .

2 **T:**    he

3 **M:** the house . . . wuh—    with his things / /

4 **T:**    with

5 **M:** And then . . . he . . .    threw his

6 **T:**    sound it out / threw

7 **M:** bu—(boat) boat/ . . . into the . . .    gahbag can / /

8    guh—

9 **T:** garbage / / Say garbage / /

10 **M:** gahbage

11 **T:** Don't say gahbage / look at me / /Say garbage / gar / Say it / /

12    everybody say it/ /

13 **CC:** garbage

14 **T:** Celena / say it/ /

15 **Ce:** garbage

16 **T:**    Right / / Marion / Liza

17 **M:** Liza . . .    was . . .    there and she was

18 **T:**    where are we Sherrie    there

19 **T:** What

20 **M:**    she was    saw what . . .

21 **T:**    no / / sss . . .    how does –j– sound / /

22 **M:** juh / /

23 **T:**    What's the boy's name / / . . . John

24 **M:** John . . . said

25 **T:**    did / / She saw what John did / / Marion / what did he do / /

26 **T:** She saw what he did / / Now what did he do / /

27 **M:** He threw his things in the gahbage

28 **T:** garbage / / Right / / Go on / /

Similarly, when Moll and his colleagues observed the reading instruction of second- and third-grade children who were taught in Spanish by one teacher and in English by another, they found that "the overriding concern of the lessons in English is decoding, pronunciation, and other forms related to the sounds of the second language."[11] Moll et al. suggested that the English reading teacher mistook nonnative pronunciation for erroneous decoding and so subverted the children's progress in reading comprehension for the sake of a pronunciation lesson in English as a second language.

Other research suggests two ways in which these kinds of differentiation of instruction can restrict the progress of the low-group children. First, there is the effect of more immediate timing of corrections. In a study similar in purpose to the wait-time research discussed in Chapter 5, New Zealand psychologists Stuart McNaughton and Ted Glynn conducted an experimental study of the effect of timing of teacher correction on beginning readers—immediate or delayed (for five to ten seconds)—on children's self-correction behavior and reading accuracy scores. Immediate correction depressed both children's self-correction and their accuracy, even on a second passage when no experimental correction occurred. McNaughton and Glynn suggest that teacher correction may interfere with children's progress by maintaining their "instructional dependence where they should be encouraging the children's self-corrections that are important both to early progress and eventual independent reading." [12]

Second, there is the effect on low-group readers of decreased attention to text meaning. According to our best understanding of the reading process, it is neither just "top-down," driven by the reader's perceptions of letters, nor just "bottom-up," driven by the reader's hypotheses about what the text might contain. Instead, processing of different levels of text structure needs to proceed simultaneously and interactively. Many beginning readers may need to have their attention focused, momentarily but explicitly, on syllables and letters. But even temporary focus at that level must be balanced by a complementary focus on higher levels of text that is essential for meaning. [13]

An important aspect of the much-used word *context* in every reader's comprehension is the mental context—the *context in the mind*—provided by the reader's understanding of a larger unit of text than is the focus of perceptual attention at any moment. Because of differences in preschool literacy experiences, children arrive at school having developed in their mind different contexts for learning to read. All children in a literate society have encountered environmental print (labels, signs, and so forth), but that experience is not functionally equivalent to being read to for building a mental context for learning to read larger units of connected texts in books. It is doubly unfortunate if attention to understanding such larger meaningful units is most neglected during instruction for the very children who need it most. [14]

### Some Final Comments on Harmful Differential Treatment

This combined picture of the all-too-common structures of inequalities at all levels of the educational system suggests that they may be the default option—how the system works unless special effort is made to change it. We can then understand why Edmund Gordon, the psychologist who was the first director of research for Head Start when it was founded in 1965, has written recently: "Being at-risk may be an iatrogenic condition"—in medicine, an illness caused by medical institutions' own actions.[15] While *differential experience* would be a more benign label, *differential treatment*, also by analogy with medicine, suggests the special responsibility of educators, teachers, and those above them who shape the contexts within which teachers and students work.

If we assume, as I do, that teachers are committed to helping all children learn, how does potentially harmful differential treatment within classrooms come about? Even if we agree that adults should tailor their instruction to the needs of their students, we are still left with the question of why the instruction is apt to be differentiated in these particular ways? In other words, what may bring about these unintended consequences?

Influences on teaching can be categorized as preactive and interactive (to use Philip Jackson's terms), depending on their temporal relationship to the teaching act.[16] *Preactive influences* are the conscious ideas that teachers bring into the classrooms, accessible in an interview and embodied in a teacher's written plans. *Interactive influences,* by contrast, are generated in the in-flight interactions with students. They are less conscious and may not result from decisions in the usual reflective sense.

Unintended but harmful kinds of differential treatment probably have their roots in both kinds of influences. Consider one more time the primary reading group research. There is an inevitable tension in all literacy teaching between holistic practice (top-down) and attention to molecular parts (bottom-up). Although our best theories of learning consistently argue for both/and rather than either/or, some teachers seem to resolve this tension differently for different groups of children. All teachers have to be careful not to differentiate their theories of learning (a preactive influence) along with their children.[17]

If we want to retain and expand the arena of professional decision making rather than letting problems be addressed in "teacher-proof" ways, such as more scripted instructional programs or computer software, we have to find ways to change. Of all educational resources, our own behavior as teachers is the most precious. Classrooms are the ultimate site for learning, and classroom talk constitutes a critical part, and the most exposed edge, of the enacted curriculum. No matter how learning groups are constituted in a curriculum area as crucial as literacy, we have to be sure that what happens within them contributes in the end to what Clay calls "different paths to common outcomes."[18]

### Making Heterogeneous Groups Work

To avoid the inequalities found in homogeneous groups, heterogeneous grouping is widely advocated. We still need far more research, especially by teacher researchers themselves, that can show in detail how to make heterogeneous groups work. Three studies by teachers or university–teacher collaborators point the way.

In reading these reports, consider social scientists Lave and Wenger's useful construct of "legitimate peripheral participation." From this perspective, it is too much to expect that children who initially vary in levels of knowledge and skills, or in self-identities as competent students, will, when grouped together, immediately participate equitably—that is, without regard to those initial differences. Some students, because of previous experiences, may initially engage in more peripheral participation. What teachers have to work for, and researchers have to watch for, is whether rates of participation and contribution to group tasks become less related over time to initial achievement status. Lave and Wenger are not writing with classrooms in mind, but their words speak to how initially peripheral students can become "empowered":

> [L]egitimate peripherality is a complex notion, implicated in social structures involving relations of power. As a place in which one moves toward more-intensive participation, peripherality is an empowering position. As a place in which one is kept from participating more fully . . . it is a disempowering position. . . . We have chosen to call that to which peripheral participation leads, *full participation*. . . .
>
> The partial participation of newcomers . . . [is] a dynamic concept. In this sense, peripherality, when it is enabled, suggests an opening, a way of gaining access to sources for understanding through growing involvement.[19]

In other words, heterogeneous groups have to be dynamic, open sites with opportunities to gain new competencies, and new identities as legitimate rather than marginal students and group members. We will see some of the different ways by which teachers work hard to make this happen.

When high school English teacher Joan Cone opened up her Advanced Placement (AP) English class to a broad range of students and began discussing *All the King's Men*, which her students had been assigned to read over the summer, Paula—who had never been in an Honors class and was the only Latina in the group—sat silent. After class, she explained:

> I can't talk like them. I just can't. I understood this book, but I can't say anything. If we get graded on discussions I'll flunk. Tony [her boyfriend

who had been in the class the year before] told me to take this class, but I've got to transfer out.[20]

Cone realized she had to do more than open the AP door. In a few pages, she tells (though without the details another teacher would need) the strategies she gradually worked out:

- "I had to spend a great deal of time modeling tasks" [like writing an essay]. . . .
- "Once I had assigned a task and my students understood what was required of them, I had to step back and let them take charge . . . " [and involve them in frequent discussions of how to make the class, and the small response groups, work better]
- "Most important, I had to use classroom talk as a vehicle for making all students feel good about themselves as learners' and contributors to others' learning. . . . "

Cone also set stricter deadlines for assignments, and she dealt with wide diversity in knowledge of "grammar and the mechanics of writing" by style sheets that "mixed complicated points with basic points so that each list was directed at writers of all levels." With changes like these, the class was a success. The last line of Cone's teacher-research article is the last line of a happy, busy letter from Paula the next year: "Hey, I'm a college student!"

David McEachen, also a high school English teacher in California, taught a junior English literature class that included previously tracked gifted and talented (GATE) and general (nonGATE) students. Although the background of two of the students was Mexican American and the rest were European American, it was the students' prior academic experience in GATE or nonGATE classes that was the significant dimension of difference. Researcher, co-author Lesley Rex analyzed eight segments of classroom interaction during the first twenty-one instructional days in which the text being discussed was *Beowulf*.[21]

Rex and McEachen were able to separate aspects of McEachen's teaching that stayed the same over the twenty-one days from aspects that changed. A continuing pattern was the teacher's probing of student comments without signaling dissatisfaction with the student's interpretation. A significant change was from a more teacher-dominated (IRE) discourse in the beginning, while McEachen was teaching the students how to "make a case," to later non-IRE discourse in which the teacher talked much less and the students talked much more.

Because the prior academic status of the students is made clear throughout the co-written article, their analysis yields a picture—more detailed than Cone's but consistent with it—of the development of a

**Figure 7–2**
Day 7: Teacher Affirms a Student Question Without Taking It Up

| Teacher | Student(s) |
| --- | --- |
| 1  Rachel what were you going to say | |
| 2 | **RS:** are we supposed to think somehow that |
| 3 | Beowulf |
| 4 | like he has a deeper understanding of everything |
| 5  maybe | |
| 6  that's an interesting point isn't it | |
| 7 | **RS:** because everyone else |
| 8 | you know all the common people |
| 9 | might have thought that it was |
| 10 | you know |
| 11 | slaves that did it |
| 12 | but are we supposed to think that maybe |
| 13 | he has deeper understanding |
| 14  pretty good | |
| 15  pretty good thinking | |
| 16  just to raise the question shows some pretty good thinking there | |
| 17  had you thought about that question Rosemary | |

(*continued*)

classroom culture in which heterogeneous grouping can work. McEachen's careful instruction in how to "make a case" for an interpretation of literature by reasoning from textual evidence enables the nonGATE students to learn how to meet his expectations, and their public identities become transformed in the process.

One important teacher strategy was to value good questions about literary interpretations more than right answers. Figure 7–2 is one example from Day 7 involving nonGATE-student Rachel and GATE-student Rosemary; "Dave" is teacher McEachen.

> In the classroom side-talk that had occurred as Dave was responding to Lia's (GATE, LL) analogy, nonGATE-student Rachel (RS) had begun

**Figure 7–2** (*continued*)

| | |
|---|---|
| 18 I hadn't really | |
| 19 | **RJ:** not really |
| 20 no | |
| 21 hmm | |
| 22 Matt, what about you | |
| 23 | **MS:** I hadn't thought about that one either |
| 24 [*T and students giggle*] | |
| 25 seriously | |
| 26 it shows | |
| 27 it suggests a greater depth of consciousness here | |
| 28 that I think might be supported by other parts of the poem | |
| 29 that's very interesting | |
| 30 | **BE:** so he might have taken the stance |
| 31 | that if the dragon hadn't come out then |
| 32 | it would have come out later |
| 33 | if it came out later he wouldn't have been there to handle it |
| 34 | and somebody else might have been there to handle it |
| 35 | who wouldn't have been able to handle it |
| 36 yeah | |

to ask a question of another student. Dave had overheard Rachel and asked her to repeat it.[22]

When the teacher affirmed the worth of Rachel's question with a brief comment (5 and 6), Rachel was evidently encouraged to offer the reasoning behind her question (7–13). The teacher then asked Rosemary (GATE) whether she had thought of that and admitted he himself had not (17 and 18). Substantive discussion of Beowulf resumed when Bobby (GATE BE) begins with "So . . . ," signaling continuity with the immediately preceding discussion (30–35). As the authors point out, questions are often considered just the way to elicit answers, which then convey the real contribution. Here, the teacher stops the movement of ideas to affirm the question itself as important cognitive work, and stays with it for eight subsequent teacher–student turns.

Rex and McEachen write modestly of *emergent inclusion*—the "gradual and tenuous process of building an inclusionary culture," and conclude that "inclusion can be achieved by shifting the focus from *what to know as an individual performer to how to know it as a member of a literate group*." [23] As evidence for the impact of this inclusive experience on individual students' future biographies, we learn that the two European American background students, who had had no previous GATE classes, "earned a satisfactory grade; went on to do well in twelfth-grade AP English; and, after graduation, attended a four-year university." [24]

The third example of ways to make heterogeneous grouping work comes from many research reports about educational psychologist Elizabeth Cohen's long-term research program on how to achieve equity in small-group instruction, which includes a science curriculum called "Complex Instruction." One report is a book by four teacher researchers at the Goddard School of Science and Technology—a public middle school in Worcester, Massachusetts, that uses Cohen's Complex Instruction science curriculum.[25]

Briefly, here are the tenets of Cohen's theory, which has been tested in many classrooms in this country and internationally:

- Students learn in small groups from their active participation as well as from each other. The rate of their participation is positively correlated with the extent of their learning. Small-group participation rates are influenced by the expectations that students in each group have for each other.

- These expectations are influenced by "status characteristics . . . defined as socially evaluated attributes of individuals." [26] Perceived differences in reading and math ability are prime examples of influential "specific" status characteristics, and "diffuse" characteristics, such as race and ethnicity, tend to correlate with them.

- Small collaborative groups will only provide opportunities for more equitable participation, and thereby for more learning, with careful teacher action of three kinds: establishing group norms about collaborative responsibilities in small group work, such as the responsibilities to both ask for help and give it when asked; using curriculum materials and tasks that require multiple skills and explaining those skills to the class; and publicly recognizing ("assigning") competence in the previously low-status students.

The first of Cohen's requirements, establishing collaborative norms, is the focus of specially designed "skill-building games," such as Master Builder. This is a referential communication task that provides practice in the norm of "explain by telling how" rather than just doing the task when a peer asks for help.[27] Establishing such norms is also the purpose of honest and specific positive feedback to students when their group works well together. Here is Worcester teacher Caryn McCrohon's feedback to one of her second-grade science groups:

> Let me tell you what I saw in this group. I saw that Mark was a good explainer, and that's on our chart [of needed skills]. Andrew asked you for help, which was his right to ask for, right? And Matt helped him, which was his duty. His duty also helped Carrie explain why two hundred centimeters went after one hundred ninety centimeters. Carrie had an answer written down, but she couldn't explain to me why she had put two hundred down. Matt explained and she understood. Then Carrie was able to take the information that Matt explained to her, and explain it to Ramone.[28]

The second requirement is a curriculum and tasks that openly require multiple skills. Here is another teacher's description to her students, before they set to work, of the multiple abilities that will be needed in the science task of figuring out how to make popcorn pop:

> Today you will find out what makes popcorn pop. The task card will show you how to heat up the popcorn. This is a task that is going to require many different intellectual abilities. Some of you will be good at *observing* very carefully what happens. Some of you may *have valuable knowledge* about what is inside the kernel of popcorn. Others will be able to *draw an accurate picture* of what happens to the corn. Still others will be good at *making hypotheses* about what has happened. Now it stands to reason that no one person will have all these abilities, but everyone will have some of these abilities. I want to see you all using one another as resources to do the best possible job.[29]

The third important kind of teacher action is making sure, when previously low-status children contribute one of these multiple skills to their group, that they receive specific, positive, public evaluation and recognition. Cohen calls this public appreciation "assigning competence." That is what teacher McEachen gave non-GATE student Rachel when he valued her *Beowulf* question, asked GATE student Rosemary whether she had thought of it, and admitted that he himself had not.

Figure 7–3 shows the interaction between the Worcester teacher McCrohon and Luke, the reporter (one of the regularly assigned group-work roles) for another second-grade small group during the "wrap-up" discussion when all the groups report on their small-group investigations to the whole class. Ross, a group member whose contribution Luke describes, is a student for whom reading (a status characteristic) was particularly difficult.

**Figure 7–3**
Interactions between teacher and student reporter

---

**Luke:** Ross, he said today was the hardest group we've ever done so far.

**Caryn:** Really, did he tell you why?

**Luke:** Cuz we messed up four times. The lines . . . we hadda stop. It was hard to draw the lines down that were all straight and everything.

**Caryn:** Well you know what, it was very hard, because you needed an accurate measurer. An accurate measurer. Was anyone in your group someone you would consider an accurate measurer?

**Luke:** Ross.

**Caryn:** Ross? So, Ross, if someone needs to turn to someone and needs accurate measuring, they would turn to Ross then. You seem to be an expert in your group on measuring.

**Child:** I know.

**Class:** And a manipulator.

**Caryn:** He's also a good manipulator.

**Child:** And he's good at sewing.

**Caryn:** And he's good at threading needles. Ross, you are just a scientist, I guess, that has a lot of abilities that can help in science group.

**Luke:** He don't think he does it good either.

**Caryn:** I know he doesn't think he does it good and that's why we tell him every day that he does.

---

In this same classroom, McCrohon had students write about their science work in dialogue journals, which she responded to with questions that elicited fuller descriptions and explanations. As all the children are writing, they come to the teacher one by one for further "challenge questions." Here is what Ross wrote during this written interaction after wrap-up was over (the teacher's questions are in italic):

I learned that we don't always guess right.

*Do guesses have to be right?*

No.

*What else did you learn?*

I learned that I could be a measurer.[30]

Probably it is more often the teacher who publicly assigns competence, but McCrohon is undoubtedly right: "It's important for students to hear these things from teachers, but it is perhaps even more mean-ingful to hear it from classmates and friends" (as McEachen's Rachel also did).[31]

These positive examples can make the challenge of teaching het-erogeneous groups seem too easy, especially in middle and high school. By that time, students' academic identities have longer autobiographies, and the perceptions of both self and others are that much harder to change.[32] That is one reason for doing everything possible to narrow the equity gap during the earlier school years, by decreasing harmful kinds of differential treatment and adding, whenever necessary, tem-porary supplemental support for learning.

## Taking Cultural Differences into Account

### Butterflies

The grandmother plaited her grandaughter's hair and then she said, "Get your lunch. Put it in your bag. Get your apple. You come straight back from school, straight home here. Listen to the teacher," she said. "Do what she say."

Her grandfather was out on the step. He walked down the path with her and out on the footpath. He said to a neighbor, "Our granddaughter goes to school. She lives with us now."

"She's fine," the neighbor said. "She's terrific with her two plaits in her hair."

"And clever," the grandfather said. "Writes every day in her book."

"She's fine," the neighbor said.

The grandfather waited with his granddaughter by the crossing and then he said, "Go to school. Listen to the teacher. Do what she say."

When the granddaughter came home from school her grandfather was hoe-ing round the cabbages. Her grandmother was picking beans. They stopped their work.

"You bring your book home?" the grandmother asked.

"Yes."

"You write your story?"

"Yes."

"What's your story?"

"About the butterflies."

"Get your book, then. Read your story."

The granddaughter took her book from her schoolbag and opened it.

"I killed all the butterflies," she read. "This is me and this is all the butterflies."

"And your teacher like your story, did she?"

"I don't know."

"What your teacher say?"

"She said butterflies are beautiful creatures. They hatch out and fly in the sun. The butterflies visit all the pretty flowers, she said. They lay their eggs and then they die. You don't kill butterflies, that's what she said."

The grandmother and grandfather were quiet for a long time, and their granddaughter, holding the book, stood quite still in the warm garden.

"Because you see," the grandfather said, "your teacher, she buy all her cabbages from the supermarket and that's why."

"Butterflies" is a short-short story by Patricia Grace, a Maori fiction writer and former primary and secondary teacher in New Zealand (see Figure 7–4).[33] Because Grace is known for her sensitive portrayals of Maori life, we should assume that the little girl is Maori and the teacher "Pakeha"—the Maori language name for New Zealanders of European (mostly British) descent. It is a fictional story, not recounting an actual event. But when the back cover of the book prepares the reader for stories in which "sunlight, childhood and nature are set against conflict and misunderstanding," we should assume that Grace has fictionalized what she perceives to be a typical event in the lives of Maori children in mainstream New Zealand schools.

Observation research in New Zealand by Marie Clay confirms that Grace's fictional account is all too accurate. In 1985, Clay reported on her observational study of five-year-olds' beginning engagement with the school curriculum during their first term in school.[34] She and her assistant spent six mornings in each of six multiethnic classrooms taught by "European" teachers. Activities observed were morning news (sharing time) and other whole-class talk, beginning reading, and some combination of individualized drawing/dictating/writing. In each classroom, they focused on six children: two Maori, two Pacific Island, and two European. By hand (without tape recorders), they recorded whether the children were "on-task," and wrote down as closely as possible any interactions with the teacher.

Positively, all three ethnic groups of these young school beginners were on-task 90 percent of the time, and teachers often initiated five to six individualized interactions with each of the children each morning. But the answer to one of Clay's questions—"How teachers provide for cultural differences in the classroom?"—was much less positive. The teachers' interactions with Maori children were shorter and less elaborated:

> Teachers started as many contacts with Maori children as with European or Pacific Island children but they asked less often for verbal elaboration [which Clay labeled *Talk More*]. These results were consistent across the two samples [of children beginning school in Term 1 and those beginning in Term 2].[35]

There are many examples in previous chapters of teachers' questions or comments that encourage students to say (or write) more about

**Table 7–2**
Incidence of Talk More, by Classroom

|  | All Children | Non-Maori | Maori |
|---|---|---|---|
| Teacher A | 5.96 (50) | 6.30 (40) | 4.40 (10) |
| Teacher B | 5.00 (58) | 5.53 (51) | 1.14  (7) |
| Teacher C | 4.74 (53) | 5.13 (32) | 4.14 (21) |
| Teacher D | 2.88 (56) | 3.46 (28) | 2.29 (28) |
| Teacher E | 2.76 (55) | 2.77 (31) | 2.50 (24) |
| Teacher F | 2.07 (55) | 1.97 (36) | 2.37 (19) |

their ideas. Just previously, for example, at the end of this chapter's section on differential treatment, are McCrohon's (written) questions to Ross in his dialogue journal.

In Clay's published report, her observational data are combined for all six teachers, but subsequently she made them available for further analysis when I arrived in New Zealand in 1987 as a Fulbright fellow to follow up her research. Table 7–2 displays the averages of Talk More (TM) per child morning for each individual classroom (identified by Teacher A–F), with terms 1 and 2 for that teacher combined.[36]

The first column gives the average for all six children in each classroom. The second and third columns separate TMs to non-Maori (European and Pacific Island, who were similar in Clay's analysis and therefore combined here) and Maori children. The numbers in parentheses show the absolute number of child mornings counted in each average.

To put the first row into words: During fifty child mornings of observations, Teacher A spoke a daily average of nearly six TM invitations to each child. Her average for the non-Maori children considered separately was about six and one-third invitations in forty child mornings, while her average for Maori children was just under four and one-half in ten child mornings. From all her data, Clay concluded:

> While the differences are small in the research tables, the sampling arithmetic [that is, considering the time observed in relation to the total morning] suggests that Maori pupils missed four teaching opportunities each per morning, six per day, thirty per week and 300 per term. That could make a difference.[37]

Two important patterns are evident in this table; first, there is a large difference among teachers in their overall use of TM invitations. Teachers A, B, and C do it more than twice as often as teachers D, E, and F. Second, the ethnic differences that result in differential treatment for the Maori children are a pervasive pattern across the classrooms. Specifically, four of the six classrooms (A, B, D, and E) fit the composite picture. In Teacher B's case, the ethnic differences are exaggerated, but the number of Maori child mornings is so low (only seven, presumably because of low attendance of the focal children) that the average may be unrepresentative. In Teacher F's case, the Maori children receive more TM invitations, but the numbers are so small for all children that none can be considered advantaged in this respect. Displayed in this way, Clay's research becomes especially valuable in showing both within-teacher and among-teacher variations on a single variable.

If Grace's teacher had realized that the child must have some ideas about butterflies different from her own, she could have asked the girl to say more about ideas she assumed in her composition. But this awareness of potential difference the teacher evidently did not have, and asking the child to "talk more" is what she did not do. Note that a different scenario, making it possible for both the teacher and the child to enlarge their knowledge about cabbages and butterflies, would not depend on the teacher's being initially as bicultural as the grandfather. It only depends on the teacher suppressing the assumption that hers is the only correct or even imaginable view.

I have placed Grace's story and Clay's observational research here, at the beginning of a discussion of cultural differences, to suggest that the New Zealand pattern is all too typical of the experiences of many children in mainstream classrooms in the United States and elsewhere, and to exemplify how student–teacher differences in cultural background can contribute to harmful differential treatment.

### Classrooms as a Meeting Place of Cultures

Classrooms and schools as preeminent spaces of cultural contact have been described in various metaphors. Each helps to call our attention to particular aspects of that complex space. Some call attention to what students bring with them in their minds, their "prior knowledge" that is such an important base for further learning.

- Moll and his Arizona border colleagues involve teachers in experiential learning about their Mexican American children's out-of-school lives and their resulting *funds of knowledge*.

- Australian educator Barbara Comber adopts a metaphor from a Canadian teacher who speaks of all children coming to school with a *virtual schoolbag* that only some children get to open and use in school.

- Two other Australian educators, Valerie Dobson and Rosalie Riley at the Yipirinia Aboriginal school in Alice Springs, call the *nonac-*

knowledgment of some children's knowledge *terra nullius* education. *Terra nullius* is the Australian legal doctrine of "empty land" that justified white settlement of Aboriginal lands until overturned in 1992 by the Australian High Court. The educational analogy would be the doctrine of Aboriginal "empty minds" until filled by white culture.

Other metaphors name the meeting place itself.

- In Los Angeles, Kris Gutierrez recommends interaction in a *third* space, different from the customary experiences of either teachers or students.

- A California high school program designed especially for Mexican American and Latino students is called Puente, Spanish for *bridge,* with curriculum materials and ideas flowing in both directions.

- Dyson describes primary classrooms in which teachers negotiate a *permeable curriculum,* implicitly arguing that school must be changed as well as the students.

- In northeast Australia, Yirrkala Community School has organized its curriculum and teaching around the local Aboriginal name for an *estuary*—the contact zone where rivers meet the sea; metaphorically, fresh river waters are indigenous student knowledge and practices, meeting the salt water of the official school knowledge and practices in changing patterns as the tides flow in and out. When the fresh and salt waters are kept in balance, this metaphor implicitly carries the potentiality of its biological source—estuaries are one of the richest environments in which diverse organisms can thrive.[38]

A final metaphor names the all-important role for teachers. In the final paragraph of her now-classic book, *Ways With Words: Language, Life, and Work in Communities and Classrooms,* Shirley Brice Heath calls for teachers to become *"cultural brokers* between communities and classrooms."[39] After examining one example from her work—how teachers can respond to cultural differences in asking and answering questions—we will turn to other examples of teacher learning and classroom change.

### Heath as Anthropologist and Teacher Educator

For nine years in the 1970s, Heath was an ethnographer in rural and middle-class black and white communities in the Southeastern United States, and simultaneously a professor in a local college, giving in-service courses for teachers. When white teachers in newly desegregated schools complained that rural black children from "Trackton" did not participate in lessons, she helped them understand what she had learned from her field work.

Heath realized that the children were not used to answering adults' known-answer questions about the labels and attributes of events. As one third-grade boy complained, "Ain't nobody can talk about things being about themselves." She encouraged teachers to observe the questions they themselves asked in their own homes and at school, and then helped them design and try out new patterns of interaction in their own classrooms. Some of the changes followed this sequence:

1. Start with content and kinds of talk familiar to the children.

2. Go on to new kinds of talk, still about familiar content, and provide peer models of children answering as the teacher expected that were audiotaped and made available for repeated hearings.

3. Provide opportunities for the Trackton children to practice the new kinds of talk, first out of the public arena and also on tape, and then in actual lessons.

4. Finally, talk with the children about talk itself.[40]

Note that in this example, teachers' new understandings and changed practices come from two sources. One source was what Heath could tell them about Trackton children's familiar questioning experiences from her years of observations in that community. A second source—less often mentioned in references to her work—is what she helped the teachers learn for and about themselves through observations in their own classrooms and homes.

In the upper grades, Heath and the teachers extended the latter more situated kind of learning by engaging students as co-researchers about contrasting language practices. So, in one class, students compared the vocabulary used in descriptions of farming in their textbook and in their home community. Students as well as teachers thereby came to understand differences between home and school discourses and validate both.

Unfortunately, generalizing from Heath's inspiring example becomes problematical. Few teachers anywhere have access to her combination of expert and personalized help.[41] Some educators writing for teachers (myself included) have tried to shortcut her process and transmit what has been learned by other ethnographers about different cultural backgrounds. But that attempt brings the danger that disembodied and generalized information about "others" may do more harm than good. Despite the best of intentions, such information may reinforce, even create, stereotypes; lower teachers' expectations; and make teachers less observant of their particular students rather than more. A comment by Ruth Landes about a teacher education project in California thirty-five years ago is still relevant today: "When educators talk more *about* pupils than *with* them and their families, separateness from the objects of discussion forfeits the experiences words should mirror."[42]

Moreover, communities themselves have changed in the quarter of a century from Heath's work until now. With increased immigration from outside the United States and increased migrations within it, classrooms throughout the country have become more diverse and less stable in cultural composition. In a time of considerable cultural change, of hybrid and overlapping identities now recognized in the "check as many as apply" list of ethnicities on the 2000 Census, and of the increasing influence of popular culture on students from all backgrounds, the dangers of reifying a set of static cultural "facts" increases.[43] Teachers still need to learn as much as they can about the background knowledge of their students, about the contents of their virtual schoolbags. But if such teacher learning can be situated in, and experienced through, the lives of their particular students, in school and out, there should be a better chance of transforming it for immediate classroom use.

### Situating Teacher Learning About Cultural Differences in the Classroom

Two very different examples of situated teacher learning are Reading Recovery, where the professional development is in the course of teaching individual children, and teacher researcher Cynthia Ballenger's self-initiated learning while teaching groups of Haitian preschool children. We then consider the difficulties that may be encountered in generalizing her model to K–12 schools.

**Reading Recovery.** Consider one more time what happens in Reading Recovery, this time in its professional development. Because any group of lowest-achieving children will include disproportionate numbers of children from nondominant language and culture groups, one might expect that such differences among children would be discussed in the Guidebook that is the basis of the intensive one-year teacher education course and periodic subsequent inservice workshops. Surprisingly, that is not so. There is accommodation to language differences in the medium of classroom Reading Recovery instruction in two countries: in Spanish in the United States and in Maori in New Zealand. But there is no mention in the English Guidebook of accommodation to cultural differences among English-speaking children.[44] Questions come to mind.

- Are such differences less important in the literacy education of young children than they will be later? That seems unlikely.

- Does the unusually high degree of individualization in the sequence and pacing of instruction take into account whatever aspects of cultural background are relevant to beginning literacy? Maybe.

- Are Reading Recovery teachers trained in ways that make the provision of group-specific cultural information unnecessary?

The first two weeks of daily Reading Recovery lessons with each child are called "Roaming around the known." During this time, the teacher's task is not to introduce any new teaching. Instead, she is to get to know, as completely as possible, each child's strengths—not weaknesses but strengths. Of special importance among such strengths, as in any literacy program, is the child's oral language, whatever it may be.

In Reading Recovery professional development, at least in the United States, special emphasis has been given to the importance of understanding each child's language as a resource for literacy learning, no matter how "nonstandard" in vocabulary or syntax that language may seem to the teacher. In the early weeks, a child's nonstandard readings of standard language texts are accepted. Then, as the child progresses, the teacher continues to appreciate the child's oral language while increasing the reading challenge: "That would make sense, but look at this," as she points to the text and asks the child to cross-check familiar oral language against the less familiar visual information on the page.

Through such professional education, the teacher is becoming her own ethnographer, so to speak, learning about what the child knows and can do through her own careful observations. She is learning how to build on the child's knowledge as an indispensable beginning, no matter how different that knowledge is from her own. During both preservice and inservice experiences, Reading Recovery teachers engage in such teaching behind a one-way mirror and receive constructive analysis from their watching colleagues.

I have used Reading Recovery once more as a positive program example because it highlights some important features of successfully taking cultural differences into account:

- assuming that all children have language and ideas relevant to school learning, and that it is the teacher's task to acknowledge and build on them.
- being open to try out alternative teaching practices.
- being helped in this important but difficult learning by being in a collaborative group of colleagues facing the same teaching problems. It is easier to make and sustain change, especially a fundamental philosophical shift, if one is not trying to do it alone.[45]

**Ballenger's learning about her Haitian children.** Cynthia Ballenger was the only non-Haitian adult in a day-care center in the Boston Haitian community. Even though she could speak Haitian Creole, she knew she was an outsider to her children's culture. Looking back on that experience in the beginning of her book-length account, *Teaching Other People's Children,* she remembers:

> I began with these children expecting deficits, not because I believed they or their background were deficient—I was definitely against such a view—but because I did not know how to see their strengths. This is the story of how I came to see them.[46]

Ballenger was familiar with Heath's work, but engaging in that kind of intensive community ethnography was out of the question. So she found ways to adapt some of Heath's ways of learning to her own situation. Her resources became careful observational records of her children when they were with her and with Haitian adults or playing with their peers, and her reflections on those observations in conversations with two separate discourse worlds outside her classroom.

One was the world of the Haitian social service agency of which the center was a part and the class on child development that she conducted for Haitian adults who hoped to get jobs in early childhood education. Here she could consult, in Creole when necessary, with Haitian parents and colleagues. The other world was the teacher–researcher group of which she had been a long-term member (the Brookline Teacher Research Seminar whose other members conducted the teacher research on nontraditional Sharing Time reported in Chapter 2).

Like the Reading Recovery teachers, Ballenger was not working alone. Conversations in the Center connected her more closely to her children and, beyond them, to Haitian culture. Conversations in the Seminar connected her to related research literature, including Heath's, and gave her a place to discuss the changes she was trying out in her classroom—changes in discipline and control, and changes in ways of teaching the heart of her curriculum, story books and the ABCs. Together, observations and conversations added up to a powerful example of informal, self-initiated, ongoing professional growth.

Admittedly, it may be difficult to approximate Ballenger's experiences in K–12 schools. Time and space are more tightly scheduled, and district and state tests can bring heavy pressures for narrowed student learning. But for those teachers who want to try, people who might help are close at hand. Whatever children's cultural backgrounds, there will be family members to talk to (as Moll and his colleagues did about "funds of knowledge"). Within the school itself, there are often colleagues from those same backgrounds and/or paraprofessional teacher aides.[47]

Robert Rueda and Lilia Monzo, two educators in southern California, have studied, through observations and interviews, the relationships that developed between thirty-two Latino "paraeducators" (some of whom were enrolled in teacher education programs) and classroom teachers in two public elementary schools with predominantly working-class Latino children. In those particular schools, they were disappointed to find little evidence of teacher learning through these relationships:

> Some teachers acknowledged that the paraeducators brought their own knowledge to the classroom but did not seem to connect it with the knowledge of the students. The idea of utilizing paraeducators' knowledge of the students' culture and community for creating lessons that draw upon prior knowledge was not brought up by any of the teachers.
>
> Furthermore, the teachers acknowledged that their paraeducators seemed to interact with students in very effective ways, but they were not aware of any specific strategies the paraeducators used in their classrooms. Interactional strategies that we found through our observations, such as the use of cariño, a demonstration of affection used commonly in the Latino community, and playful language to minimize the negative effects of correcting students' academic and behavioral errors, were neither acknowledged nor adopted by teachers.[48]

The paraprofessionals, all of whom were bilingual, did report being asked for help with Spanish, but we don't know in what context or what the Spanish was about.

With or without access to adult members of their children's home cultures, teachers can always learn from their students. With younger children, careful classroom observations (like those of the Reading Recovery teachers and Ballenger) are always possible; and teachers can always ask individual children to "talk more," as some of the New Zealand teachers did. With older children, teachers can plan assignments that involve their students as researchers of language and cultures, as one of Heath's collaborating teachers did.[49]

In classrooms with bilingual students, teachers can welcome their knowledge of languages other than English as a resource for the whole class in understanding complex concepts in the curriculum. One vivid example comes from South African researcher Marsalidh Kilalea's observations in a university class for teachers on "Language and Learning" in South Africa (where there are 11 official languages).[50] The teachers had been watching a videotape of a school science class on electricity, and a question had been raised about whether the students understood the concept of "circuit," which the teacher had defined as "path," or were just "parroting" him. In the Bakhtinian terms discussed in Chapter 6, was the teacher's scientific language about electricity "internally persuasive" or merely "authoritative"? One professor asked the teachers, "What words could children use for 'circuit' in their own language?" Teachers who knew Zulu, Sotho, and Xhosa as well as Greek (an immigrant language) contributed terms from their languages and the nearest English equivalent. Moments later, the two professors who taught the class (pseudonyms: MIRiam and DEBbie) each commented on the lively discussion:

**MIR:** My own position on it, and I know it's a controversial position, is that when you are working with some of these really difficult concepts, work with the multilingual resources of the class, get your kids to articulate in their home languages what they understood those to be, even if no one else speaks the other language. I suppose what we're really saying is that part of coming to understand the language or the discourses of these different disciplines is beginning to articulate in your own words what these scientific labels actually mean, and there are different paths to doing it.

**DEB:** I want to add one more thing. When I put up on the board what's another word for "circuit," he gave "path" and Tula gave us "channel," and then it died. There was nothing else coming up. But the minute we went into African languages we got "road," we got "road for electricity," we got "circle," "circle for electricity," all of a sudden we got more of the English equivalents as well as more of the African languages' equivalents. So it also helps the children with getting back into the medium of instruction if the medium is English. That's really using the children's own language for their own resources to make sure they understand the concept.[51]

As with the metaphors for multicultural classrooms, these metaphors for "circuit" focus on different aspects of a complex whole. "Path," "channel," and "road" bring the meaning of passageway; "circle" omits that meaning but calls attention to the essential closed circularity.

## Final Comments on Differential Treatment and Cultural Differences

Nigerian American anthropologist John Ogbu separates cultural differences into primary and secondary characteristics:

> *Primary cultural differences* are those different cultural features that existed *before* two populations came into contact, such as those brought by immigrant minorities from their countries of origin to the United States. . . . *Secondary cultural characteristics* are, on the other hand, those different cultural features that came into existence *after* two populations have come into contact, especially in contact involving the subordination of one group to another.[52]

Ogbu's primary cultural characteristics are what most of the cultural difference literature is about, and it is what Heath analyzed in Trackton and Ballenger studied in the Haitian Center. Ogbu attributes secondary cultural characteristics only to groups he calls "castelike minorities" such as Native Americans, Mexican Americans, and African Americans in the United States. The "secondary" experience of "subordination" is what

children from all such groups share in the differential treatments analyzed in the first part of this chapter. That is why I have emphasized how
important it is for teachers to face those aspects of differential treatment
that are within their sphere of influence, whether or not they can come
to understand the more particular aspects of their children's primary
cultures.

I also want to suggest an extension of Ogbu's secondary cultural
characteristics to the dominant group (including myself) as well. Just
as nondominant groups take on certain behaviors (such as silence or resistance) and internalize certain self-perceptions (such as images of in-
feriority) from prolonged, sometimes multigenerational experiences of
low-status contact, so dominant group members adopt certain behaviors and internalize certain self-perceptions in response to prolonged,
multigenerational experiences of high-status contact, more monocul-
tural lives, and frequent white privileges.

The little Maori girl who wrote her story about butterflies might not
have felt able to question, or disagree with, her teacher's interpretation.
If so, such silence could be less a characteristic of primary Maori culture
and more a secondary characteristic of prolonged colonial and post-
colonial New Zealand life. Although her teacher's nonconscious mono-
culturalism may be partly a residue of British cultural inheritance, that
inheritance is, at least partly, a secondary residue of even more prolonged
colonial domination. Even though relationships between U.S. white
teachers and their students of color may seem less obviously colonial,
we are no less influenced by such secondary characteristics, and no less
in need of initiating change. Only with such changes can we achieve
the goal invisioned in the introduction to this edition: Classroom discourse as the drama of teaching and learning with speaking parts for all.

## Notes

1. Interview with Clay 2000, 22.

2. E.g., Fountas and Pinnell 1996.

3. E.g., Juel and Minden-Cupp 2000.

4. Darling-Hammond 1995.

5. Duke 2000.

6. Darling-Hammond op cit., 473.

7. Nystrand et al. 1997, 47–48. *See* Perry (1988) for an African American
high school student's reflections on her experiences in private and public schools.

8. Allington 1980, Tables 2–4.

9. Collins unpublished manuscript(n.d.).

10. Collins 1996.

11. Moll, Estrada, Diaz, and Lopez 1980, 57.

12. McNaughton and Glynn 1981.

13. For two thorough but very different presentations of this integrated view of the reading process, see Clay 1991 and Snow et al. 1998.

14. Heath 1982a and Purcell-Gates 1995, especially Ch. 8.

15. Gordon 1999, 35. This chapter is authored by Gordon "with Constance Yowell."

16. Jackson 1968.

17. In a still insightful analysis of primary classrooms in England, Berlak and Berlak (1981) call this and other tensions "dilemmas of teaching." In thinking about these patterns of differential treatment, the literature on teacher expectations may come to mind. Whereas expectations differ simply in amount—a teacher expects more of some children, less of others—describing specific tensions or dilemmas helps us to see how the realizations of such expectations in situated teaching behaviors can vary in qualitative ways.

18. Clay 1998.

19. Lave and Wenger 1991, 36–37. The contrast with "marginality" in the next paragraph comes from Holmes and Meyerhoff's (1999) special journal issue that explores the relationship of Lave and Wenger's concept of Community of Practice to related terms and theories and to research on language and gender. A fourth study of heterogeneous grouping (not included in this chapter) is a collaborative report on a ninth-grade world literature class in Montclair, New Jersey. Here one group of sometimes marginalized students are African American boys. They "move toward more intensive participation," in Lave and Wenger's terms, when the class is allowed to discuss their literature assignment in friendship groups before being redistributed into groups balanced by race, gender, and achievement (Fine et al. in press).

20. Cone 1992, 712–13; subsequent quotes from 716, 717. Too late for inclusion here, I discovered a book entirely about Cone's AP class with a Bakhtinian analysis (Knoeller 1998).

21. Rex and McEachen 1999.

22. Ibid., Appendix B, 129. This one transcript is given in two formats. Rex first made the one reproduced here, dividing the speech by lines according to "message units." Reading it may give insights into the speaker's cognitive processes. A more conventional prose format appears on 102.

23. Ibid., 118, 122 (emphasis in the original).

24. Ibid., 76.

25. Reddy et al. (1998) contains the teacher researcher reports from the Goddard school. For other Cohen research, *see* Cohen and Lotan 1995, Cohen and Lotan (eds.) 1997. Written for teachers are Cohen 1994, and 1998. Shulman et al. 1998 is a "casebook for educators," among which 4, 5, 11, and 16 are from classes using Cohen's Complex Instruction (as well as 1, 6, and 12 from Brown's Community of Learners classrooms).

26. Cohen and Lotan 1995, 100–101.

27. Reddy et al., op cit., 23–24, referring to skill games described in Cohen 1994.

28. Reddy et al., op cit., 42–43.

29. Cohen 1998 (emphases added for multiple abilities).

30. Reddy et al. (op cit., 46–48) includes both transcriptions and dialogue journal entry. *See* Ch. 2, n. 29, for book references on dialogue journals. Assigning recurring and rotating roles like "reporter" are an important part of Cohen's program. As Ehrlich and Zack explain, the roles "not only encourage learning by facilitating groupwork processes, but they encourage it through their very implementation as well" (1997, 44).

31. Sarah Michaels, who began the research on sharing time (*see* Chapter 2) has been working with the Goddard teachers during their implementation of Cohen's program. She notices that the practice of consistently speaking of children's *status* seems to help shift teachers' thinking about children away from fixed abilities and toward situated positioning that is more open to change (personal communication, March 31, 2000).

32. One example is Case 11 in Shulman et al., op cit.: an eighth-grade teacher's report of his failure to change Dennis's status and participation during his implementation of Complex Instruction.

33. Grace 1987, 61.

34. Clay 1985.

35. Ibid., 31.

36. My reanalysis and follow-up explorations were first reported in Cazden 1988 (published by the Auckland, New Zealand, Reading Association). Versions of that report appear in Cazden 1990 and Cazden 1992, Ch. 15.

37. Clay op cit., 31.

38. References for these metaphors: Moll et al. 1992; Comber 1999 (personal communications); Gutierrez et al. 1999; Dyson 1993; for more about Puente, educators Dobson and Riley, and Yirrkala Community School, *see* Cazden 2000, Chs. 12 and 16.

39. Heath 1983. Recent sociocultural discussions of teaching are using a related term *mediation* and its variants *mediator* and *mediating.*

40. Ibid and Heath 1982b. This sequence of kinds of assistance to Trackton children is another example of scaffolds at the curriculum level, similar to Hillocks' "gateway activities" described in Chapter 4. It also can be grouped with Cone's style sheets and McEachen's teaching of "how to make a case" (included in the discussion of successful heterogeneous grouping work earlier in this chapter); all are examples of *explicit* instruction called for by Delpit (1995).

41. At the end of Heath's acknowledgments is a little-noticed item that indicates the unusual depth of her relationship to the African American communities she was working in: "In a manner rarely shown an outsider, black churches allowed me the unique privilege of being in their midst as worshiper and as sometime preacher. Their members heard before any others, aside from students in my courses, portions of this book and discussions of its purposes" (1983, xi–xii).

42. Landes 1965, 64. My discussion here draws on Cazden and Mehan (1989).

43. The 1996 (twelfth) and subsequent reprintings of Heath (1983) include a new Epilogue (370–76) that discusses changes in the lives of Trackton's children, now grown and parents themselves, and consequently changes in her ethnographic methods in her more recent research on youth in arts-based organizations that includes the reciprocal 'critiques' described in Chapter 6. *See also* Heath 1995 for her discussion of "race, ethnicity, and the defiance of categories," and Rampton 1995, Introduction for similar comments from England.

44. Clay 1993.

45. In these ways, Reading Recovery validates each child as an individual learner, but does not validate their group identity as members of a particular cultural community. Toward this end, some Reading Recovery teachers have urged more attention to the group (race, gender, etc.) characteristics of characters and themes in the books selected for Reading Recovery lessons. *See* discussion in Cazden 2000, Ch. 12.

46. Ballenger 1999.

47. Paley's two books, published sixteen years apart, *White teacher* (1979; new Preface in 2000 edition) and *Kwanzaa and Me* (1995) give vivid accounts of what she learned about race and racism from parents, colleagues, and a visiting African American adult in *Kwanzaa and Me* who had been a child in the *White Teacher* classroom. Cazden 1992, Chapter 17, describes one multiethnic and multilingual New Zealand elementary school, Richmond Road, where the adult staff members were continuously learning from each other.

48. Rueda and Monzo 2000 (to be available also through ERIC and on the website of the Center for Applied Linguistics: *www.cal.org*). This research is an important reminder that cross-cultural relationships among adults can be as problematical as between teachers and their students. In Australia's Northern Territory (which has the highest proportion of Aborigines of any state), the NT Department of Education (1986) published a unique resource, "Team Teaching in Aboriginal Schools." This booklet stresses how the white teachers need to give up dominating the conversation and listen and learn, while the Aboriginal teachers (often in the status of aides) need to learn to give up silently resisting and speak up and talk back. Everyone has to learn new ways of talking together if adults of unequal status in the larger society are to work effectively together in helping children learn.

49. One of the programs of the Alaska Native Knowledge Network (*www.ankn.uaf.edu*) is an annual set of science fairs in which students are encouraged to incorporate both Western science and indigenous knowledge and values into their projects, which are then judged by two groups of judges: scientists and science teachers, and Native Elders. For example, in 1998, Kelsey Peterson, a fifth grader in Kodiak tested three types of stitches for parkas: cotton, gut-skin, and traditional rye grass. Whenever students will be interviewing members of a community of which the teacher is not a member, ways of interviewing need to be planned carefully. In addition to role-playing in class, parents can be asked for advice, and the results shared in class as themselves important insights into cross-cultural communications.

50. Kilalea 2000.

51. Ibid., 329. I have edited Kilalea's transcript segments for easier reading in just the way Vivian Paley edited her transcriptions of children's speech (Ch. 5, n. 5). Miriam and Debbie (pseudonyms) are both formulating ideas as they speak, and verbatim transcriptions of such exploratory talk of even the most formally educated adults (with all the sentence fragments, repetitions, and "ums" included) will look inarticulate on the printed page.

52. Ogbu and Matute-Bianchi, 1986, 96, 97.

# Chapter Eight

# New Contexts for Students' Language Development

This book is all about changes in classroom language use, about language planning at the microlevel of interpersonal interaction. The recommended changes add up to powerful new contexts for students' language development.

For reasons already set forth, students' continued language development throughout their years in school is important. In the short run—here and now—on the path to clarification and new knowledge, articulating ideas more clearly and completely is important for speakers themselves. Moreover, as classrooms change toward a community of learners, all students' public words become part of the curriculum for their peers. In the longer run, oral, as well as written, communication skills are increasingly important in the worlds of work and civil society. This chapter reviews changes in student language use already described in Chapters 2 through 7, but here re-presented under new names.

## Exploratory Talk and Final Drafts

Many years ago, British educator Douglas Barnes called our attention to the analogy between first drafts, now an accepted first step toward fluent writing, and exploratory talk as a first step toward fluent and elaborated talk.[1] Simon's utterances while playing a computer game with Roger in Chapter 6 are examples of exploratory talk.

While watching one of Eleanor Duckworth's interviews with children working on a geometric problem, a teacher said, "I guess for the first time clearly I saw children learning—the process of learning without the answers fully intact." *Exploratory talk* is speaking "without the answers fully intact."

When students (and adults too) try to formulate ideas as they are speaking, the resulting utterances are often not well articulated. Usually, such utterances are incomplete and often have disfluencies that indicate cognitive load. Ellie's problem (Chapter 3) in expressing a convincing explanation of why she thought that eight minus a half is four is just one example. She was listened to by her teacher and her peers, and her explanation gradually became more complete over the course of the extended interaction with her teacher and her peers. Just as first drafts are an important beginning toward an eventual more complete and coherent final written text, so opportunities for exploratory talk, and for subsequent help toward oral fluency and completeness, are important in speaking as well.

## Accountable Talk

More complete, well-formulated student utterances also contribute to the whole learning community. *Accountable talk* is the name given by Lauren Resnick and her colleagues at the University of Pittsburgh to the kinds of talk needed in a community of learners. They identify three criteria (for researchers) and norms (for participants).[2]

Two norms refer to intellectual, academic qualities of student utterances:

- *Accountability to knowledge:* Participants make use of specific and accurate knowledge, . . . provide evidence for claims and arguments, . . . [and] recognize the kind of knowledge or framework required to address a topic.

- *Accountability to standards of reasoning:* Participants use rational strategies to present arguments and draw conclusions . . . [and] challenge the quality of each other's reasoning.

Knowledge and reasoning often go together, but it is important to maintain the distinction between them. In one second-grade class, I observed an African American boy asking his teacher how to spell "funner." She told him to check the dictionary, which it turned out he was very adept at using. While his spelling was inadequate (a matter of knowledge), his reasoning was excellent: If we form many comparatives by adding *er*, such as bigger and faster, dirtier and sunnier, why not "funner"?

The third norm of accountable talk is actually first on Pittsburgh's list:

- *Accountability to the learning community:* Participants are engaged in talk, . . . listen attentively to one another, . . . [and] ask each other questions aimed at clarifying or expanding a proposition.

In his Afterword to an edited volume about teacher research in the United States, Barnes speaks to this principle:

> Much learning is not a matter of accepting received knowledge; uncertainty and disagreement are a normal part of life. Since most people become anxious in the face of uncertainty, students need support in looking at alternative explanations and actions. The necessary learning includes finding out how to disagree with another student without making it a personal attack and how to receive criticism without feeling rejected. This is indeed social learning, but it is social learning in the service of the topic under discussion.[3]

We saw in the nontraditional lessons in Chapter 3 and the discussion of listening responsibilities in Chapter 5 examples of students learning how to ask, add to, and even disagree with what their peers have said, and to do so politely, in ways most likely to be heard.

Further examples are given in the CD-ROM that accompanies the Primary Literacy Standards (also developed under the guidance of Lauren Resnick). They show how even young students can be accountable to their learning communities in these ways.[4] For example, in a first-grade discussion of the book, *William's Doll,* the teacher suggests that William's father, who tries to distract William from wanting a doll by bringing him a basketball and an electric train, is like the father in another book they had discussed. Hannah speaks up: "I have two things to say. One is that I disagree with, with, you a little bit" and proceeds to give her different opinion. The commentary on the CD-ROM describes Hannah's speech act as a "challenge," but her phrase "a little bit" mitigates the interpersonal force of her disagreement, here not with a peer but with the teacher.[5]

Later, the discussion turns to William's grandmother, who wants to get him the doll. Another girl, Ashanti, says, "Maybe his grandmother, um, knows that it doesn't matter if a boy has a girl thing and if a girl has a boy thing. It's sort of like my life, because my brother plays with my dolls." As the CD's commentary points out, "Ashanti justifies her interpretation by citing an example from personal experience." In this primary classroom, Ashanti's evidence from personal experience and Hannah's evidence from textual sources both are valued. (In later grades and in college, students may find that teachers value text-based evidence more highly.)

## Academic Language

In Accountability to Knowledge, "Recognizing the kind of . . . framework required to address a topic" can refer to what Wertsch calls the "speech genre of formal instruction." This is explained by Wertsch in his discussion about the way the teacher shifted Danny's sharing-time narrative about his piece of lava away from his personal experience of getting it from his mother and to the geology of its formation (see Chapter 2). I am calling these expectations and norms for language use simply *academic language*.[6] Here again are some examples from preceding chapters of contrasting speech norms and teachers' responses to them.

Remember how second graders Roberto and Maria, in the first nontraditional math lesson in Chapter 3, explained how they calculated the difference in two children's heights:

**Roberto:** I shrunk the big guy down by taking away the little guy from him.

**Maria:** I subtracted Paolo from Jorge . . .

Both children's formulations accurately describe what they (correctly) did, but only Maria uses the mathematical term "subtracted," thereby shortening her words for the same meaning to five in contrast to Roberto's fourteen. This is an example of how academic language can often express meaning in a condensed way. It is not a criticism of the teacher to point out that, with these young children, her attention at least at the moment is only on the mathematical operations and not on ways of talking about them.

Gutierrez, whose metaphor of a 'third space' where student cultures meet the official curriculum was mentioned in Chapter 7, describes a discussion in that space where conversational and academic terms are both used deliberately by the teacher. A bilingual and bicultural teacher used both "formal" terms (*busto* and *pecho*) for bust and chest and colloquial language ("chi-chis"—boobs) to show, according to Gutierrez, how different ways of speaking can be used to make meaning.[7] Remember how the teachers working with Heath in Appalachia got their students to compare the vocabulary of farming in their community and in the school textbooks.

In the science lessons analyzed by Wells in his reevaluation of the IRE structure in Chapter 3, the teacher takes time in both the planning and review sessions to reinforce the importance of making a "fair test," and she repeatedly uses terms related to it. We even have evidence that some of the children begin to appropriate her academic terms: "What we kept constant was . . . " (review 48) and even the less familiar complex noun phrase for one of their variables, "release height" (review 60–62).

Finally, there is Lampert's explicit explanation to Ellie (and the whole fifth grade) about how to talk clearly about "eight minus a half is four," and more generally about the importance of conventions in ways of speaking:

> One of the things that is a kind of convention in mathematics is that when we just talk about numbers and we don't associate them with any object or group of objects, that the symbol means half of one whole. So if, if you were gonna communicate to the rest of the world who uses mathematics, they would take this [pointing to the expression "8½" on the chalkboard] to mean eight wholes minus one-half of a whole. . . . If, if you had said that the number that comes out is half the numbers that goes in, it would be easier for you to understand?

Not surprisingly for a fifth grader, Ellie responds, "I just couldn't put it in there, but that's what was in my mind."

One semester when I was teaching a course on Classroom Discourse at Harvard, Native Alaskan teacher Martha Demientieff introduced her take-home exam with an unusually thoughtful reflection on her own language habits:

> As I began work on this assignment, I thought of the name of the course and thought I had to use the word *discourse*. The word felt like an intruder in my mind, displacing my word *talk*. I could not organize my thoughts around it. It was like a pebble thrown into a still pond disturbing the smooth water. It makes all the other words in my mind out of sync. When I realized that I was using too much time agonizing over how to write the paper, I sat down and tried to analyze my problem. I realized that in time I will own the word and feel comfortable using it, but until that time my own words were legitimate. Contrary to some views that exposure to the dominant culture gives an advantage in learning, in my opinion it is the ownership of words that gives one confidence. I must want the word, enjoy the word and use the word to own it.[8]

Demientieff is writing as an adult about written language use. But perhaps her reflections speak also for less self-consciously aware younger students whose language development we hope to support. The task is not easy, for them or for us. To quote Bakhtin one last time:

> Language is not a neutral medium that passes freely and easily into the private property of the speaker's intentions; it is populated—overpopulated—with the intentions of others. Expropriating it, forcing it to submit to one's own intentions and accents, is a difficult and complicated process.[9]

In the spirit of Demientieff's last sentence, our task in schools is to create the conditions in which students will want these new ways with words, enjoy them, use them, and thereby come to feel them as their own.

## Dialect Differences

In the traditional sharing-time stories told by Deena in California and Leona in the Boston area, we heard examples of nonstandard verb forms that no one commented on:

We *was walking* around by my house . . . (Deena)

We *was having* / *we was* / she paid ten dollars. . . . (Leona)

My puppy / he always *be following* me . . . (Leona)

Of all the aspects of student language use discussed in this chapter, questions about dialect differences are arguably the most important to many teachers; so, more needs to be said here.

*Dialects* are varieties of a language associated with a regionally or socially defined group of people. Each dialect is characterized by a cluster of features—including accent, vocabulary, syntax—and often differences in use as well. The dialect that is now called "standard English" started out as the speech of the people of southeastern England. When they gained political dominance, the way they spoke gained linguistic dominance in the whole country and subsequently the whole British empire. Still-identifiable regional dialects in the United States include Bostonian and Southern.[10]

For reasons that have to do with controversies over race and racism more than linguistic differences themselves, the most discussed dialect in this country is African American Vernacular English (AAVE). Controversies over possible relationships between AAVE and low academic achievement seem to erupt periodically into the national media. In my professional memory, this has happened three times.

The first was during the late 1960s in the context of President Johnson's War on Poverty. In the Mississippi Headstart program, the Child Development Group of Mississippi (CDGM) proudly created books using the children's language: "If a toad *hop* up on you and *wet* on you he *make* a big blister on your feet [*italics added*]." When Southern senators attacked CDGM for its political militancy, their quotes from such books became part of their arguments in Congress against budget appropriations.

In 1979, some fifteen years later, what came to be called the "Black English" court case was brought in Ann Arbor, Michigan, on behalf of black students who were failing in school. The judge's decision in favor of the plaintiffs ordered the school system to take dialect differences into account in their reading instruction. More recently, in the late 1990s the "Ebonics"controversy developed over attempts by the Oakland, California, school board to help African American students learn standard English.[11]

From the 1960s until now, the focal educational issues are how to take dialect differences into account in teaching beginning reading, and how to help students learn to write consistently in standard English (except, of course, when portraying nonstandard-speaking characters) and speak it when appropriate.

On teaching beginning reading, the authoritative report to the National Research Council, "Preventing reading difficulties in young children," has sound advice. They list the principles recommended by linguist William Labov, which start with:

- "distinguish between mistakes in reading and mistakes in pronunciation" [in contrast to one teacher's persistent correction of "garbage" in Chapter 7].

- "give more attention to the ends of words" (where variation in pronunciation is most apparent). . . .

Then the NRC committee adds:

> The linguistic principles must be embedded in a larger perspective that recognizes these [nonstandard-dialect-speaking children] as intelligent, well-adjusted products of their own culture, still full of aspiration and promise. It is only in such a perspective that the standard language can be presented as an avenue toward educational advancement and the improvement of economic opportunity.[12]

Well said.

Two African American educators discuss the second issue about how (even whether) to deliberately help students to become more bidialectal. Lisa Delpit directly addresses the controversy:

> I have met many radical or progressive teachers of literacy who attempt to resolve the problem of students who chose to "not learn" by essentially deciding to "not teach." They appear to believe that to remain true to their ideology, their role must be to empower and politicize their most disenfranchised students by refusing to teach what Gee calls the superficial features (grammar, form, style, and so forth) of dominant Discourses. . . .
>
> There are several reasons why students- and parents-of-color take a position that differs from the well-intentioned position of the teachers I have described. First, they know that members of society need access to dominant Discourses to (legally) have access to economic power. Second, they know that such Discourses can be and have been acquired in classrooms because they know individuals who have done so. And third, and most significant to the point I want to make now,

they know that individuals have the ability to transform dominant Discourses for liberatory purposes.[13]

Foster describes one example of how standard English can be taught:

> When I lived in North Carolina, I visited an elementary school . . . [where] each week the fourth- and fifth-grade classes produced, wrote, and staged a news program that was broadcast to the entire school and taped for further analysis [by the students]. The idea behind this curriculum was to provide students with an authentic social and speech context in which to use more mainstream forms of English.[14]

From this brief description, we have to imagine classroom discussions of contrasting dialect forms, both in preparation of the broadcast and in reviewing it afterward, and we have to infer two additional design principles for this activity: positioning students to speak with authority and providing motivated opportunities for repeated "practice."

Teachers are engaged in language planning not only when they make considered decisions about whether and how to teach standard dialect, but also when they make much less consciously considered responses, moment-to-moment, to student speech in official classroom "airtime." At such moments, it is important to remember that, except in the rare moments of private teacher–student conferences, students always speak before a dual audience of teacher and peers.

One acknowledgment of the power of this dual audience is a brief autobiographical comment by white linguist Roger Shuy:

> Personally I can remember very clearly my school conflicts between peer pressure and teacher expectations. One strategy to avoid this conflict is to give the right answer to the teacher but to do so in either nonstandard or informal English.

Shuy suggested that an example of a bidialectal oral response might be, "La Paz ain't the capital of Peru."[15]

What should be the teacher's response to such an utterance?—to revoice it in standard English, or, to recognize silently, even with admiration, that the student has found what the Berlaks (discussed in Chapter 7) call a "transformational solution" to a student dilemma? Such a transformational solution might help prevent the student speaker from making a forced choice between the values and expectations of peer group and school.

In all discussions with students about their language, remember the importance of respect and trust (discussed at the end of Chapter 4), and try to avoid moralizing in words or tone of voice. Developing students' language resources by helping them learn another dialect of English can become a battleground because of the power of language attitudes, our students' and our own. The more we can keep "talking *proper*" a matter of practical (and for older students, political) reality rather than morality, the better.[16]

## Transferring Language Forms
## Across Situations of Use

For almost the last decade, Shirley Brice Heath has been conducting a national research project on the participation of teenagers and young adults in community-based organizations that sponsor sports, arts, and social entrepreneurship projects (the source of Soep's critique report in Chapter 6). The varied roles that young people take on in these projects—as planners, actors, and critics, always in collaboration with more knowledgeable adults and peers—call on specific language resources. Heath's examples include hypothetical *if-then* constructions; modal auxiliary verbs, such as *can* and *could*, for projecting possibilities into the future (not asking for permission); and mental-state verbs, such as *think* and *believe*. She selects these particular language forms for research analysis not only for what their use accomplishes interactionally and practically, but for what she believes they do for the speakers cognitively as well.[17]

In her discussion, Heath raises an important question about how language use—whether in community-based organizations or the classroom—affects the development of the speakers' language resources. In their introduction to the book on older children's language, which contains a chapter by Heath on this work, editors Hoyle and Adger wisely warn that, in research on language development, "it is difficult to tease apart developmental progress and new opportunities for its display."[18] Heath agrees with the editors that syntactic constructions with if-then clauses, modals, and mental-state verbs are not initially acquired at this late age.

Her hypothesis is more interesting and more important for thinking about language use in the classroom. I read Heath's preliminary report as suggesting that frequent and varied opportunities for practicing such language structures and the thinking processes that they express while in their project roles increases the likelihood that the speakers will transfer these communicative and cognitive strategies to other situations, as well as to their own internal monitoring. In other words, increased transferability of complex language/cognitive structures across contexts of use, so important in a world of ever-changing demands, is one important dimension of language development—one that can be stimulated by practice.[19]

Note that the all-important word *practice* has two essential complementary meanings here and throughout this book. First, there is *practice* in the social sense of a Community of Practice in which young people participate with more knowledgeable others as "apprentices," so to speak. Second, there is *practice* in the individual sense of repeated opportunities for meaningful use.

## Notes

1. Barnes 1976.

2. Institute for Learning, July 1996.

3. Barnes, op cit.

4. New Standards 1999 (quotes from the first grade are on 107).

5. Such a mitigating phrase is one of many politeness strategies. *See* Brown and Levinson (1987) for a comprehensive cross-cultural analysis, and Cazden 1979b for analysis of classroom language (in two Chicago bilingual/bicultural classrooms) in their terms.

6. Readers will find other terms with overlapping meanings in widespread use: Bakhtin speaks of "social languages," but that term would include dialect (to be discussed next in this chapter), whereas I want to keep the educational issues of dialect (defined by social groups who speak them) separate from academic language (defined by social situations in which they are spoken); *register* and *genre* are conventional terms in sociolinguistics, but the boundary between them is becoming fuzzier; Gee has coined the term *Discourse* with a capital D, but that carries the connotations of his particular theory, which has raised important criticisms (for instance, by Delpit (1993)—quoted later in this chapter). So, I am using the nontechnical, nontheoretical term, *academic* language. Hicks (1995) provides an excellent review.

7. Gutierrez et al. 1999, 297.

8. Demientieff 1988 (take-home exam, Harvard Graduate School of Education). British writers refer to the quotation marks around "discourse" as *scare* quotes. Bakhtin (1981) explains that when not reporting the speech of another person, they are written signals that a word or phrase still retains for the writer some vestige of its alien origin. In a study of the journals of twenty adult interns in second- and foreign-language teaching, Donald Freeman and I (1991) found sixty-eight instances of such quotation marks. They seemed to signal the writer's continuing but still incomplete socialization into new professional ways of thinking and talking about language learning and teaching. It is my subjective impression, as a reader, that such marks are increasing in academic writing, and I wonder if it is because writers feel immersed in so many alternative ways with words, from some of which they want publicly and visibly to maintain their distance.

9. Bakhtin 1981, 294. In Virginia Woolf's (1942) vivid description of one of her writing problems, words "have too many famous marriages."

10. In 1999, for no apparent reason, *The Boston Globe* (Bombardieri, 1999) featured the local accent on the first page of its second section, with the headline, "It's still a mahk [*sic*] of distinction: The accent sets Bostonians apart." Read-

ers elsewhere may know it as the way President Kennedy talked. Sad to say, it's often harder for speakers of other dialects to feel so proud. Jenny, an Appalachian woman now living in a more Northern city who came to Victoria Purcell-Gates' reading clinic with her son Donny to ask for reading help for both of them, told Purcell-Gates: "I couldn't learn to read. . . . 'cause I talk different. 'Cause I'm you know . . . countrified, and my words don't come out the way they're supposed to." And a teacher at Donny's school said to Purcell-Gates, "I *knew* she [Jenny] was ignorant as soon as she opened her mouth" (Purcell-Gates, 1995, 26, 134). Even Shirley Brice Heath, who had grown up in rural Virginia, remembers being reminded of her own marginalized identity when she applied for a doctorate degree and was admonished to replace her Southern accent with "general American pronunciation" (personal communication, 1988, while preparing her biography in Spolsky 1999, 762–63). Wolfram et al.'s (1999) book, *Dialects in Schools and Communities,* gives an excellent and very accessible overview.

11. Prompted by this controversy, there are now two excellent edited books on AAVE. *The Real Ebonics Debate: Power, Language, and the Education of African American Children,* edited by two African American educators (Perry and Delpit 1998), began as a special issue of the periodical *Rethinking Schools. Making the Connection: Language and Academic Achievement Among African American Students,* edited by a biracial trio of linguists (Adger et al. 1999), began as a conference sponsored by thirteen professional organizations. Baugh (1997) explains that the term *Ebonics* was coined in 1973 by a group of black scholars by combining *ebony* (black) with *phonics* (speech sounds).

12. Snow et al., 1998, 241–42.

13. Delpit 1993, 291–92. Her reference is to Gee 1989. *See* Gee (1996, 137) for his response. Her book, *Other People's Children* (1995) is essential reading on the education of students of color.

14. Foster 1997, 10–11. For further teaching suggestions, see the articles about Carrie Secret (African American fifth-grade Oakland teacher) and by Terry Meier (white teacher educator) in Perry and Delpit (op cit.). For more discussion about "the language of African American students in classroom discourse," *see* Cazden (in Adger et al., op cit.). Simmons (1991) reminds us from Oklahoma that all these dialect-teaching issues also confront teachers of "predominantly white, lower-to-middle class students."

15. Quote from Shuy 1981; example from personal communication (1985, from his memory long after the fact).

16. The term "talkin' proper" is the title of the language autobiography of Mississippi teacher researcher Bette Ford (1998). In his study of language attitudes among African American students in Oakland before the Ebonics controversy, anthropologist John Ogbu (1999) emphasizes the emotions of ambivalence and resistance.

17. Heath 1998. *See also* Heath 1993 and Heath and Smyth 1999 from the same research. Projects are not, of course, confined to community-based organizations. Producing the school news broadcast reported by Foster is one example. Two national school programs that encourage projects are the Rural Challenge Research and Evaluation Program (1999) and Expeditionary Learning

Outward Bound (Cousins et al., 2000; Udall and Medrick, 1996). To my knowledge, only Heath has analyzed the effects of project participation on student language use and development.

18. Hoyle and Adger 1998, 4.

19. Readers who are familiar with arguments between context-specific ("situated") and general (transferable) cognitive skills will be interested in the words of Michael Cole, reflecting back on his pioneering research with Sylvia Scribner on literacy in Liberia: "When technological, social, and economic conditions create many activities where reading and writing are instrumental, the range of literacy skills can be expected to broaden and increase in complexity. Under these conditions, the 'context-specific' and 'general-ability' interpretations of literacy's consequences converge" (1996, 235). Heath seems to be suggesting that, with multiple opportunities for challenging practice, the same convergence applies to oral language.

# Afterword

Creating the conditions for the interdependent goals of academic and language development for all students requires changes in classroom language use, which is what this book has been all about.

It's a big job, and teachers can't make these changes alone. Contexts are nested, from the most immediate to the act of speaking to the more distant: classroom, school, district, and so on. Plus, the classroom context is never wholly of the participants' making.[1] Bracketing out such influences, as we have done here, and considering classroom discourse as if it were autonomous, is expedient for teachers and researchers. But those who help to shape the contexts that surround the classroom have to realize their responsibility as well.

Some teachers will want to take on the added work of trying to influence policies that affect their work. That's where teacher research comes in. In addition to refining education in their own classrooms, teachers' research can contribute local evidence to discussions about educational policies in their schools and districts. That evidence, like the evidence from text or personal experiences provided by student speakers, makes teachers' statements in such forums "accountable" too.[2]

Finally, a word from one teacher to others. Thinking about the research reported in this book inevitably will lead to greater self-consciousness, at least temporarily. It has for me, when teaching in San Diego and since, and I wish it didn't have to happen. I wish we as teachers could be as successful as so many parents on intuition alone. But as anthropologist Edward Sapir explains: "It is sometimes necessary to become conscious of the forms of social behavior in order to bring about a more serviceable adaptation to changing conditions." Or, in his blunter words, analysis and conscious control are "the medicine of society, not its food."[3]

Because of conditions both within the classroom and outside it, we need the "medicine" of more careful analysis and conscious control so that our *implicit* theories of the language of teaching and learning can be open to continual re-vision. Nothing less does justice to our profession and our children.

# Notes

1. Heath's two Epilogues to *Ways With Words* mentioned in Chapter 7, note 23, give vivid examples of contextual influences. The first Epilogue is about influences from within the world of education, about why new language arts strategies devised by the Appalachian teachers had all but disappeared by the time the book was published in 1983. The second Epilogue, in the 1996 and subsequent reprintings, is about influences in the world of families, about how the lives of Trackton's children had changed by the time they became parents themselves.

2. Keresty, O'Leary, and Wortley (1998) is an account of one such successful effort around early literacy policies.

3. Sapir 1951.

# References

Adger, C. T., D. Christian, and O. Taylor, eds. 1999. *Making the Connection: Language and Academic Achievement Among African American Students.* McHenry, IL: Delta Systems. (Also available through National Council of Teachers of English.)

Airasian, P. W., and M. E. Walsh. 1997. *Constructivist Cautions. Phi Delta Kappan* 78: 444–49.

Alaska Native Knowledge Network. 1998. *Alaska Standards for Culturally Responsive Schools.* Fairbanks, AK: Author. <www.ankn.uaf.edu>.

Allen, S. 1992. "Student-Sustained Discussion: When Students Talk and the Teacher Listens." In *Students Teaching, Teachers Learning,* ed. N. A. Branscombe, D. Goswami, and J. Schwartz, 81–92. Portsmouth, NH: Boynton/Cook.

Allington, R. L. 1980. "Teacher Interruption Behaviors During Primary Grade Oral Reading." *Journal of Educational Psychology* 72: 1–37.

Alvermann, D. E., J. P. Young, C. Green, and J. M. Wisenbaker. 1999. "Adolescents' Perceptions and Negotiations of Literacy Practices in After-School Read and Talk Clubs." *American Educational Research Journal* 36: 221–64.

Anderson, E. S. 1978. "Learning to Speak with Style: A Study of the Sociolinguistic Skills of Children." Doctoral dissertation, Stanford University, Stanford, CA (UMI 78–8755).

Anderson, R. C. 1999. "Foreword: Theoretical Foundations for Literacy Acquisition." In *Stirring the Waters: The Influence of Marie Clay,* ed. J. S. Gaffney and B. J. Askew, vi–viii. Portsmouth, NH: Heinemann.

Aronson, E. A. 1978. *The Jigsaw Classroom.* Beverly Hills, CA: Sage.

Atwell, N. 1998. *In the Middle: New Understandings About Writing, Reading, and Learning* (second edition). Portsmouth, NH: Heinemann.

Baker, C. D. 1997. "Transcription and Representation in Literacy Research." In *Handbook of Research on Teaching Literacy Through the Communicative and Visual Arts,* ed. J. Flood, S. B. Heath, and D. Lapp, 110–20. New York: Simon and Schuster/Macmillan.

Bakhtin, M. 1981. *The Dialogic Imagination.* Austin, TX: University of Texas Press.

———. 1986. *Speech Genres and Other Late Essays.* Austin, TX: University of Texas Press.

Ball, D. L. 1991. "What's All This Talk About 'Discourse'?" *Arithmetic Teacher.* 39(3): 44–48.

———— and S. M. Wilson. 1996. "Integrity in Teaching: Recognizing the Fusion of the Moral and the Intellectual." *American Educational Research Journal* 33: 155–92.

Ballenger, C. 1999. *Teaching Other People's Children: Literacy and Learning in a Bilingual Classroom.* New York: Teachers College Press.

Barnes, D. 1976. *From Communication to Curriculum.* London: Penguin. (Also available from Boynton/Cook, Upper Montclair, NJ.)

————, J. Britton, and H. Rosen. 1969. *Language, the Learner and the School.* Baltimore: Penguin. (Revised ed., 1971.)

———— and F. Todd. 1995. *Communication and Learning Revisited: Making Meaning Through Talk.* Portsmouth, NH: Heinemann.

Bartlett, E. J., and S. Scribner. 1981. "Text and Context: An Investigation of Referential Organization in Children's Written Narratives." In *Writing: The Nature, Development and Teaching of Written Communication,* ed. C. H. Frederiksen and J. F. Dominic. Hillsdale, NJ: Erlbaum.

Baugh, J. 1997. "What's In a Name? That by Which We Call the Linguistic Consequences of the African Slave Trade." *The Quarterly of the National Writing Project* 19(1): 9.

Beck, I. L., M. G. McKeown, R. L. Hamilton, and L. Kucan. 1998. *American Educator* (Spring/Summer): 66–85.

Bereiter, C. 1994. "Constructivism, Socioculturalism, and Popper's World 3." *Educational Researcher* 23(7): 21–23.

Berlak, A., and H. Berlak. 1981. *Dilemmas of Schooling: Teaching and Social Change.* London: Methuen.

Berman, R. 1995. "Narrative Competence and Storytelling Performance: How Children Tell Stories in Different Contexts." *Journal of Narrative and Life History* 5: 285–313.

————, D. I. Slobin, et al. 1994. *Relating Events in Narrative: A Cross-Linguistic Developmental Study.* Hillsdale, NJ: Erlbaum.

Bernstein, B. 1971. *Class, Codes, and Control, Vol. I.* London: Routledge and Kegan Paul.

————. 1990. *Class, Codes, and Control, Vol. IV: The Structuring of Pedagogic Discourse.* London: Routledge.

Black, S. D., J. A. Levin, H. Mehan, and C. N. Quinn. 1983. "Real and Non-Real Time Interaction: Unraveling Multiple Threads of Discourse." *Discourse Processes* 6: 59–75.

Bombardieri, M. 1999. "It's Still a Mark of Distinction: The Accent Sets Bostonians Apart." *The Boston Globe* 9/23, B1, B9.

Bransford, J. D., A. L. Brown, and R. R. Cocking, eds. 1999. *How People Learn: Brain, Mind, Experience, and School.* Washington, DC: National Academy Press.

Brown, A. L. 1992. "Design Experiments: Theoretical and Methodological Challenges in Creating Complex Interventions in Classroom Settings." *The Journal of the Learning Sciences,* 2(2), 141–178.

———. 1994. "The Advancement of Learning." *Educational Researcher,* 23(8) 4–12.

———, Ash, M. Rutherford, K. Nakagawa, A. Gordon, and J. C. Campione. 1993. "Distributed Expertise in the Classroom." In *Distributed Cognitions: Psychological and Educational Considerations,* ed. G. Salomon, 188–228. New York: Cambridge University Press.

——— and J. C. Campione. 1994. "Guided Discovery in a Community of Learners." In *Classroom Lessons: Integrating Cognitive Theory and Classroom Practice,* ed. K. McGilly, 229–70. Cambridge, MA: MIT Press.

———, S. Ellery, and J. C. Campione. 1998. "Creating Zones of Proximal Development Electronically." In *Thinking Practices in Mathematics and Science Learning,* ed. J. G. Greeno and S. V. Goldman, 341–67. Mahwah, NJ: Erlbaum.

———, and A. S. Palincsar. 1989. "Guided, Cooperative Learning and Individual Knowledge Acquisition." In *Knowing, Learning, and Instruction: Essays in Honor of Robert Glaser,* ed. L. Resnick, 393–490. Hillsdale, NJ: Erlbaum.

Brown, P., and S. Levinson. 1987. *Politeness: Some Universals in Language Usage.* New York: Cambridge University Press.

Brown, R. and U. Bellugi. 1964. "Three Processes in the Child's Acquisition of Syntax." *Harvard Educational Review* 34: 133–51.

Bruer, J. T. 1994. "Classroom Problems, School Culture, and Cognitive Research." In *Classroom Lessons: Integrating Cognitive Theory and Classroom Practice,* ed. K. McGilly. Cambridge, MA: MIT Press.

Carrasco, R. L., A. Vera, and C. B. Cazden. 1981. "Aspects of bilingual student's communicative competence in the classroom: A case study." In *Latino Language and Communicative Behavior,* 237–69. ed. R. Duran. Norwood, NJ: Ablex.

Cazden, C. B. 1972. *Child Language and Education.* New York: Holt, Rinehart and Winston.

———. 1976. "How Knowledge About Language Helps the Classroom Teacher—Or Does It: A Personal Account." *Urban Review* 9: 74–90. (Reprinted in Cazden 1992.)

———. 1979a. "Peekaboo as an Instructional Model: Discourse Development at Home and at School." *Papers and Reports on Child Language Development No. 17,* 1–29. Stanford University, Dept. of Linguistics.

———. 1979b. "Language in education: Variation in the teacher-talk register." In *Language in Public Life,* Georgetown University Round Table on Languages and Linguistics, J. Alatis and G. R. Tucker, eds., 144–162. Washington, DC: Georgetown University Press.

————. 1986a. "Classroom Discourse." In *Handbook of Research on Teaching*, 3d ed., ed. M. C. Wittrock. 432–63. New York: Macmillan.

————. 1986b. "Language in the Classroom." In *Annual Review of Applied Linguistics, Vol. 7*, ed. R. Kaplan, 18–33. Rowley, MA: Newbury House.

————. 1988. "Environmental Assistance Revisited: Variation and Functional Equivalence." In *The Development of Language and Language Researchers*, ed. F. Kessel, 281–97. Hillsdale, NJ: Erlbaum.

————. 1990. "Differential Treatment in New Zealand: Reflections on Research in Minority Education." *Teaching and Teacher Education* 6: 291–303.

————. 1992. *Whole Language Plus: Essays on Literacy in the United States and New Zealand*. New York: Teachers College Press.

————. 1994. "Situational Variation in Children's Language Revisited." In *Sociolinguistic Perspectives on Register*, ed. D. Biber and E. Finegan, 277–93. New York: Oxford University Press.

————. 2000. "Taking Cultural Differences into Account" (Ch. 12); "Four Innovative Programmes: A Postscript from Alice Springs" (Ch. 16). In *Multiliteracies: Literacy Learning and the Design of Social Futures*, ed. B. Cope and M. Kalantzis, 249–66 and 321–32. London and New York: Routledge.

————, M. Cox, D. Dickinson, Z. Steinberg, and C. Stone. 1979. "You All Gonna Hafta Listen": Peer Teaching in a Primary Classroom. In *Children's Language and Communication: Twelfth Annual Minnesota Symposium on Child Development*, ed. W. A. Collins. Hillsdale, NJ: Erlbaum.

————, V. P. John, and D. Hymes, eds. 1972. *Functions of Language in the Classroom*. New York: Teachers College Press. (Reprinted by Waveland Press, 1985.)

———— and H. Mehan. 1989. "Principles from Sociology and Anthropology: Context, Code, Classroom, and Culture." In *Knowledge Base for the Beginning Teacher*, ed. M. Reynolds, 47–57. Oxford and New York: Pergamon.

————, S. Michaels, and P. Tabors. 1985. "Self-Repair in Sharing Time Narratives: The Intersection of Metalinguistic Awareness, Speech Event, and Narrative Style." In *The Acquisition of Writing: Revision and Response*, ed. S. W. Freedman. Norwood, NJ: Ablex.

Chafe, W. 1986. "Evidentiality in English Conversation and Academic Writing." In *Evidentiality: The Linguistics of Epistemology*, ed. W. Chafe and J. Nichols, 261–72. Norwood, NJ: Ablex.

Chaudron, C. 1980. "Those Dear Old Golden Rule Days." *Journal of Pragmatics* 4: 157–72.

Chomsky, N. 1957. *Syntactic Structures*. The Hague: Mouton.

Christian, S. 1997. *Exchanging Lives: Middle School Writers Online*. Urbana, IL: National Council of Teachers of English.

Christie, F. 1990. "The Morning News Genre." *Language and Education* 4: 161–79.

Citrino, A., and B. Gentry. 1999. "Beat Farmers, Bombs from Baghdad, and the Northern Lights: Crossing Cultures, Sharing Stories." In *Electronic Net-*

*works: Crossing Boundaries/Creating Communities,* ed. T. Howard and C. Benson, 112–32. Portsmouth, NH: Heinemann.

Clay, M. M. 1985. "Engaging with the School System: A Study of Interactions in New Entrant Classrooms." *New Zealand Journal of Educational Studies* 20(1): 20–38.

———. 1991. *Becoming Literate: The Construction of Inner Control.* Portsmouth, NH: Heinemann.

———. 1993. *Reading Recovery: A Guidebook for Teachers in Training.* Portsmouth, NH: Heinemann.

———. 1997. "International Perspectives on the Reading Recovery Program." In *Handbook of Research on Teaching Literacy Through the Communicative and Visual Arts,* ed. J. Flood, S. B. Heath, and D. Lapp, 655–67. New York: Macmillan.

———. 1998. *By Different Paths to Common Outcomes.* York, ME: Stenhouse.

———. 2000. "Interview." In *Reading Recovery in North America: An Illustrated History,* 22. Columbus, OH: Reading Recovery Council of North America (February, www.readingrecover.org).

———, and C. B. Cazden. 1990. "A Vygotskian Interpretation of Reading Recovery." In *Vygotsky and Education: Instructional Implications and Applications of Sociohistorical Psychology,* ed. L. C. Moll, 206–22. New York: Cambridge University Press

Cobb, P. 1994. "Where Is the Mind? Constructivist and Sociocultural Perspectives on Mathematical Development." *Educational Researcher* Oct.: 13–20.

——— and H. Bauersfeld, eds. 1995. *The Emergence of Mathematical Meaning: Interaction in Classroom Cultures.* Hillsdale, NJ: Erlbaum.

——— and J. Whitenack. 1996. "A Method for Conducting Longitudinal Analyses of Classroom Videorecordings and Transcripts." *Educational Studies in Mathematics* 30: 213–28.

———, T. Wood, and E. Yackel. 1993. "Discourse, Mathematical Thinking, and Classroom Practice." In *Contexts for Learning: Sociocultural Dynamics in Children's Development,* ed. E. A. Forman, N. Minick, and C. A. Stone, 91–119. New York: Oxford University Press.

Cognition and Technology Group at Vanderbilt. 1997. *The Jasper Project: Lessons in Curriculum, Instruction, Assessment, and Professional Development.* Hillsdale, NJ: Erlbaum.

Cohen, E. G. 1994. *Designing Group Work Strategies for the Heterogeneous Classroom.* New York: Teachers College Press.

———. 1998. "Making Cooperative Learning Equitable." *Educational Leadership* Sept.: 18–21.

——— and R. A. Lotan. 1995. "Producing Equal-Status Interaction in the Heterogeneous Classroom." *American Educational Research Journal* 32: 99–120.

———. 1997. *Working for Equity in Heterogeneous Classrooms: Sociological Theory in Practice.* New York: Teachers College Press.

Cole, M. 1996. *Cultural Psychology: A Once and Future Discipline.* Cambridge, MA: Harvard University Press.

Collins, J. P. 1996. "Socialization to Text: Structure and Contradiction in Schooled Literacy." In *Natural Histories of Discourse,* ed. M. Silverstein and G. Urban, 203–28. Chicago: University of Chicago Press.

Cone, J. K. 1992. "Untracked Advanced Placement English: Creating Opportunity Is Not Enough." *Phi Delta Kappan* 73: 712–17.

Cope, B., and M. Kalantzis. 2000. *Multiliteracies: Literacy Learning and the Design of Social Futures.* London and New York: Routledge.

Cousins, E., A. Mednick, and M. Campbell, eds. 2000. *Literacy All Day Long.* Dubuque, IA: Kendall/Hunt.

Cremin, L. A. 1961. *The Transformation of the School.* New York: Knopf.

Crook, C. 1994. *Computers and the Collaborative Experience of Learning.* London and New York: Routledge.

Cummins, J., and D. Sayers. 1997. *Brave New Schools: Challenging Cultural Illiteracy.* New York: St. Martin's Press.

Danielewicz, J., D. L. Rogers, and G. Noblit. 1996. "Children's Discourse Patterns and Power Relations in Teacher-led and Child-led Sharing Time." *Qualitative Studies in Education* 9: 311–31.

Darling-Hammond, L. 1995. "Inequality and access to knowledge." In *Handbook of Research on Multicultural Education,* ed. J. A. Banks and C. A. M. Banks, 465–83. New York: Macmillan.

de la Cruz, E. and L. Brandt. 1995. "When is writers' workshop Writers' Workshop? Key events affecting organizational patterns in first grade." *Journal of Classroom Interaction* 30(1): 21–28.

Delpit, L. 1993. "The Politics of Teaching Literate Discourse." In *Freedom's Plow: Teaching in the Multicultural Classroom,* ed. T. Perry and J. W. Fraser, 285–95. New York: Routledge.

———. 1995. *Other People's Children: Cultural Conflict in the Classroom.* New York: New Press.

Dewey, J. 1938/1963. *Experience and Education.* New York: Collier.

Diamondstone, J. 2000. "A view of what a text can be: Encouraging novel perspectives." *Journal of Adolescent and Adult Literacy,* 44(2), 108–20.

Dinsmore, D. F. 1986. "'Has Anyone Got Any News?': The Nature of 'New Times' in an Infants Class." Manuscript. Lancaster, UK: University of Lancaster.

Dorr-Bremme, D. W. 1982. "Behaving and Making Sense: Creating Social Organization in the Classroom." Doctoral dissertation, Harvard University, Cambridge, MA (UMI #82–23, 203).

Driver, R., H. Asoko, J. Leach, E. Mortimer, and P. Scott. 1994. "Constructing Scientific Knowledge in the Classroom." *Educational Researcher* Oct.: 5–12.

Duckworth, E. 1981. "Understanding Children's Understandings." Paper presented at the Ontario Institute for Studies in Education, Toronto, Canada.

Duke, N. K. 2000. "For the Rich it's Richer: Print Experiences and Environments offered to Children in very low- and very high-socio-economic status first-grade classrooms." *American Educational Research Journal*, 37, 441–78.

Dyson, A. H. 1993. *Social Worlds of Children Learning to Write in an Urban Primary School*. New York: Teachers College Press.

Eckert, P. 1998. "Entitled to Know." In *Thinking Practices in Mathematics and Science Learning*, ed. J. G. Greeno and S. V. Goldman, 147–51. Mahwah, NJ: Erlbaum.

Edgar, C., and S. N. Wood, eds. 1996. *The Nearness of You: Students and Teachers Writing Online*. New York: Teachers and Writers Collaborative.

Edwards, A. D., and J. J. Furlong. 1978. *The Language of Teaching: Meaning in Classroom Interaction*. London: Heinemann.

———, and D. P. G. Westgate. 1994. *Investigating Classroom Talk*, 2d ed. Bristol, PA: Falmer Press.

Edwards, D., and N. Mercer. 1987. *Common Knowledge: The Development of Understanding in the Classroom*, 2d ed. London and New York: Methuen.

Ehrlich, D. E., and M. B. Zack. 1997. "The Power in Playing the Part." In *Working for Equity in Heterogeneous Classrooms: Sociological Theory in Practice*, ed. E. G. Cohen and R. A. Lotan, 44–57. New York: Teachers College Press.

Erickson, F. E. 1982. "Classroom Discourse as Improvization: Relationships Between Academic Task Structure and Social Participation Structures in Lessons." In *Communicating in the Classroom*, ed. L. C. Wilkinson, 153–82. New York: Academic Press.

———. 1996. "Going for the Zone: The Social and Cognitive Ecology of Teacher–Student Interaction in Classroom Conversations." In *Discourse, Learning, and Schooling*, ed. D. Hicks, 29–62. New York: Cambridge University Press.

Everhart, R. B. 1983. *Reading, Writing and Resistance: Adolescence and Labor in a Junior High School*. Boston: Routledge and Kegan Paul.

Fecho, B. 2000. "Critical Inquiry into Language in the Urban Classroom." *Research in the Teaching of English* 34: 368–95.

Fine, M., B. Anand, C. Jordan, and D. Sherman. in press. "Before the bleach gets us all." In *Construction sites: excavating race, class, and gender among urban youth*, ed. L. Weiss and M. Fine. New York: Teachers College Press.

Ford, B. 1998. "Talkin' Proper." *American Quarterly*, 50(1) 125–29.

Forman, E. A., N. Minick, and C. A. Stone, eds. 1993. *Contexts for Learning: Sociocultural Dynamics in Children's Development*. New York: Oxford University Press.

Foster, M. 1997. "Ebonics and all that Jazz: Cutting through the Politics of Linguistics, Education, and Race." *The Quarterly of the National Writing Project*, 19(1) Winter, 7–8, 10–12.

Fountas, I. C., and G. S. Pinnell. 1996. *Guided Reading: Good First Teaching for All Children*. Portsmouth, NH: Heinemann.

Franklin, M. C. 1999. "Lessons in the millenium." *The Boston Sunday Globe*, Nov. 14, P5 and P8.

Freeman, D., and C. B. Cazden. 1991. "Learning to Talk Like a Professional: Some Pragmatics of Foreign Language Teacher Training." In *Pragmatics and Language Learning* 2: 225–45. Urbana, IL: University of Illinois, Division of English as an International Language.

Gallas, K. 1992. "When Children Take the Chair: A Study of Sharing Time in a Primary Classroom." *Language Arts* 69: 172–82. (Reprinted as Ch. 2 in K. Gallas. 1994. *The Languages of Learning: How Children Talk, Write, Dance, Draw, and Sing Their Understanding of the World*. New York: Teachers College Press.)

———. 1998. *"Sometimes I Can Be Anything": Power, Gender, and Identity in a Primary Classroom*. New York: Teachers College Press.

———, M. Anton-Oldenburg, C. Ballenger, C. Beseler, S. Griffin, R. Pappenheimer, and J. Swaim. 1996. "Talking the Talk and Walking the Walk: Researching Oral Language in the Classroom." *Language Arts* 73: 608–17.

Gee, J. P. 1985. "The Narrativization of Experience in the Oral Style." *Journal of Education* 167: 9–35.

———. 1986. "Units in the Production of Discourse." *Discourse Processes* 9: 391–422.

———. 1989. *Literacy, Discourse, and Linguistics: Essays by James Paul Gee*. Special issue of *Journal of Education* 171(1).

———. 1996. *Social Linguistics and Literacies: Ideology in Discourses*, 2d ed. Bristol, PA: Taylor and Francis.

———, S. Michaels, and M. C. O'Connor. 1992. "Discourse Analysis." In *The Handbook of Qualitative Research in Education*. San Diego: Academic Press.

Goffman, E. 1974. *Frame Analysis: An Essay on the Organization of Experience*. New York: Harper and Row.

———. 1981. *Forms of Talk*. Philadelphia: University of Pennsylvania Press.

Gordon, E. W. 1999. *Education and Justice: A View from the Back of the Bus*. New York: Teachers College Press.

Grace, P. 1987. *Electric City and Other Stories*. Auckland, NZ: Penguin.

Griffin, P., and H. Mehan. 1981. "Sense and Ritual in Classroom Discourse." In *Conversational Routine: Explorations in Standardized Communication Situations and Pre-patterned Speech*, ed. F. Coulmas. The Hague: Mouton.

Groves, S. 1997. "Making progress through scientific dialogue." Paper presented at annual meeting of the American Educational Research Association, Chicago, March.

Grubb, N. 1999. *Honored But Invisible: An Inside Look at Teaching in Community Colleges*. New York and London: Routledge.

Gutierrez, K., D. Baquedano-Lopez, and C. Tejeda. 1999. "Rethinking Diversity: Hybridity and Hybrid Language Practices in the Third Space." *Mind, Culture, and Activity* 6(4): 286–303.

Halliday, M. A. K. 1978. *Language as Social Semiotic: The Social Interpretation of Language and Meaning.* Baltimore: University Park Press.

Hardcastle, J. 1985. "Classrooms as Sites for Cultural Making." *English in Education* Autumn: 8–22.

Heath, S. B. 1982a. "What No Bedtime Story Means: Narrative Skills at Home and School." *Language in Society,* 11, 49–76.

———. 1982b. "Questioning at Home and at School: A Comparative Study." In *Doing the Ethnography of Schooling: Educational Anthropology in Action,* ed. G. Spindler, 102–31. New York: Holt, Rinehart and Winston.

———. 1983. *Ways with Words: Language, Life, and Work in Communities and Classrooms.* Cambridge: Cambridge University Press. (The 1996 edition and subsequent reprintings have a new Epilogue.)

———. 1993. "Inner City Life Through Drama: Imagining the Language Classroom." *TESOL Quarterly* 27: 177–92.

———. 1995. "Race, Ethnicity, and the Defiance of Categories." In *Toward a Common Destiny: Improving Race and Ethnic Relations in America,* ed. W. D. Hawley and A. W. Jackson, 39–70. San Francisco: Jossey-Bass.

———. 1998. "Working Through Language." In *Kids Talk: Strategic Language Use in Later Childhood,* ed. S. M. Hoyle and C. T. Adger, 217–40. New York: Oxford University Press.

——— and L. Mangiola. 1991. *Children of Promise: Literate Activity in Linguistically and Culturally Diverse Classrooms.* Washington, DC: National Educational Association.

——— and L. Smyth. 1999. *Art Show: Youth and Community Development, a Resource Guide.* Washington, DC: Partners for Livable Communities (*www.livable.com*).

Heider, E. R., C. B. Cazden, and R. Brown. 1968. "Social Class Differences in the Effectiveness and Style of Children's Coding Ability." *Project Literacy Reports,* No. 9. Ithaca, NY: Cornell University.

Hemphill, L. 1986. "Context and Conversation Style: A Reappraisal of Social Class Differences in Speech." Doctoral dissertation, Harvard University, Cambridge, MA (UMI #86–20, 273).

Hicks, D. 1995. "Discourse, Learning and Teaching." *Review of Research in Education, Vol. 21,* ed. M. Apple, 49–95. Washington, DC: American Educational Research Association.

Hiebert, J., T. P. Carpenter, E. Fennema, K. Fuson, P. Human, H. Murray, A. Oliver, and D. Wearne. 1996. "Problem-Solving as a Basis for Reform in Curriculum and Instruction: The Case of Mathematics." *Educational Researcher* 23 (May): 12–21.

Hillocks, G. Jr. 1995. *Teaching Writing as Reflective Practice.* New York: Teachers College Press.

Holmes, J., and M. Meyerhoff. 1999. "The Community of Practice: Theories and Methodologies in Language and Gender Research." *Language in Society* 28: 173–83.

Howard, T., and C. Benson, eds. 1999. *Electronic Networks: Crossing Boundaries/ Creating Communities.* Portsmouth, NH: Heinemann.

Hoyle, S. M., and C. T. Adger. 1998. *Kids Talk: Strategic Language Use in Later Childhood.* New York: Oxford University Press.

Hunt, V. 1996. "The Raptor Project." In *The Nearness of You: Students and Teachers On-line,* ed. C. Edgar and S. N. Wood, 231–40. New York: Teachers and Writers Collaborative.

Hymes, D. 1996. *Ethnography, Linguistics, Narrative Inequality: Toward an Understanding of Voice.* Bristol, PA: Taylor and Francis.

Institute for Learning. 1996. Accountable Talk Scoring Rubric (Condensed Version). Pittsburgh: University of Pittsburgh, Learning Research and Development Center, July.

Irvine, J. T. 1979. "Formality and Informality in Communicative Events." *American Anthropologist* 81: 773–90.

Istomina, Z. M. 1975. "The Development of Voluntary Memory in Pre-school Age Children." *Soviet Psychology* 13: 5–64.

Jackson, P. W. 1968. *Life in Classrooms.* New York: Holt, Rinehart and Winston.

James, W. 1958. *Talks to Teachers.* New York: Norton (talks delivered in 1892).

Jimenez, R. T., and R. Gersten. 1999. "Lessons and Dilemmas Derived From the Literacy Instruction of Two Latina/o Teachers." *American Educational Research Journal* 36: 265–301.

Juel, C., and C. Minden-Cupp. 2000. "Learning to Read Words: Linguistic Units and Instructional Strategies." *Reading Research Quarterly,* 35, 458–93.

Kamler, B. 1980. "One Child, One Teacher, One Classroom: The Story of One Piece of Writing." *Language Arts* 57: 680–93.

Keresty, B., S. O'Leary, and D. Wortley. 1998. *You Can Make a Difference: A Teacher's Guide to Political Action.* Portsmouth, NH: Heinemann.

Kilalea, M. 2000. "Patterns of Communication in Collaborative Teaching." Unpublished doctoral dissertation, University of the Witwatersrand, Johannesburg.

Knoeller, C. 1998. *Voicing Ourselves: Whose Words We Use When We Talk About Books.* Albany: State University of New York Press.

Kohl, H. 1994. *I Won't Learn From You.* New York: The New Press.

Kucan, L., and I. L. Beck. 1997. "Thinking Aloud and Reading Comprehension Research: Inquiry, Instruction, and Social Interaction." *Review of Educational Research* 67: 271–99.

Lambert, W. E., R. C. Hodgson, R. C. Gardner, and S. Fillenbaum. 1960. "Evaluational Reactions to Spoken Languages." *Journal of Abnormal and Social Psychology* 60: 44–51.

Lampert, M. 1990. "When the Problem Is Not the Question and the Solution Is Not the Answer: Mathematical Knowing and Teaching." *American Educational Research Journal* 27(1): 29–64.

————, P. Rittenhouse, and C. Crumbaugh. 1996. "Agreeing to Disagree: Developing Sociable Mathematical Discourse." In *The Handbook of Education and Human Development: New Models of Learning, Teaching and Schooling,* ed. D. R. Olson and N. Torrance 731–64. Cambridge, MA: Blackwell.

Landes, R. 1965. *Culture in American Education.* New York: Wiley.

Lashley, K. S. 1961. "The Problem of Serial Order in Behavior." In *Psycholinguistics: A Book of Readings,* ed. S. Saporta 180–98. New York: Holt, Rinehart and Winston.

Lave, J., and E. Wenger. 1991. *Situated Learning: Legitimate Peripheral Participation.* New York: Cambridge University Press.

Leinhardt, G. 1987. "Development of an Expert Explanation: An Analysis of a Sequence of Subtraction Lessons." *Cognition and Instruction* 4: 225–82.

Lemke, J. L. 1990. *Talking Science: Language, Learning, and Values.* Norwood, NJ: Ablex.

Leont'ev, A. N. 1981. "The Problem of Activity in Psychology." In *The Concept of Activity in Soviet Psychology,* ed. J. V. Wertsch. Armonk, NY: M. E. Sharpe.

Levinson, S. 1979. "Activity Types and Language." *Linguistics* 17: 365–99.

Lewis, C. 1997. "The Social Drama of Literature Discussions in a Fifth/Sixth Grade Classroom." *Research in the Teaching of English* 31: 163–204.

Linde, C. 1999. "The Transformation of Narrative Syntax into Institutional Memory." *Narrative Inquiry* 9(1): 139–74.

Lortie, D. C. 1975. *Schoolteacher: A Sociological Study.* Chicago: University of Chicago Press.

Lundgren, U. P. 1977. *Model Analysis of Pedagogical Discourse.* Stockholm: Stockholm Institute of Education, Department of Educational Research.

Manuilenko, Z. V. 1975. "The Development of Voluntary Behavior in Preschool-age Children." *Soviet Psychology* 13(4): 65–116.

Martin, G. 1987. "A Letter to Bread Loaf." In *Reclaiming the Classroom: Teacher Research as an Agency for Change,* ed. D. Goswami and P. S. Stillman, Upper Montclair, NJ: Boynton/Cook.

McCarthey, S. J. 1994. "Teachers, Text, and Talk: The Internalization of Dialogue from Social Interaction During Writing." *Reading Research Quarterly* 29: 201–40.

McLeod, A. 1986. "Critical Literacy: Taking Control of Our Own Lives." *Language Arts* 63: 37–50.

McNaughton, S., and T. Glynn. 1981. "Delayed Versus Immediate Attention to Oral Reading Errors: Effects on Accuracy and Self-Correction." *Educational Psychology* 1(1): 57–65.

McNeill, D. 1992. *Hand and Mind: What Gestures Reveal about Thought.* Chicago: University of Chicago Press.

Mehan, H. 1979. *Learning Lessons.* Cambridge, MA: Harvard University Press.

————, I. Villanueva, L. Hubbard, and A. Lintz. 1996. *Constructing School Success: The Consequences of Untracking Low-achieving Students.* New York: Cambridge University Press.

Mercer, N. and E. Fisher, 1997. "Scaffolding through talk." In *Computers and talk in the primary classroom,* ed. R. Wegerif and P. Scrimshaw, 196–210. Clevedon (UK) and Bristol, PA: Multilingual Matters.

Michaels, S. 1981. "Sharing Time: Children's Narrative Styles and Differential Access to Literacy." *Language in Society* 10: 423–42.

————. 1985a. "Classroom Processes and the Learning of Text Editing Commands." *Quarterly Newsletter of the Laboratory of Comparative Human Cognition* 7: 70–79.

————. 1985b. "Hearing the Connections in Children's Oral and Written Discourse." *Journal of Education* 167: 36–56.

———— and C. B. Cazden. 1986. "Teacher–Child Collaboration as Oral Preparation for Literacy." In *The Acquisition of Literacy: Ethnographic Perspectives,* ed. B. B. Schieffelin, 132–54. Norwood, NJ: Ablex.

Minstrell, J. A. 1989. "Teaching Science for Understanding." In *Toward the Thinking Curriculum: Current Cognitive Research* (1989 Yearbook of the Association for Supervision and Curriculum Development), ed. L. Resnick and L. E. Klopfer, 131–49. Alexandria, VA: ASCD.

Moll, L. C., C. Amanti, D. Neff, and N. Gonzalez. 1992. "Funds of Knowledge for Teaching: Using a Qualitative Approach to Connect Homes and Classrooms." *Theory into Practice* 31: 132–41.

————, E. Estrada, E. Diaz, and L. M. Lopez. 1980. "The Organization of Bilingual Lessons: Implications for Schooling." *Quarterly Newsletter of the Laboratory of Comparative Human Cognition* 2: 53–58.

Morson, G. S. and C. Emerson. 1990. *Mikhail Bakhtin: Creation of a Prosaic.* Stanford: Stanford University Press.

Murnane, R. J., and F. Levy. 1996. *Teaching the New Basic Skills: Principles for Educating Children to Thrive in a Changing Economy.* New York: The Free Press.

National Council of Teachers of Mathematics. 1989. *Curriculum and Evaluation Standards for School Mathematics.* Reston, VA: Author.

————. 1991. *Professional Standards for Teaching Mathematics.* Reston, VA: Author.

————. 2000. *Principles and Standards for School Mathematics.* Reston, VA: Author.

National Institute of Education. 1974. Conference on Studies in Teaching, Report of Panel 5. *Teaching as a Linguistic Process in a Cultural Setting* (ED 111 805).

New London Group. 1996. "A Pedagogy of Multiliteracies: Designing Social Futures." *Harvard Educational Review* 66: 60–92.

Newman, D., P. Griffin, and M. Cole. 1989. *The Construction Zone: Working for Cognitive Change in School.* Cambridge, MA: Cambridge University Press.

New Standards. 1999. *Reading and Writing Grade by Grade: Primary Literacy Standards for Kindergarten Through Third Grade.* Washington, DC: National Center for Education and the Economy and the University of Pittsburgh (info@ncee.org).

Northern Territory Department of Education. 1986. *Team Teaching in Aboriginal Schools.* Darwin, AU: Author.

Nystrand, M., A. Gamoran, R. Kachur, and C. Prendergast. 1997. *Opening Dialogue: Understanding the Dynamics of Language and Learning in the English Classroom.* New York: Teachers College Press.

Ochs, E. 1979. "Transcription as Theory." In *Developmental Pragmatics,* ed. E. Ochs and B. B. Schieffelin. New York: Academic Press.

O'Connor, M. C. 1998. "Can We Trace the 'Efficacy of Social Constructivism'?" In *Review of Research in Education Vol. 23,* ed. P. D. Pearson and A. Iran-Nejad. 25–71. Washington, DC: American Educational Research Association.

———. 1996. "Managing the Intermental: Classroom Group Discussion and the Social Context of Learning." In *Social Interaction, Social Context and Language: Essays in Honor of Susan Ervin-Tripp,* ed. D. I. Slobin, J. Gerhardt, A. Kyratzis, and J. Guo, Hillsdale, NJ: Erlbaum.

——— and S. Michaels. 1996. "Shifting Participant Frameworks: Orchestrating Thinking Practices in Group Discussion." In *Discourse, Learning, and Schooling,* ed. D. Hicks, 63–103. New York: Cambridge University Press

Ogbu, J. U. 1999. "Beyond Language: Ebonics, Proper English, and Identity in a Black-American Speech Community." *American Educational Research Journal* 36: 147–84.

——— and M. E. Matute-Bianchi. 1986. "Understanding Sociocultural Factors: Knowledge, Identity, and School Adjustment." In *Beyond Language: Social and Cultural Factors in Schooling Language Minority Students,* 73–142. Sacramento: California State Department of Education.

Ogburn, J., G. Kress, I. Martins, and K. McGillicuddy. 1996. *Explaining Science in the Classroom.* Buckingham and Philadelphia: Open University Press.

Paley, V. 1979. *White Teacher.* Cambridge, MA: Harvard University Press.

———. 1981. *Wally's Stories.* Cambridge, MA: Harvard University Press.

———. 1990. *The Boy Who Would Be a Helicopter.* Cambridge, MA: Harvard University Press.

———. 1992. *You Can't Say You Can't Play.* Cambridge, MA: Harvard University Press.

———. 1995. *Kwanzaa and Me.* Cambridge, MA: Harvard University Press.

———. 1997. *The Girl with the Brown Crayon.* Cambridge, MA: Harvard University Press.

Palincsar, A. S. 1986. "The Role of Dialogue in Providing Scaffolded Instruction." *Educational Psychologist* 21: 73–98.

————. 1998. "Keeping the metaphor of scaffolding fresh: A response to C. Addison Stone's 'The metaphor of scaffolding: Its utility for the field of learning disabilities.'" *Journal of Learning Disabilities,* 31, 370–73.

Perez, C., and H. Tager-Flusberg, 1998. "Clinicians' Perceptions of Children's Oral Personal Narratives." *Narrative Inquiry* 8: 181–201.

Perry, I. 1988. "A Black Student's Reflections on Public and Private Schools." *Harvard Educational Review* 58(1): 332–36.

Perry, T., and L. Delpit. 1998. *The Real Ebonics Debate: Power, Language, and the Education of African American Children.* Boston: Beacon Press.

Peyton, J. K., and J. Staton. 1993. *Dialogue Journals in the Multilingual Classroom: Building Language Fluency and Writing Skills Through Written Interaction.* Stamford, CT: Ablex.

Poole, D. 1990. "Contextualizing IRE in an Eighth-Grade Quiz Review." *Linguistics and Education* 2: 185–211.

————. 1994. "Routine Testing Practices and the Linguistic Construction of Knowledge." *Cognition and Instruction* 12: 125–90.

Poveda, D. in press. "*La ronda* in a Spanish Kindergarten Classroom (and a Cross-Cultural Comparison with "Sharing Time" in the U.S.A.)." *Anthropology and Education Quarterly.*

Pratt, M. L. 1977. *Towards a Speech Act Theory of Literary Discourse.* Bloomington: Indiana Universitiy Press.

Purcell-Gates, V. 1995. *Other People's Words: The Cycle of Low Literacy.* Cambridge, MA: Harvard University Press.

Putnam, R. T., M. Lampert, and P. L. Peterson. 1990. "Alternative Perspectives on Knowing Mathematics in Elementary Schools." In *Review of Research in Education, Vol. 16,* ed. C. B. Cazden, 57–150.

Quinn, C. N., H. Mehan, J. A. Levin, and S. D. Black. 1983. "Real Education in Non-real Time: The Use of Electronic Message Systems for Instruction." *Instructional Science* 11: 313–27.

Rampton, B. 1995. *Crossing: Language and Ethnicity Among Adolescents.* London: Longman.

Reddy, M., P. Jacobs, C. McCrohon, and L. R. Herrenkohl. 1998. *Creating Scientific Communities in the Elementary Classroom.* Portsmouth, NH: Heinemann.

Resnick, L. B. 1985. "Cognition and instruction: Recent theories of human competence and how it is acquired." In *Pscyhology and Learning: The Masser Lectures Series.* Vol. 4, ed. B. L. Hammond. Washington, DC: American Psyhological Association.

Rex, L. A. and D. McEachen. 1999. "If Anything Is Odd, Inappropriate, Confusing, or Boring, It's Probably Important." *Research in the Teaching of English,* 34: 65–129.

Rogoff, B. 1995. "Observing Sociocultural Activity on Three Planes: Participatory Appropriation, Guided Participation, and Apprenticeship." In *Sociocultural Studies of Mind,* ed. J. V. Wertsch, P. del Rio, and A. Alvarez, 139–64. Cambridge, UK: Cambridge University Press.

Rose, M. 1999. "'Our Hands Will Know': The Development of Tactile Diagnostic Skill—Teaching, Learning and Situated Cognition in a Physical Therapy Program." *Anthropology and Education Quarterly* 30: 133–60.

Rosen, H. 1984. *Stories and Meanings.* Sheffield, England: National Association for the Teaching of English. (Also available from Boynton/Cook Publishers, Upper Montclair, NJ.)

———. 1985. "Review of S. B. Heath, *Ways with Words.*" *Harvard Educational Review* 55: 448–56.

Rosenshine, B., and C. Meister. 1994. "Reciprocal Teaching: A Review of the Literature." *Review of Educational Research* 64: 479–530.

Rowe, M. B. 1986. "Wait Time: Slowing Down May Be a Way of Speeding Up!" *Journal of Teacher Education* 37: 43–50.

Rueda, R. S., and L. D. Monzo. 2000. *Apprenticeship for Teaching: Professional Development Issues Surrounding the Collaborative Relationship Between Teachers and Paraeducators.* Santa Cruz: University of California at Santa Cruz, Center for Research on Education, Diversity, and Excellence (www.cal.org).

Rural Challenge Research and Evaluation Program, Harvard Graduate School of Education. 1999. *Living and Learning in Rural Schools and Communities: A Report to the Annenberg Rural Challenge.* Cambridge, MA: Author.

Rutherford, M. 1992. "Second Language Learning in a 'Community of Learners' Classroom." Manuscript written at the University of California School of Education.

Sacks, H., E. A. Schegloff, and G. Jefferson. 1974. "A Simplest Systematics for the Organization of Turn-taking in Conversation." *Language* 50: 696–735.

Sapir, E. 1951. "The Unconscious Patterning of Behavior in Society." In *Selected Writing of Edward Sapir,* ed. D. G. Mandelbaum, Berkeley: University of California Press.

Saunders, W. and C. Goldenberg. 1996. "Four Primary Teachers Work to Define Constructivism and Teacher-Directed Learning: Implications for Teacher Assessment." *The Elementary School Journal* 97: 139–162.

———, C. Goldenberg, and J. Hamann. 1992. "Instructional Conversations Beget Instructional Conversations." *Teaching and Teacher Education* 8: 199–218.

Sayers, D. 1994. "Bilingual Team-Teaching Partnerships Over Long Distances: A Technology-Mediated Context for Intra-group Language Attitude Change." In *Cultural Diversity in Schools: From Rhetoric to Practice,* ed. C. Faltis, R. DeVillar, and J. Cummins, 299–331. Albany: State University of New York Press.

Schifter, D. 1997. "Learning mathematics for teaching: Lessons in/from the domain of fractions." Newton, MA: Education Development Center, Center for the Development of Teaching, Paper Series.

Schlegel, J. 1998. "Finding Words, Finding Meanings: Collaborative Learning and Distributed Cognition." In *Kids Talk: Strategic Language Use in Later*

*Childhood,* ed. S. M. Hoyle and C. T. Adger, 187–204. New York: Oxford University Press.

Schoenbach, R., C. Greenleaf, C. Cziko, and L. Hurwitz. 1999. *Reading for Understanding: A Guide to Improving Reading in Middle and High School Classrooms.* San Francisco: Jossey-Bass.

Sfard, A. 1998. "On Two Metaphors for Learning and the Dangers of Choosing Just One." *Educational Researcher* 27(2): 4–13.

———. In press. "Balancing the Unbalanceable: The NCTM Standards in the Light of Theories of Learning Mathematics." In *A Research Companion for NCTM Standards,* ed. J. Kilpatrick, G. Martin, and D. Schifter, Reston, VA: National Council of Teachers of Mathematics.

Sheeran, Y., and D. Barnes. 1991. *School Writing.* Bristol, PA: Open University Press.

Shulman, J. H., R. A. Lotan, and J. A. Whitcomb, eds. 1998. *Groupwork in Diverse Classrooms: A Casebook for Educators.* New York: Teachers College Press.

Shulman, L. 1987. "Knowledge and teaching: Foundations of the new reform." *Harvard Educational Review,* 57(1), 1–22.

Shuy, R. 1981. "Learning to Talk Like Teachers." *Language Arts* 58: 168–74.

Simmons, E. A. 1991. "Ain't We Never Gonna Study No Grammar?" *English Journal* Dec.: 48–51.

Sinclair, J. McH., and R. M. Coulthard. 1975. *Towards an Analysis of Discourse: The English Used by Teachers and Pupils.* London: Oxford University Press.

Sittnick, P. 1999. "A School at the Crossroads." In *Electronic Networks: Crossing Boundaries/Creating Communities,* ed. T. Howard and C. Benson, 193–204. Portsmouth, NH: Heinemann.

Smitherman, G. 1977. *Talkin' and Testifyin': The Language of Black America.* Boston: Houghton Mifflin. (Reprinted in 1986, Detroit: Wayne University Press.)

Snow, C. E. 1977. "Mothers' Speech Research: From Input to Interaction." In *Talking to Children: Input and Acquisition,* ed. C. E. Snow and C. A. Ferguson, New York: Cambridge University Press.

———, S. B. Burns, and P. Griffin, ed. 1998. *Preventing Reading Difficulty in Young Children.* Washington, DC: National Academy Press.

——— and B. A. Goldfield. 1981. "Building Stories: The Emergence of Information Structures from Conversation." In *Analyzing Discourse: Text and Talk. Georgetown University Round Table on Language and Linguistics 1981,* ed. D. Tannen, (127–41). Washington, DC: Georgetown University Press.

———. 1983. "Turn the Page Please: Situation-Specific Language Acquisition." *Journal of Child Language* 10: 551–69.

Soep, E. M. 1996. "An Art in Itself: Youth Development Through Critique." *New Designs for Youth Development* 12(4): 42–46.

Solsken, I., J. Willett and J. Wilson-Keenan. 2000. "Cultivating hybrid texts in multicultural classrooms: Promise and challenge." *Research in the Teaching of English,* 35, 179–212.

Spolsky, B. 1999. *Concise Encyclopedia of Educational Linguistics.* Oxford: Pergamon.

Staton, J., R. Shuy, J. K. Peyton, and L. Reed. 1988. *Dialogue Journal Communication: Classroom, Linguistic, Social and Cognitive Views.* Norwood, NJ: Ablex.

Steinberg, Z., and C. B. Cazden. 1979. "Children as teachers—of peers and ourselves." *Theory into Practice,* 18, 258–66.

Stires, S. *Beyond Show and Tell: Developing Oral Texts.* Unpublished manuscript.

Stone, A. 1993. "What Is Missing in the Metaphor of Scaffolding." In *Contexts for Learning: Sociocultural Dynamics in Children's Development,* ed. E. A. Forman, N. Minick, and C. Addison Stone, 167–83. New York: Oxford University Press.

Tannen, D. 1984. *Conversational Style: Analyzing Talk Among Friends.* Norwood, NJ: Ablex.

Tharp, R. G., and R. Gallimore. 1988. *Rousing Minds to Life: Teaching, Learning and Schooling in Social Context.* Cambridge, UK: Cambridge University Press.

Tizard, B. 1986. "The Care of Young Children: Implications of Recent Research." London: Institute of Education, Thomas Coram Research Unit Working and Occasional Papers.

——— and M. Hughes. 1984. *Young Children Learning.* Cambridge, MA: Harvard University Press.

Tobin, K. 1986. "Effects of Teacher Wait Time on Discourse Characteristics in Mathematics and Language Arts Classes." *American Educational Research Journal* 23: 191–200.

Tracy, K. 1984. "Staying on Topic: An Exploration of Conversational Relevance." *Discourse Processes* 7: 447–64.

Tunstall, P., and C. Gipps. 1996. "Teacher feedback to young children in formative assessment: A typology." *British Educational Research Journal,* 22, 389–404.

Udall, D., and A. Mednick. 1996. *Journey Through Our Classrooms.* Dubuque, IA: Kendall/Hunt.

Ulichny, P. 1996. "Performed Conversations in an ESL Classroom." *TESOL Quarterly* 30: 739–64.

Vygotsky, L. S. 1962. *Thought and Language.* Cambridge, MA: MIT Press.

———. 1978. *Mind in Society: The Development of Higher Psychological Processes.* Cambridge, MA: Harvard University Press.

Warschauer, M. 1999. *Electronic Literacies: Language, Culture, and Power in Online Education.* Mahwah, NJ: Erlbaum.

———, K. Donaghy, and H. Kuamoyo. 1997. *Computer-Assisted Language Learning* 10(4): 349–61.

Webb, N. M., and A. S. Palincsar. 1996. "Group Processes in the Classroom." In *Handbook of Educational Psychology,* ed. D. C. Berliner and R. C. Calfee, 841–73. New York: Simon and Shuster/Macmillan.

Wegerif, R., and N. Mercer. 1996. "Computers and Reasoning Through Talk in the Classroom." *Language and Education* 10(1): 47–64.

———— and P. Scrimshaw, eds. 1997. *Computers and Talk in the Primary Classroom.* Clevedon, UK and Bristol, PA: Multilingual Matters.

Wells, G. 1986. *The Meaning Makers: Children Learning Language and Using Language to Learn.* Portsmouth, NH: Heinemann.

————. 1993. "Reevaluating the IRF Sequence: A Proposal for the Articulation of Theories of Activity and Discourse for the Analysis of Teaching and Learning in the Classroom." *Linguistics and Education* 5: 1–37.

Wenger, E. 1998. *Communities of Practice: Learning, Meaning, and Identity.* Cambridge, UK: Cambridge University Press.

Wertsch, J. V. 1984. "The Zone of Proximal Development: Some Conceptual Issues." In *New Directions for Child Development, Vol. 23: Children's Learning in the "Zone of Proximal Development,"* ed. B. Rogoff and J. V. Wertsch, San Francisco: Jossey-Bass.

————. 1985. *Vygotsky and the Social Formation of Mind.* Cambridge, MA: Harvard University Press.

————. 1991. *Voices of the Mind: A Sociocultural Approach to Mediated Action.* Cambridge, MA: Harvard University Press.

———— and C. A. Stone. 1985. "The Concept of Internalization in Vygotsky's Account of the Genesis of Higher Mental Functions." In *Culture, Communication and Cognition: Vygotskian Perspectives,* ed. J. V. Wertsch. Cambridge, MA: Cambridge University Press.

Wolfram, W., C. T. Adger, and D. Christian. 1999. *Dialects in Schools and Communities.* Mahwah, NJ: Erlbaum.

Wood, D. J., J. S. Bruner, and G. Ross. 1976. "The Role of Tutoring in Problem Solving." *Journal of Child Psychology and Psychiatry* 17(2): 89–100.

Woolf, V. 1942. "Craftsmanship." In *The Death of the Moth and Other Essays.* New York: Harcourt Brace.

# Subject Index

Academic language, 172–174
  *See also* under Frames of Reference; *See also* Register
Accountable talk, 170–172
Affirmative interaction, *See* under Equity issues
Appropriation, 26, 75–77
Audience
  as "addressivity" of utterances, 116
  expanded in telecommunication, 127, 128
  dual, of teachers and peers, 12–13, 176
  role in writing conferences, 116–117

Bilingual/multilingual learning and teaching, 79*n*.23, 103, 127–128,134*n*.10, 142–144, 160–162, 163, 172

Changes in classroom discourse, 81, 131, 169
  advocated by NCTM standards, 48–49, 55–56
  initiated by students, 23, 25
  pressures on teachers for, 5, 8*n*.7
  *See also* Teacher research
Common knowledge, as teaching objective, 41, 47, 75, 130, 136*n*.38, *n*.40
Communicative competence, 3, Ch. 8 passim
  as new basic skill, 4–5
  required in nontraditional lessons, 48, 50, 55
  self-corrections as evidence of, 15
Community of learners, 78, 89, 131, 169
  in Ann Brown's literacy/science program, 68, 109–110, 132–133

contrasted with isolated individuals, 48–49, 74–75, 131
  revoicings as contributing to, 91
Complex Instruction in Elizabeth Cohen's science program, 150–153
Computers, interaction with, 123–134 passim
  diffusion of computer expertise in the classroom, 132–134
  dislocated from rest of curriculum, 129–131
  hypertext assistance, 97
Constructivism, 76–77
  *See also* Internalization
Contexts
  in the mind, 75, 92, 130, 136*n*.38, *n*.40, 144
  nested, 181, 182*n*.1
Contextualization cues, 101
Contextualized/decontextualized tasks, 74–75
Cultural contact in classrooms
  among adults, 160–162, 167*n*.48
  metaphors for, 156–157
Cultural differences, 153–163 passim
  contrasting with differential treatment, 137
  disembodied information about, 158–159
  primary and secondary characteristics, 163–164
  situated learning about, 159–161, 167*n*.49
Curriculum
  actual vs. intended curriculum, 2
  as scaffold, 69–71
  discourse ground rules as, 6
  requiring multiple skills and abilities, 150–153

Default option
  differential treatment as, in educational system, 144–145
  IRE as, in classroom interaction, 31
Dialects, 174–177, 178*n*.6, 178–79*n*.10
  and learning to read, 175
  becoming bidialectal, 175–177
  Ebonics, 174–175, 179*n*.11, 179*n*.16
Dialogue journals, 27, 29*n*.29, 152
Differential treatment, 137–153 passim
  as default option, 144–145
  as unintended consequences, 145
  causing secondary cultural differences, 163–164
  related to cultural differences, 137, 156
  contrasted with differential experience, 145
  helpful or harmful, 137–138
  *See also* Tracking
Dilemmas
  for students, 176
  for teachers, 54–56, 58*n*.31, 165*n*.17
Discourse(s)
  Gee's discourse vs. Discourse, 178*n*.6
  home vs. school, 6, 16–17, 77–78, 158
  indicated by quotation marks, 178*n*.8
  influenced by high-stakes testing, 103–105
  internally persuasive vs. authoritative, 76, 110–111, 118
  multivocal vs. univocal, 121
  of power, 6
  oral/written hybrid in telecommunication, 127
  *See also* Language, Register, Structures of Discourse
Dynamic assessment, 69, 79*n*.14

Ebonics, *See* under Dialects
Equity issues, 5, 81, 133–134
  affirmative interaction, 84
  deregulation, 83–84
  dilemma for teachers about, 54–55

  in peer discourse, 150
  speaking parts for all, 5, 8
  *See also* Cultural differences, Differential treatment, Gender Differences, Social class differences

Exploratory talk, 125, 168–170
  and final drafts, 237–238

Frames of reference
  academic, 20–22
  of teachers vs. discourse analysts, 16, 28*n*.7
  of teachers vs. parents, 16–17
  *See also* Reconceptualization/recontextualization

Gender differences, 84, 86
Genres, *See* Narratives
Gestures, 111–113, 134*n*.4

Heterogeneous groups, 146–153, 165*n*.19, 166*n*.40

Identities, 2, 27, 106*n*.10, 159
  language variations and, 1–2
  roles and, 6, 8*n*.9, 68
  transformations of, 26–27
  *See also* Roles for speaking
Improvisation, *See* under Structures of discourse
Initiation-Response-Evaluation/Feedback (IRE/F), 30, 49, 123–124
  as default option, 43
  criticism of, 46
  functions of, 41, 47, 59*n*.35
  contrasted with telecommunication lessons, 128–129
Internalization, 75–77, 80*n*.33
  and appropriation, 75–76
  and transformation of participation, 80*n*.33
Interruptions, *See* under Speaking rights

Jigsaw groups, 68, 102, 103, 113–114

Language
  academic language, 172–174; *See also* Frames of reference

attitudes toward, 127–128, 176–177
development, 27, Ch. 8 passim
form-function relationships, 38–39, 47
functions, 3
intonation, 77–78
variations, 2–3, 6, 20, 22, 38–39, 172, 173, 178n.8
*See also* Dialects, Discourse(s), Register
Learning, Ch. 5 passim
affective aspects of, 77–78
assessment of, by more than discourse, 68–69
longitudinal research for documenting, 130
of language/discourse(s), Chapter 8 passim
Legitimate peripheral participation, 146, 165n.19
Lessons, Chapter 3 passim
complementarity of traditional and nontraditional, 56
differences between traditional and nontraditional, 49–50, 55–56
Listening responsibilities, 26, 88–91, 119; *See also* Revoicing

Narratives
as universal genre, 19
children's self-corrections in, 15
cultural differences in, 17–19, 29n.18
conversational vs. institutional, 13, 28n.7

Participation structures, *See* Changes in classroom discourse, Lessons, Peer discourse, Sharing time
Pedagogical content knowledge, 54, 71
Peer discourse, 109–123 passim
contributions of, to learning, 66, 110–111, 150
new opportunities in teacher-led lessons, 109–110
influences on, 123
student perceptions of, 113, 121–123, 132
*See also* Audience, Heterogeneous groups, Jigsaw

Practice, two meanings of, 177–178
Preactive vs. interactive influences on teaching, 145

Reading Recovery, 63–66, 76–77, 95–96, 159–160, 167n.45
Reciprocal Teaching, 66–69, 74, 96, 109
Reconceptualization/Recontextualization, 71–75; *See also* under Revoicing
Register(s), 178n.6
of science, 44, 45–46
of math, 72–73
Relevance, 17, 37
Resistance to learning, 179n.16
Re-voicing, 89–91, 107n.16, 109
as reconceptualization, 91
two functions of, 90–91
Roles for speaking, 8n.9, 125, 166n.30
in community-based organizations, 177
in Complex Instruction, 166n.30
in tutoring, 114–115
Routines, 101–103, 108n.35, 108n.36

Scaffolds, 60–71 passim
curriculum (not only interaction) as, 61–71, 166n.40
in computer software, 124, 126
Sharing time, Ch. 2 passim
changes in, initiated by children, 23, 25
in other countries, 28n.2, 29n.22
significance of, 10–11
similarities to other curriculum activities, 27
*See also* Narratives
Situated vs. transferable cognitive and language skills, 180n.19
Social
constructivism, 77, 116
languages , 178n.6
meanings of, 116
relationships in learning, 131–134, 171
socially-shared cognition, 113
united with cognitive, 2, 17, 26–27, 60, 75
Social class differences, 18, 86–87, 107n.12

Speaking rights, 82–88 passim, 125, 144*n*.2
  interruptions, 86–87, 107*n*.12
  student self-selection as deregulation, 83–84
Structures of discourse
  and rules, scripts, schemata, 57*n*.8
  as claims about participants' communicative competence, 40, 57*n*.8
  default (unmarked) option in, 31
  design principles for, 81
  dual dimensions of (sequential and selectional), 37–39
  improvisation, 39–40
  nested in larger activity structures, 81–82
  related to functions, 38, 47
Student perspectives, *See* under Peer discourse

Tape recordings
  advice for making, 9*n*.12, 134*n*.9
  analysis of, vs. listening in real time, 16, 28*n*.7
  transcriptions of, 12, 58*n*.23, 106*n*.5, 165*n*.22
  value of, for teachers, 6–7
Teacher expectations, 94, 115, 124
Teacher feedback/evaluation, 41, 44–45, 107
  assigning competence, 150–163, 166*n*.31
  differential treatment in, 213–218
  in higher and lower reading groups, 139–144
  in Topically Related Sets, 32

timing of, 51, 95–100
  valuing student questions, 148–150
  *See also* Revoicing
Teacher questions, 92–93
  authentic and known-answer, 46–47
  in higher and lower tracked classes, 139
  open and closed, 92–93
  process (metacognitive), 46, 92
  that assist and/or assess, 107*n*.22
  *See also* Wait time
Teacher research, 6, 135*n*.16, 181
  in early childhood education, 83–84, 167*n*.47
  in heterogeneous groups, 146–147, 150–153
  in language arts, 84, 118–119
  in math lessons, 49, 58*n*.23
  in sharing time, 22–27
  on cultural differences, 160–161, 167*n*.47
  special features of, 22
  with student co-researchers, 158
Topically related sets (TRS), 32, 37
Tracking, 138–144
Transcriptions, *See* under Tape recordings

Wait time, 94–95
Writing conferences, 27, 29*n*.29, 116–119

Zone of proximal development (ZPD), 63, 66

# Name Index

Adger, C. T., 107*n*.16, 108*n*.32, 177, 179*n*.14, 179*n*.11, 180*n*.18
Airasin, P. W., 80*n*.34
Allen, S., 84, 106*n*.8
Allington, R. L., 140, 164*n*.8
Alvermann, D. E., 132
Anderson, R., 108*n*.35
Aronson, E. A., 79*n*.11
Atwell, N., 97, 108*n*.33, 118–19, 135*n*.16

Baker, C. D., 28*n*.5
Bakhtin, M., 26, 29*n*.27, 75, 76, 80*n*.32, 80*n*.31, 110, 116, 134*n*.1, 134*n*.11, 173, 178*n*.8, 178*n*.9, 178*n*.6
Ball, D. L., 49, 54, 55, 57*n*.1, 58*n*.30, 58*n*.31, 58*n*.32, 58*n*.21
Ballenger, C., 159–61, 167*n*.46
Barnes, D., 1–2, 6, 9*n*.12, 9*n*.10, 60, 80*n*.31, 93, 103, 108*n*.24, 169, 171, 178*n*.1, 178*n*.3,
Bartlett, E. J., 28*n*.10
Bauersfeld, H., 135*n*.17
Baugh, J., 179*n*.11
Baxter, S., 85
Beck, I. L., 69, 79*n*.16, 108*n*.25
Bellugi, U., 72, 79*n*.22
Benson, C., 135*n*.27–28
Bereiter, C., 80*n*.34
Berlak, A., 58*n*.31, 165*n*.17, 176
Berlak, H., 58*n*.31, 165*n*.17, 176
Berman, R., 28*n*.10
Bernstein, B., 57*n*.14, 107*n*.12, 108*n*.35
Black, S. D., 135*n*.34
Bombardieri, M., 178*n*.10
Brandt, L., 108*n*.37
Bransford, J. D., 78*n*.2, 80*n*.35, 97
Brown, A. L., 67–68, 69, 76, 78*n*.2, 79*n*.9, 79*n*.8, 79*n*.14, 79*n*.12, 79*n*.22, 82, 101, 103, 105*n*.1,

108*n*.36, 109, 113–14, 132–33, 136*n*.44
Brown, P., 178*n*.5
Brown, R., 72, 86, 107*n*.11
Bruer, J. T., 75, 80*n*.29
Bruner, J. S., 78*n*.2

Campione, J. C., 79*n*.8, 108*n*.36
Cazden, C. B., 8*n*.5, 8*n*.1, 18, 28*n*.9, 28*n*.4, 29*n*.15, 57*n*.3, 59*n*.34, 78*n*.2, 79*n*.7, 79*n*.14, 80*n*.38, 86, 107*n*.12, 107*n*.11, 108*n*.29, 114, 134*n*.9–10, 136*n*.38, 166*n*.38, 166*n*.36, 167*n*.45, 167*n*.42, 179*n*.14
Chafe, W., 108*n*.39
Chaudron, C., 29*n*.22
Chomsky, N., 57*n*.4
Christian, D., 108*n*.32
Christian, S., 126–27, 135*n*.28
Christie, F., 28*n*.2
Citrino, A., 129, 130, 135*n*.35
Clay, M. M., 63, 79*n*.7, 108*n*.29, 137–38, 141, 145, 153–56, 164*n*.1, 165*n*.18, 165*n*.13, 166*n*.37, 166*n*.34, 167*n*.44
Cobb, P., 73, 80*n*.25, 80*n*.34, 80*n*.24, 119, 121, 135*n*.17
Cocking, R. R., 78*n*.2
Cognitition and Technology Group at Vanderbilt, 108*n*.34
Cohen, E. G., 150–51, 165*n*.26, 165*n*.25, 166*n*.29–31
Cole, M., 74, 78*n*.2, 80*n*.26, 180*n*.19
Collins, J. P., 141–43, 164*n*.9–10
Comber, B., 156, 166*n*.38
Cone, J. K., 146–47, 165*n*.20, 166*n*.40
Cope, B., 59*n*.34
Coulthard, R. M., 38, 57*n*.6
Cremin, L. A., 54, 58*n*.29

Crook, C., 129–30, 135*n*.23, 136*n*.36–40
Crumbaugh, C., 58*n*.26
Cummins, J., 128, 135*n*.33, 135*n*.30
Cunningham, J. R., 8*n*.7

Danielewicz, J., 29*n*.20
Darling-Hammond, L., 138–39, 164*n*.6, 164*n*.4
Dawes, L., 126
de la Cruz, E., 108*n*.37
Delpit, L., 6, 29*n*.15, 166*n*.40, 175–76, 178*n*.6, 179*n*.13
Demientieff, M., 173, 174, 178*n*.8
Dewey, J., 54, 58*n*.29
Diamondstone, J., 29*n*.29
Diaz, E., 165*n*.11
Dinsmore, D. F, 28*n*.3, 28*n*.2
Dobson, V., 156–57, 166*n*.38
Donaghy, K., 135*n*.31
Dorr-Bremme, D. W., 12, 27*n*.1, 28*n*.13
Douglas, N., 107*n*.10
Driver, R., 80*n*.34
Duckworth, E., 92, 107*n*.22, 169–70
Duke, N. K., 138, 164*n*.5
Dyson, A. H., 157, 166*n*.38

Eckert, P., 84, 106*n*.7
Edgar, C., 135*n*.28–29
Edwards, A. D., 9*n*.13, 28*n*.5, 92, 108*n*.23
Edwards, D., 47, 57*n*.17, 80*n*.28, 130, 136*n*.38
Ehrlich, D. E., 166*n*.30
Ellery, S., 108*n*.36
Emerson, C., 80*n*.32
Erickson, F. E., 39–40, 57*n*.9, 106*n*.8, 134*n*.4
Estrade, E., 165*n*.11

Fairclough, N., 59*n*.34
Fine, M., 165*n*.19
Fisher, E., 124, 135*n*.24
Ford, B., 179*n*.16
Forman, E. A., 80*n*.37
Foster, M., 176, 179*n*.17, 179*n*.14
Fountas, C., 164*n*.2
Franklin, M. C., 134*n*.6
Freeman, D., 178*n*.8
Furlong, J. J., 92, 108*n*.23

Gallas, K., 9*n*.11, 23–27, 29*n*.25–28, 76, 109
Gee, J. P., 8*n*.9, 28*n*.7, 59*n*.34, 178*n*.6, 179*n*.13
Gentry, B., 129, 130, 135*n*.35
Gersten, R., 108*n*.28
Glynn, T, 144, 165*n*.12
Godfrey, L., 90
Goffman, E., 107*n*.16
Goldenberg, C., 59*n*.34
Goldfield, B. A., 62, 79*n*.6
Goodnow, J., 80*n*.37
Gordon, E. W., 145, 165*n*.15
Grace, P., 153, 156, 166*n*.33
Griffin, P., 57*n*.8, 74, 80*n*.26
Groves, S., 58*n*.25
Grubb, N., 134*n*.12
Gutierrez, K., 157, 166*n*.38, 172, 178*n*.7

Halliday, M. A. K., 2, 8*n*.4, 57*n*.11, 58*n*.22
Hardcastle, J., 87, 88, 107*n*.14
Hamann, J., 59*n*.34
Haselkorn, S., 62
Heath, S. B., 8*n*.9, 28*n*.14, 114, 134*n*.7–8, 135*n*.14, 157–59, 161, 165*n*.14, 166*n*.39–41, 167*n*.43, 177, 179*n*.10, 179–80*n*.17, 180*n*.19, 182*n*.1
Heider, E. R., 86, 107*n*.11
Hemphill, L., 87, 107*n*.12
Hicks, D., 9*n*.13, 178*n*.6
Hiebert, J., 49, 58*n*.24, 134*n*.2
Hillocks, G., Jr., 61, 69–70, 79*n*.20, 79*n*.18, 81, 101
Holmes, J., 165*n*.19
Howard, T., 135*n*.27–28
Hoyle, S. M., 107*n*.16, 177, 180*n*.18
Hughes, M., 28*n*.11
Hunt, V., 127, 135*n*.29
Hymes, D., 5–6, 8*n*.8, 8*n*.1, 28*n*.7

Institute for Learning, 178*n*.2
Irvine, J. T., 106*n*.4
Istomina, Z. M., 80*n*.27

Jackson, P. W., 145, 165*n*.16
James, W., 101, 108*n*.35
Jefferson, G., 106*n*.4
Jimenez, R. T., 108*n*.28
Johnson, L. B., 174

Jones, E., 80*n*.23
Juel, 164*n*.3

Kalantzis, M., 59*n*.34
Kamler, B., 116–17, 135*n*.13
Keresty, B., 182*n*.2
Kilalea, M., 162–63, 168*n*.50
Kohl, H., 80*n*.39
Kress, G., 59*n*.34
Kuamoyo, H., 135*n*.31
Kucan, L., 69, 79*n*.16

Labov, W., 175
Lambert, W. E., 29*n*.16
Lampert, M., 49, 51–54, 58*n*.26, 58*n*.27, 58*n*.21, 72–73, 77, 80*n*.36, 109, 132, 133, 136*n*.42, 173
Landes, R., 158–59, 167*n*.42
Lashley, K. S., 57*n*.4
Lave, J., 146, 165*n*.19
Leinhardt, G., 59*n*.35
Lemke, J. L., 38, 57*n*.7, 57*n*.15, 58*n*.22, 107*n*.14
Leont'ev, A. N., 57*n*.11, 75–76, 80*n*.30
Levinson, S., 108*n*.23, 178*n*.5
Levy, F., 8*n*.6
Lewis, C., 121–23, 132, 135*n*.20
Linde, C., 28*n*.7
Lionni, L., 83, 106*n*.5
Lopez, L. M., 165*n*.11
Lortie, D. C., 57*n*.10, 80*n*.39
Lotan, R. A., 165*n*.26, 165*n*.25
Luke, A., 59*n*.34
Luke, C., 59*n*.34
Lundgren, U. P., 93, 108*n*.25

Mackey, S., 8*n*.7
Mangiola, L., 114, 134*n*.7–8
Manuilenko, Z. V., 80*n*.27
Martin, G., 29*n*.18
Matute-Bianchi, M. E., 168*n*.52
McCarthy, F., 113
McCreddy, 107*n*.16
McCrohon, C., 151–52, 155
McEachen, D., 59*n*.35, 147–50, 150, 151, 165*n*.21–24, 166*n*.40
McLaughlin, M., 135*n*.14
McLeod, A., 88, 107*n*.14
McNaughton, S., 144, 165*n*.12
McNeill, D., 134*n*.4

Medrick, A., 180*n*.17
Mehan, H., 1, 8*n*.2, 31, 32, 39, 40, 46, 47, 57*n*.1, 57*n*.2, 57*n*.8, 73, 82, 105–6*n*.3, 114, 128, 167*n*.42
Meier, T., 179*n*.14
Meister, C., 108*n*.30
Mercer, N., 47, 57*n*.17, 80*n*.28, 124, 130, 135*n*.24–25, 136*n*.38
Meyerhoff, M., 165*n*.19
Michaels, S., 11–12, 18, 20, 28*n*.4, 28*n*.9, 29*n*.19, 29*n*.29, 29*n*.15, 47, 57*n*.18, 59*n*.34, 68, 79*n*.13, 90–91, 106*n*.9, 107*n*.17–21, 133, 136*n*.45, 166*n*.31
Minden-Cupp, 164*n*.3
Minick, N., 80*n*.37
Minstrell, J. A., 94, 108*n*.27
Moll, L. C., 143, 156, 161, 165*n*.11, 166*n*.38
Monzo, L. D., 161–62, 167*n*.48
Morson, G. S., 80*n*.32
Murnane, R. J., 8*n*.6

Nakata, M., 59*n*.34
National Institute of Education, 8*n*.4
National Research Council, 89, 175
Newman, D., 74, 80*n*.26
New Standards, 178*n*.4
Nystrand, M., 139–40, 164*n*.7

Ochs, E., 28*n*.5
O'Connor, C., 90–91
O'Connor, M. C., 47, 57*n*.18, 80*n*.34, 107*n*.17–21, 131, 136*n*.41
Ogbu, J. U., 163–64, 168*n*.52, 179*n*.16
Ogburn, J., 57*n*.14
O'Leary, S., 182*n*.2

Paley, V., 26, 29*n*.27, 59*n*.32, 83, 84, 87, 88, 106*n*.6, 106*n*.5, 135*n*.16, 167*n*.47, 168*n*.51
Palincsar, A. S., 66, 69, 79*n*.8, 79*n*.17, 96, 103, 123, 135*n*.22
Perez, C., 29*n*.17
Perry, T., 29*n*.15, 164*n*.7, 179*n*.14, 179*n*.11
Peyton, J. K., 29*n*.29
Pinnel, G. S., 164*n*.2
Poole, D., 103–5, 108*n*.39, 108*n*.38
Poreda, D., 28*n*.2

Pratt, M. L., 13, 28*n*.6
Purcell-Gates, V., 165*n*.14, 179*n*.10
Putnam, R. T., 58*n*.19

Quinn, C. N., 135*n*.34

Rampton, B., 167*n*.43
Reddy, M., 29*n*.29, 165*n*.25,
    166*n*.30, 166*n*.27
Resnick, L. B., 69, 76, 79*n*.15,
    170–71
Rex, L. A., 59*n*.35, 147, 150,
    165*n*.21–24
Richards, J., 90
Riley, R., 156–57, 166*n*.38
Rittenhouse, P., 58*n*.26
Rogoff, B., 60, 78*n*.1, 80*n*.33
Rose, M., 79*n*.21
Rosen, H., 19, 29*n*.18
Rosenshine, B., 96, 108*n*.30
Ross, G., 78*n*.2
Rowe, M. B., 94, 108*n*.26
Rueda, R. S., 161–62, 167*n*.48
Rutherford, M., 101–2, 103,
    108*n*.37, 108*n*.36

Sachs, H., 106*n*.4
Sapir, E., 181, 182*n*.3
Saunders, W., 59*n*.34
Sayers, D., 128, 135*n*.33, 135*n*.30
Scary, R., 62
Schegloff, E. A., 106*n*.4, 136*n*.40
Schifter, D., 58*n*.23, 89, 107*n*.15
Schlegel, J., 111, 134*n*.4, 134*n*.5,
    134*n*.3
Schoenbach, R., 79*n*.10
Scribner, S., 28*n*.10
Scrimshaw, P., 135*n*.26, 135*n*.23
Secret, C., 179*n*.14
Sfard, A., 56, 59*n*.33, 80*n*.34
Sheeran, Y., 9*n*.10
Shulman, J. H., 165*n*.25, 166*n*.32
Shulman, L., 54, 58*n*.28
Shuy, R., 176, 179*n*.15
Simmons, E. A., 179*n*.14
Sinclair, J. McH., 38, 57*n*.6
Sittnick, P., 126, 127, 128, 135*n*.29,
    135*n*.27
Slobin, D. I., 28*n*.10
Smitherman, G., 18, 29*n*.15
Smyth, L, 135*n*.14, 179*n*.17
Snow, C. E., 61, 62, 79*n*.6, 79*n*.4,
    165*n*.13, 179*n*.12

Soep, E. M., 117, 135*n*.15, 135*n*.14,
    177
Sohmer, R., 68, 79*n*.13, 85, 106*n*.9
Solsken, I., 28*n*.7
Staton, J., 29*n*.29
Steinberg, Z., 114–15, 134*n*.9–10
Stires, S., 22–23, 29*n*.24
Stone, A., 78, 80*n*.37, 80*n*.30, 131
Stone, C. A., 79*n*.5, 80*n*.37
Sullivan, J., 113

Tabors, P., 28*n*.9, 28*n*.4
Tager-Flusberg, H., 29*n*.17
Tannen, D., 87, 107*n*.13
Tizard, B., 28*n*.11
Tobin, K., 108*n*.26
Todd, F., 9*n*.12, 80*n*.31, 103
Tracy, K., 17, 28*n*.12

Udall, D., 180*n*.17
Ulichny, P., 96–97, 108*n*.31

Vygotsky, L. S., 21, 58*n*.31, 63, 75,
    76, 78, 78*n*.2, 79*n*.14, 80*n*.31,
    134*n*.4

Walsh, M. E., 80*n*.34
Warschauer, M., 135*n*.31
Webb, N. B., 123, 135*n*.22
Wegerif, R., 126, 135*n*.23, 135*n*.25–
    26
Weiner, L., 167*n*.42
Wells, G., 40–47, 47, 57*n*.16,
    57*n*.18, 57*n*.11–13, 130, 172
Wenger, E., 68, 79*n*.13, 146,
    165*n*.19
Wertsch, J. V., 20–22, 29*n*.23,
    29*n*.21, 61–62, 79*n*.5, 80*n*.31,
    80*n*.30, 172
Westgate, D. P. G., 9*n*.13, 28*n*.5
Wilson, S. M., 55, 58*n*.30
Wolfram, W., 108*n*.32, 179*n*.10
Wood, D., 78*n*.2
Wood, S. N., 135*n*.28–29
Wood, T., 80*n*.24
Woolf, V., 178*n*.9
Wortley, D., 182*n*.2

Yackel, E., 80*n*.24
Yowell, C., 165*n*.15

Zack, M. B., 166*n*.30